american
TROUBADOURS

Backbeat Books

american
TROUBADOURS

groundbreaking singer-songwriters of the 60s

by Mark Brend
FOREWORD BY TOM RAPP

Backbeat
Books

american troubadours
by Mark Brend

A BACKBEAT BOOK
First edition 2001

Published by Backbeat Books
600 Harrison Street,
San Francisco, CA 94107
www.backbeatbooks.com

An imprint of The Music Player Network United
Entertainment Media, Inc.

Produced for Backbeat Books by Outline Press Ltd,
115J Cleveland Street, London W1T 6PU, England.
www.balafon.dircon.co.uk

ISBN 0-87930-641-6

Art Director: Nigel Osborne
Design: Paul Cooper
Editor: Tony Bacon
Production: Phil Richardson

Origination by Global Colour (Malaysia)
Print by Colorprint Offset Ltd. (Hong Kong)

01 02 03 04 05 5 4 3 2 1

I have the honour of writing these few words to introduce *American Troubadours* because I was a singer-songwriter and made some records in the 1960s, then disappeared for decades, and did not die.

Of the nine artists in this book, sadly the majority are dead: David Ackles, David Blue, Tim Buckley, Tim Hardin and Phil Ochs. The survivors are Fred Neil, Tim Rose, Tom Rush and, I'm pretty sure, Tom Rapp. Survival is greatly aided, apparently, by having the initials TR.

Having somehow survived from this period, I am often asked what the Lessons from this time are. I have developed a list of Six Lessons. All of them are things the singer-songwriters in this book stood for. One I got directly from Phil Ochs in a conversation we had in Los Angeles in 1971: Governments Always Lie.

"They have no morals – you have to kick their ass to get them to do the right thing," he said.

The other five are: Love is Real; Justice is Real; Honesty is Possible and Necessary; Everything is Not for Sale; and, of course, Never Buy Drugs from a Policeman.

One of my great memories from the period this book covers is of a time I played with Ramblin' Jack Elliott at The Bitter End club in Greenwich Village, New York. Dylan had been hanging around all week. "Don't talk to Dylan!" was the firm instruction from the club's managers.

After the last show, Jack asked Dylan to come up and play, which he did (using my guitar – I still have the strings). Tim Buckley had just died, and that was mentioned. Dave Van Ronk was asked up and he sang. Phil Ochs was there and Dylan and Jack asked him to come up and sing, but he gestured that he couldn't sing, pointing to his throat.

A few weeks later, Phil was dead. But for the time that he and we were all enjoying the glow of the club and the people in it, a kind of grace surrounded everything. Some of that survives in the music that didn't die and will always be there to listen to, if we want it. **TOM RAPP, NEW JERSEY, DECEMBER 2000**

introduction

For a few years in the early 1960s, before The Beatles and The Rolling Stones, rock'n'roll had lost much of its vital force. The energy that had at first made the new music so appealing and so threatening seemed to have evaporated. The best of the first generation of rockers were either dead, emasculated by establishment forces, or lost on some tangent taking them ever further away from the source of their inspiration. Buddy Holly and Eddie Cochran were killed in accidents; Elvis Presley went into the army; Chuck Berry had problems with the law; Jerry Lee Lewis incurred public and media wrath when he married his teenage cousin; Little Richard found God; Gene Vincent turned to drink.

Sensing this vacuum, the faceless middle-aged powers behind the music business did what they always do. They took aspects of the rebellious style, and manufactured teen idols. The new stars – Frankie Avalon, Fabian and the like – had something of the appearance of the originators, but none of the danger, energy or power. Rock'n'roll had been drained of its blood. American teenagers who had been so excited by Elvis in 1956 were now looking elsewhere for substance, for authenticity, and for the means with which to hit out at convention. Many of them found an unlikely outlet for their energies.

There had been folk revivals before, and there have been others since, but none so widespread and influential as the one that swept the US in the late 1950s and early 1960s. Rather than one particular, specific event, it was more like a gradual coming together of strands that had been present in American life for years, even decades, before. But as this happened, something grew that attracted bored teenagers who had grown tired of rock'n'roll. Generally, though not exclusively, these teenagers were white and middle-class, with intellectual, liberal, left-wing proclivities.

As a musical term the word "folk" was too vague to have much meaning. It encompassed black blues, white country, British and Irish 19th-century ballads, and a whole lot else. You'd be equally welcome in the folk fraternity if you could pick Leadbelly songs on a 12-string guitar, strum your way through a Woody Guthrie anthem, or play traditional Appalachian tunes on a dulcimer.

Yet in spite of this apparent eclecticism there were rules about what was and what was not acceptable. It was often less than clear exactly what the rules were and who made them, but they tended to centre on notions of authenticity, community and anti-commercialism. In time these rules would seem to many of the young iconoclasts initially drawn to the movement like restrictive narrow-mindedness dressed up as idealism, but for a short while they offered a framework for the inarticulate rage of disaffected youth.

Just as with early rock'n'roll, the folk scene offered something spontaneous, genuine and untainted, as opposed to the manufactured, the contrived and the commercial. Unlike rock'n'roll, it occupied itself overtly and unselfconsciously with more than music and style. Peter Knobler of *Crawdaddy* magazine wrote: "The Folk Movement [was] perhaps the first of this generation's Capitalised causes to merge politics and culture." [1]

The new folk music fostered a sense of beleaguered community. A particular attraction to youthful malcontents was the sense of "us" (liberal, left-leaning pacifists) against "them" (Republicans and bland, middle-class materialists). It was "of the people". It had intellectual pretensions. It was serious. It was critical of comfortable Middle America. It was anti-establishment. And folk music was also easy to play. All you needed was a guitar or a banjo or a washtub bass, a few chords, and a nasal whine that could just about hold a tune.

Woody Guthrie was the doyen of American folk singers. Through the 1930s and 1940s he had travelled across America, and sometimes further afield, writing hundreds of songs about displaced migrants, poverty, unionisation and the rest. He was later struck down by Huntington's chorea, a progressive wasting disease, and was all but inactive by the time the seeds he had sown flowered in the late-1950s revival. But Guthrie hovered over the new generation of folk performers like a benign god, a universally respected symbol of credibility and a source of material and inspiration. People felt he was what a folk singer should be, which is why so many dressed like him and sang like him.

On the route to the new revival there were a few key reference points from Guthrie's heyday two decades before. For a few years around the start of the 1950s folk music had enjoyed a surge of popularity on the back of the success of The Weavers group. They were unusual in that they had hit records while retaining what would today be called roots credibility. The commercial highpoint of their career was a US number-one hit in 1950 with 'Goodnight Irene'. But as the decade wore on they were pressurised into inactivity because of their political radicalism, at a time when the American establishment saw the spirit of communism in the skin of every liberal.

One of The Weavers was Pete Seeger, a gaunt livewire of humanistic fervour. He had earlier worked with Guthrie, and – despite being politically blacklisted – continued as best he could to carry the torch for folk music and all its normally attendant political causes following the demise of The Weavers.

When folk music captured the minds and hearts of a much younger generation, Seeger was present as a link back to that earlier age – or at least a romanticised perception of it – that exercised such a powerful hold on the collective imagination of the movement. Seeger became a father figure to younger performers, always ready to encourage, guide and correct. Later, when his young charges grew sufficiently confident and competent to cut loose from the influence of their elders, he sometimes seemed reluctant to let the torch pass to the next generation.

Other events contributed to the momentum that eventually propelled the revival into the national arena. Harry Smith's six-LP *Anthology Of American Folk Music,* released in 1952, preserved dozens of obscure recordings that had originally been released on 78rpm records in the 1920s and 1930s. It became a treasure-trove into which aspiring performers of the new generation would delve, and consequently a means by which traditional music was passed from one generation to the next. For folk purists like Pete Seeger this was an important principle.

In 1958 a neatly-dressed, commercial folk group, The Kingston Trio, had a massive hit with 'Tom Dooley', the strongest showing in the charts for a folk record since the heyday of The Weavers. Although they never matched that first success, The Kingston Trio scored many more hits for the rest of the decade and well into the 1960s. Purists thought that they were too commercial, but the Trio highlighted the continued existence of folk music, presenting it as an option to American youth just at the time when the power of rock'n'roll was beginning to wane.

By 1959 folk clubs were opening all over America, but the revival became centred on two geographical areas. Greenwich Village in New York City had for years been attracting a bohemian set: artists, students, intellectuals, beat poets. Then a group of coffee-houses on Bleecker and MacDougal streets began to present folk music, and became the epicentre of the folk music world, a place toward which virtually every aspiring young performer would gravitate in the coming years. Bob Dylan, Tim Hardin, Phil Ochs, Tim Rose, Fred Neil and David Blue all arrived there shortly after the start of the 1960s, and for a few short years exchanged songs, tunings, ideas, jokes and audiences as they honed their craft and established their respective styles.

In Boston and neighbouring Cambridge in Massachusetts a parallel scene sprang up. Joan Baez was the dominant figure in terms of commercial success and fame, emerging from a group of performers that included Tom Rush and Eric Von Schmidt. The Boston/Cambridge camp came to represent one side of a split between the traditionalists and the innovators in the folk revival.

While the Boston and Cambridge musicians tended to maintain a notion of purity, their New York compatriots were quicker to question the orthodox conventions of folk music and preferred instead to use it as a springboard to new sounds and new directions. Tom Rush says: "[Boston] was a more amateur scene than Greenwich Village – amateur in the positive sense. Not many of us had careers in mind – I didn't, in fact – and very few of us went on to become career professional musicians. They were much more career orientated in Greenwich Village; in Cambridge you had typewriter repairmen, pharmacologists and English majors plugging along for the fun of it."[2]

As the new decade wore on many of the Boston/Cambridge performers, particularly Baez, remained primarily folk singers, while the majority of the better known Greenwich Village-based artists achieved recognition with music that had grown out of the folk revival, but which could no longer be called folk music. Despite this tension there was cross-pollination between the two scenes. "There was a good deal of traffic back and forth," suggests Tom Rush. "There was an avid audience in the Boston area, and for those of us with the time and inclination, the next obvious step in expanding that audience was to go to New York."[3]

While this was happening, other smaller enclaves formed throughout America. There was one in Coconut Grove in Miami, for example, where folk singers met and exchanged ideas. It was a time when friendships, rivalries and repertoires would overlap. Dylan had a relationship with Baez. Tom Rush performed in both Greenwich Village and Florida, and eventually went to settle in New York. Tim Hardin went to Boston for a while. Fred Neil and Vince Martin both moved between Greenwich Village and Florida.

The folk movement of the late 1950s and early 1960s seems impossibly distant and antiquated now. The power and relevance of songs that were at least 20 years old in 1960 and which hailed from cultures, circumstances and environments which even then were historical has diminished. Today, the rock'n'roll of 1956 seems much closer in time than the folk music of 1961.

In an era when boundaries between different forms of popular music have all but disappeared, questions like "Can a white boy sing the blues?" seem quaintly irrelevant. Not only do white boys sing their version of the blues, but middle-class white boys from English and American suburbs sing their versions of soul, reggae, country and many other types of music previously thought of as "ethnic" in some sense, and nobody really thinks that much about it. But in the late 1950s and early 1960s it was a question that vexed the burgeoning folk movement in America, clawing at its well-intentioned but confused ideals of authenticity.

Tom Rush says: "What struck me as strange was having college kids singing about how tough it was working in the coal mines – singing these songs with a great deal of fervour and intensity."[4] Apparently it was authentic for middle-class white teenagers to sing traditional songs and the blues of black Depression-era America, but somehow frivolous to write their own songs about their own experiences. Middle-aged black bluesmen were being "rediscovered" and touted by their young champions in what was benign but ultimately patronising cultural imperialism.

The whole scene was a curious blend of radical politics and musical conservatism. Peter Knobler describes it as "an alternating current of progressive thinking and reverse psychology".[5] It was hardly surprising that when pop music emerged revitalised in the hands of The Beatles and The Rolling Stones, the folk revival as a youth movement died a rapid death. There was an irony in all this, of course. The British "invasion" bands were themselves all reinterpreting many of the forms that prospered in the folk revival. It's just that they were reinterpreting, not trying slavishly to recreate.

The folk revival was an anachronism, a throwback to an imagined era of gritty authenticity that stood in stark contrast to the commercialism of late-1950s and early-1960s pop. Although it filled a gap in popular culture until the next new movement came along, folk's importance resides less in the actual music it generated and more in the influence it had on a generation of songwriters and performers. It taught these songwriters that politics and music can mix, that songs don't have to be just about the usual girl-meets-boy, and that there are narrative possibilities in songwriting that were as yet untapped in the realms of popular music.

And then there was Bob Dylan. Phil Ochs said: "My basic view of Dylan was that I was impressed with him immediately."[6] When the faux hobo from Minnesota first appeared on the already burgeoning scene, almost everyone in Greenwich Village gained a similar impression of Dylan – and certainly any folk singer operating on that circuit would have heard and seen him. Dylan's influence was undeniable, and the twists and turns of his career path from then on were mirrored by those of many of his contemporaries. In the words of David Blue, "He was the symbol of the time, the spearhead."[7]

Dylan had risen to prominence with a vocal style and a look that owed a considerable debt to Woody Guthrie. Although Dylan's derivative first album initially sold poorly, his reputation as a writer became established when Peter Paul & Mary had a worldwide hit with his 'Blowin' In The Wind' in 1963.

The folk movement hoped that in Dylan they had found a true champion to articulate their collective rage against the forces of commercialism, oppression and bigotry. With Joan Baez at his side, Dylan was royalty. And for a very short while he seemed happy with this role. He linked arms and sang with Seeger at the Newport folk festival, he wrote the strident, sloganeering early songs, he performed with Baez and other stalwarts. But then he heard The Beatles, The Byrds, and The Animals… and he started to remember why it was that he loved rock'n'roll.

No one thing inspired Dylan to go electric. It is known that he was impressed with The Animals' arrangement of 'House Of The Rising Sun', a song he had recorded early in his career. He talked of the impact The Beatles had on him, and of realising the possibilities of playing with other musicians. And, external influences aside, the ever-questioning, confrontational Dylan was bound to have tired of the restrictive conventions of folk music sooner or later.

Dylan wasn't the first folk artist to pick up an electric guitar. But he was the first of his generation of writers thrown up by the folk revival to distance himself from that same movement. First he wrote his own songs, which some folk traditionalists thought questionable, but he got away with it because songs like 'The Times They Are A Changin'' could serve as rallying cries for the movement. Then, when he started to write allusive, alliterative free-verse and surreal narratives in place of the black-and-white them-and-us certainties expected in the folk revival, people started to feel threatened. He was going against the grain, but going electric was the final betrayal – even if doubts had been festering in the minds of purists for some time.

It seems incredible and comical now that Dylan's brief electric set at the Newport folk festival in 1965 should have caused such upheaval among folk fans and players. Did the gentle, avuncular Pete Seeger really try to cut the power cables as Dylan's electric band rocked through 'Maggie's Farm'? Witnesses say he did.

The folk magazine *Sing Out* reviewed the performance with barely concealed contempt. "Dylan emerged from his cult-imposed aura of mystery to demonstrate the new 'folk-rock', an expression that has already begun to find its way into the 'top forty' charts by which musical success is measured. To many it seemed that it was not very good 'rock', while other disappointed legions did not think it was very good Dylan."[8]

Half the Newport audience booed Dylan in self-righteous indignation; the other half cheered. It was the end of the folk revival as a meaningful force in American popular culture, a symbolic marker of a transition that had taken place in Dylan's career, and a culmination of the long-running rift between folk purists and innovators. Dylan had outgrown the movement that had spawned him. He was moving on, developing as an artist and alienating traditionalists. Others were following.

Through all the turbulence of this phase of his career, it was acknowledged that Dylan set the creative standards among his young contemporaries. He couldn't be avoided. As Tom Rapp says: "Dylan was an influence, in the way that air is an influence if you breathe."[9] So when Dylan stepped out of the folk revival, many of his erstwhile folk-singing contemporaries followed.

It's impossible to say who first thought of playing folk songs with electric guitars, drums and a rock'n'roll attitude, inventing folk-rock in the process. Like many developments in music, the collision of events and circumstances made it inevitable that different people in different places would have similar ideas.

The Byrds were a group of West Coast folkies that included David Crosby – who had been active on the Coconut Grove scene in Florida with Fred Neil and Vince Martin. Very early on he and the other Byrds saw the potential for merging the harmonies and jangling guitars of Merseybeat with folk songs. Their first hit single was a Dylan song, 'Mr Tambourine Man', that in its original form was an obtuse solo narrative stretching over many verses.

For their 1965 hit The Byrds stripped 'Tambourine Man' down to just two verses and a repeated chorus of soaring harmonies, alongside leader Roger McGuinn's chiming electric 12-string Rickenbacker guitar – a gloriously incandescent and uplifting sound. It was a hugely influential record on the new generation of folk singers. Not that each of them immediately rushed off to make similar recordings of their own songs. But it gave an indication of what an electric band could do to an acoustic folk song.

When The Byrds repeated the trick with Pete Seeger's 'Turn, Turn, Turn' a few months later they sent a clear message to the folk movement and the music business: folk songs played by young pop bands with electric guitars sold more records than folk songs strummed on acoustic guitars by earnest folk-singers. The cultural shift was complete, and folk music – as a style, an idea, a movement – never again had such commercial influence or such a foothold in youth culture.

For a very brief period, "folk-rock" as defined by the music business became a craze, and unlikely artists made cash-in records. Barry McGuire's 'Eve Of Destruction' single was a huge worldwide hit in 1965 – top-five in the US and top-20 in the UK. Penned by PF Sloan, a songwriter and sometime performer quick to spot a trend, it was an ill-focused rant about an impending apocalypse, effectively roared by the gravel-throated McGuire over a quintessential jangling folk-rock backing. It was a good record, but one that Phil Ochs thought marked the end of folk-rock as a viable genre. Surely this was the point at which the music business hijacked an emerging style for its own commercial ends, just as it had with rock'n'roll nearly a decade earlier?

People continued to make folk-rock records, although the term became less widely used. It was later applied to British groups like Fairport Convention, but in its original American form was a brief transitional phase that served to connect some of the values of folk music to the pop world. When folk-rock ceased to be in vogue as a genre, the true influence of folk music continued to be felt in less obvious ways.

The folk music revival was restrictive and conservative, and folk-rock proved to be a shortlived hybrid. But after both these movements had peaked, the artists who lived through both stages with their creative faculties intact went on to do their best work. Dylan is the obvious example.

From the traditional material on his first album, through his own early excursions into songwriting, and on to the transitional *Bringing It All Back Home* album, he was an artist in development. He reached the first great creative phase of his maturity with *Highway 61 Revisited* (1965) and *Blonde On Blonde* (1966). These records drew on folk and folk-rock, but could not really be classified as either.

Shortly afterward, those contemporaries of Dylan whose artistic development in some senses paralleled his own also started to produce records that finally broke free of the constricting codes of folk and folk-rock. They are now identified as the first generation of singer-songwriters.

The origins of the term "singer-songwriter" are not clear. By the time Elektra released their *Singer-Songwriter Project* compilation album in 1965 it was already in use, but this album more than any other single event established the term as a label for a particular type of folk-influenced artist.

Like most music-genre labels – punk, psychedelia, R&B and so on – "singer-songwriter" doesn't stand up to close examination. Buddy Holly and Bob Marley were singer-songwriters in the literal sense that they wrote songs and they sang them. But nobody calls them singer-songwriters: one is a rock'n'roll artist, the other is a reggae artist. But despite the looseness of the term, it is fair to say that over the past 35 years "singer-songwriter" has come to be attached to a particular type of artist in the minds of most fans of pop and rock.

The first defining feature of the work of the singer-songwriters is in the lyrics, where there is a broad tendency toward the poetic and the confessional or autobiographical. There are also, in some cases, attempts to tackle broader social, personal and political themes, usually avoided in pop music. It was part of what Tom Rapp was referring to when he said: "I think that the big change in music in the 1960s was that people were starting to write about other things than boys and girls."[10]

Musically, the songs have roots in folk and country music, but incorporate other styles, often with a traditional pop sensibility, and thus have gone beyond being either country or folk songs. Acoustic and electric instruments are used together. There is a strong emphasis on melody, and an inclination toward ballads rather than up-tempo songs.

In a more general sense, the work of the singer-songwriter is mature, adult music. It aspires to be literary, to have substance. It is not intended as throwaway teen pop.

The nine artists featured in this book – David Ackles, David Blue, Tim Buckley, Tim Hardin, Fred Neil, Phil Ochs, Tom Rapp, Tim Rose, and Tom Rush – were to an extent eclipsed by a second wave of singer-songwriters such as James Taylor and Jackson Browne who came to prominence in the early 1970s. Many of the first generation saw their careers start to slide, and some started to back out of the race. Phil Ochs only recorded a handful of tracks in the 1970s. Fred Neil's last release was in 1971. Others, notably Tim Hardin, David Ackles and Tim Buckley, responded by experimenting radically in an attempt to move beyond the generally accepted confines of popular song.

In the cases of Ackles and Buckley these experiments resulted in some of their best-regarded work – *American Gothic* (1972) and *Starsailor* (1971) respectively. Hardin's earlier *Suite For Susan Moore* (1969) was less successful, although not without merits. None of these albums resulted in any sort of sustained commercial breakthrough, however, and each marked in different ways the beginning of the end of their creator's careers. These were fascinating creative roads to travel, but commercial dead-ends. Ackles felt unable to sustain an output to match the acclaim heaped on *American Gothic*; Buckley was dismayed by the public bewilderment that greeted *Starsailor*; and Hardin never again recorded an album of new, original material.

By the mid 1970s the careers of all our nine featured singer-songwriters were in decline. Some like Tom Rush, Tim Rose, Tim Hardin and even Tim Buckley had once seemed close to pop stardom, with minor hit singles, albums scraping the lower reaches of the charts, television appearances, and critical adulation. That might now have seemed like a distant memory, but not distant enough for each to make desperate attempts at commercial success as inspiration and audiences dwindled.

Rose's *The Musician,* Hardin's *Nine,* Rush's *Ladies Love Outlaws* and Buckley's *Sefronia* were all made between 1973 and 1975. Each was littered with trappings designed to provide commercial allure – strings, female backing vocals, brass sections, slick production – and each was far removed from the inspired heights the artists had achieved only a few years before.

Toward the end of the decade they were all yesterday's men. The tidal wave of punk energy in 1976 and 1977 was meant to sweep away the lingering survivors of the 1960s generation. For a while it looked like it had, and most of the big-name survivors were forced into retreat for a short while. Many lesser names saw their careers blown away altogether. It's difficult to imagine somebody like Tim Rose, a 30-something folk-influenced singer-songwriter, competing on the London pub circuit with the emerging generation of teenage three-chord thrashers.

"Singer-songwriter" became a term of contempt, a byword for middle-aged, limp self-indulgence. Even the careers of previously successful role-models – Leonard Cohen, for example – were in the doldrums, and Dylan, for so long the guiding star to a generation of performers, had stepped off the map altogether. Cohen became a comedy-writer's cipher for bedsit gloom and depression, and could not get a major label to issue his albums in the States. Dylan, with his conversion to a particularly strident version of evangelical Christianity, once again alienated his audience. By this time the careers of the nine artists in this book either ended or went into abeyance.

By the late 1970s Tim Buckley and Phil Ochs were dead. Tim Hardin and David Blue followed them shortly afterward. Fred Neil had retreated into seclusion, Tim Rose and Tom Rapp found other ways to make a living and had left the music business, and within a few years David Ackles followed suit. Tom Rush retired for a while, before emerging to continue a low-key career through the 1980s and beyond – the only member of this group to do so.

But in time the angry youth of the 1970s discovered the expressive possibilities of crafted songwriting. Some of the forgotten masters began the long climb out of the bargain basement. Nick Cave started to champion Tim Rose, and covered one of his songs on an album in the mid 1980s. Elvis Costello sometimes performed a David Ackles song live, and mentioned him reverently in interviews. This Mortal Coil took Tim Buckley's 'Song To The Siren' into the UK charts in 1984 and also recorded a Tom Rapp song. Cover versions of songs by Tom Rush, Fred Neil and Tim Hardin once more appeared in the charts. Long-deleted albums were reissued on CD in the 1990s, and Tim Rose and Tom Rapp even started to record again.

At the time of writing, eight of our nine American Troubadours have been "rediscovered", their back-catalogues reissued and their reputations reassessed. Only David Blue remains largely forgotten. Tim Buckley is the best known, and is now firmly established as a pioneering figure. The others are still known only to relatively small groups of enthusiasts – critics, knowledgeable collectors, and other musicians. These are their stories.

[1] Peter Knobler sleevenotes to Fantasy reissue (Fantasy 24709) of Rush's two Prestige albums
[2] Author's interview August 30th 2000
[3] Author's interview August 30th 2000
[4] Author's interview August 30th 2000
[5] Peter Knobler sleevenotes to Fantasy reissue (Fantasy 24709) of Rush's two Prestige albums
[6] *Guitar Player* October 1970
[7] *ZigZag* 41 1974
[8] Irwin Silber *Sing Out* 1965
[9] Author's Interview August 1st 2000
[10] *Ptolemaic Terrascope* 1993

DAVID ACKLES

1		2	3	4
5	6			

A publicity still for the vaudeville duo of David Ackles and his sister Sally in 1945 (1). Ackles in Wargrave, England (2) during preparations for making his *American Gothic* album in 1972. On stage at US venue The Boarding House in 1971 (3). Ackles at the University of Southern California (USC) School of Theater (4) where he worked in the mid 1990s. An Elektra publicity shot (5) from around 1969. Front cover picture (6) from the 1971 Elektra reissue of Ackles's first album, retitled as *The Road To Cairo*.

| 1 | | 2 | | 3 |
| 4 | | 5 | | |

David Blue (1, far left) – then known as David Cohen – in the shortlived Unicorn Jook Band, standing next to folk-singer Eric Andersen. Blue in Dylanesque pose (2) on the sleeve of his 1968 album *These 23 Days In September*, and again in the studio in the mid 1970s (3). Front and back cover shots (4, 5) from his first album, released in 1966 on the Elektra label.

DAVID BLUE

DAVID BLUE

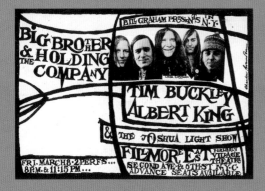

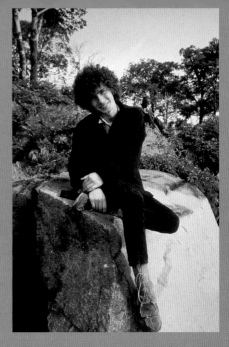

TIM BUCKLEY

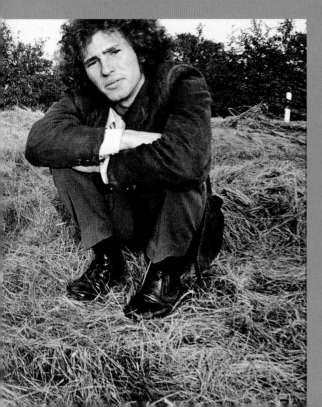

| 1 | 2 | 3 |
| 4 | | 5 |

Publicity (1) for the opening night of the Fillmore East venue in New York, featuring Tim Buckley supporting Janis Joplin's Big Brother & The Holding Company. From the gatefold sleeve of the *Blue Afternoon* LP (3), released in 1970. Three late-1960s press shots when the photogenic Buckley (2, 4, 5) seemed on the cusp of pop stardom.

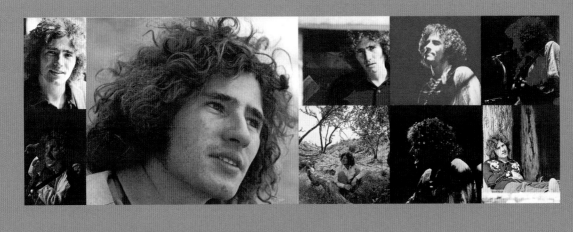

Tim Buckley on stage in the late
1960s. Several live recordings
from this period have since been
issued, providing evidence of his
musical development between
studio albums.

| 1 | | 2 | | 3 |
| | 4 | |

This Is Tim Hardin appeared in 1967, although it consisted of demo material recorded some years earlier – and featured a similarly early cover shot (1). An ad (2) for 1973's *Nine*, Hardin's last complete studio album. Two shots of Hardin on-stage (3) and backstage (4) in the late 1960s.

Sometimes you get lucky and you come across a singer who sees things his own way and sings things his own way and sounds like nobody else in this copycat world of music.

Tim Hardin on-stage in the late 1960s (1) and again in the UK in 1973 (3). A *Billboard* ad (2) for Hardin's first US single, released in 1966. Hardin had the look of a desolate and troubled man by the time his second Columbia album, *Bird On A Wire* (4), appeared in 1971. Hardin in the last year of his life (5) pictured with his grandmother, from the sleeve of his posthumous live album *The Homecoming Concert*.

Fred Neil and Vince Martin (1, 2) collaborated on the 1964 Elektra album, *Tear Down The Walls*. Neil on-stage (3) in the 1960s, and in classic singer-songwriter pose on the corner of Bleecker and MacDougal streets (4), the epicentre of the folk revival. A poster (5) for rare live appearances by Neil in Berkeley and San Francisco in 1967.

FRED NEIL

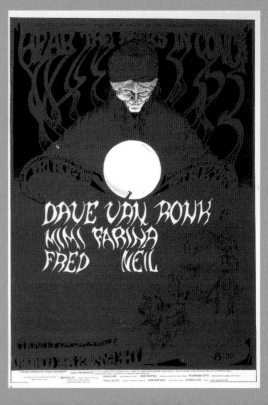

Fred Neil had already withdrawn
from regular live performing when
he was tempted to appear at the
1975 Montreux jazz festival,
where he played several songs
he'd never recorded.

PHIL OCHS

Phil Ochs pictured (1) for the cover of his second Elektra album, *I Ain't Marching Anymore*, on-stage (2) during his "topical songs" period in the mid 1960s, and in Canada (3) toward the end of the decade. The *Rehearsals For Retirement* LP (4) of 1968 featured a mock tombstone, an eerie portent of Ochs's death eight years later.

| 1 | 2 | | 3 |

| | | 4 | |

Phil Ochs pictured (3) in the late 1960s. A composite picture (1) has Allen Ginsberg (left) and Ochs (right) wearing the same gold suit: Ginsberg at the Ochs memorial concert in 1976, Ochs pictured in 1970. Ochs had reinvented himself as a Che Guevara/Elvis Presley hybird (4) for this *Greatest Hits* album of 1970. Ochs (2, fourth from left) with Melanie, Bob Dylan, Dave Van Ronk and Arlo Guthrie at a Chile benefit concert in 1974, the first time that Ochs and Dylan had appeared on stage together since falling out nearly a decade before.

TOM RAPP

Three line-ups of Tom Rapp's Pearls Before Swine: the original band (2) in 1967 consisted of Lane Lederer and Roger Crissinger (standing, left to right), Rapp (seated) and Wayne Harley (kneeling); in 1971 (1) Gordon Hayes, Jon Tooker, Mike Krawitz and Rapp (left to right); and in 1973 (5) Rapp, Art Ellis and Bill Rollins (left to right). Rapp is pictured (3) in 1975. A handbill (4) announces a week's residency at the Los Angeles Troubadour in 1971.

Tom Rapp in 1998.

TIM ROSE

1		2	3	4
5		6		

Tim Rose in the studio (5) with Al Kooper recording the 'Long Haired Boy' single, performing in a TV studio (1), and posing for a publicity shot (2), all around 1968. Rose in 1972 (3) from the photo-shoot for his fourth album, on-stage in 1999 (4) during his comeback, and adopting a macho pose for the sleeve of his debut album (6) released in 1967.

TOM RUSH

1 2 3

4

Tom Rush at the start of his career in the early 1960s, pictured on the British release of his second album (1) and on a reissue (4). Two Elektra shots from later in the decade, one taken on-stage (2), the other (3) from the photo-session for *The Circle Game* LP.

TOM RUSH

An ad (2) for Tom Rush's eponymous first Columbia album, released in 1970, along with two shots from the same session (3, 5). Rush around the time of his *Ladies Love Outlaws* album of 1974 (1, 4), his last for Columbia, and pictured in the 1990s (6).

DAVID ACKLES

CHAPTER 1

Times change, times change I know,
But it sure goes slow
Down river
When you're locked away.

FROM 'DOWN RIVER' BY DAVID ACKLES, *WEA International Inc 1968*

By 1975 David Ackles was without a record deal, and would never make another LP. Yet only three years earlier he had released *American Gothic*, an album that was acclaimed by the London *Sunday Times* and *The Los Angeles Free Press* among others as heralding a whole new direction in popular music.

When Phil Collins appeared on *Desert Island Discs*, the British radio programme on which celebrities choose records they would take with them if they were marooned on a desert island, he chose a song called 'Down River' by little-known American singer-songwriter David Ackles. Many years earlier Elton John had also expressed his admiration, describing himself as the number one Ackles fan.

The respect of such mainstream artists fosters the expectation that Ackles himself must have been the writer of slick, palatable, radio-friendly piano ballads. Ackles did indeed write piano ballads, but his songs about prostitution, religious doubt, racism and divorce were not destined for the radio playlists.

The music of David Ackles remains a well kept secret among a small group of devotees. These include Elvis Costello and Elektra boss Jac Holzman in addition to Collins and John, as well as scattered enthusiasts of the musically esoteric. Collectively they are a disparate bunch. Mainstream chart regulars, an admired practitioner of literate songwriting, a music mogul of perceptive taste and judgement, and fans who probably don't have Phil Collins records in their collections. Taken together they point to something unclassifiable in the work of Ackles.

Ackles the man proves to be as hard to categorise as his music. He signed his first recording contract when he had turned 30, was always reluctant to tour, and never embraced the rock'n'roll lifestyle. He was a happily married family man. He retained throughout his life the Christian faith passed to him by his parents. He was successful in many other fields of endeavour, and as far as the music business was concerned he was always an outsider. His story is one of an uncomfortable shifting between the hope of mainstream success and cult status – and ultimately of not fitting into either category.

David Ackles was born in Rock Island, Illinois, the heart of the American Midwest, on February 20th 1937. "Not a bad place for an incipient songwriter to get a start,"[1] he said later. He came from a well-established showbusiness tradition. His mother, who was born in the UK, came from a line of music-hall performers, while his father was an accomplished amateur musician. As a young child Ackles formed a vaudeville duet with his sister, and later acted in a series of b-movies about Rusty The Dog in the late 1940s. His film career came to a premature end at the age of 12 or 13 when his voice broke and he started to grow a moustache.

Ackles was never wholly caught up in the folk revival that entranced the likes of Tom Rush and Phil Ochs, but the vaudeville duet with his sister did later mutate into a folk duet. "[We sang] the most obscure folksongs we could find," he said. "The more obscure they were, the more people liked them."[2] However, this was a dalliance and not a defining rite of passage, American folk music simply becoming one of many forms he absorbed into the eclectic style of his musical maturity, albeit an important one. Much later, Ackles said: "You must tap into the roots of your music – if you don't know the earliest songs of your people, you won't be in the continuum."[3] And for Ackles, "roots" meant more than just folk music.

In his late teens, Ackles went to study English Literature at the University of Southern California, and for a further year in Edinburgh, Scotland. After graduating he spent the rest of his 20s supporting himself with a number of odd jobs, including private detective, security guard and circus roustabout, all the while continuing to work irregularly in theatre and TV. This period was later romanticised in an Elektra press release for his first album, and as a result Ackles endured questions from journalists for years about his early exploits. He also began composing seriously – musicals, ballet scores and choral pieces. These early experiences and enthusiasms were to leave a mark on his songwriting, and helped form a distinctively theatrical singing style.

His prevailing creative ambitions, nurtured during this period, were directed toward stage musicals, or "musical theatre" as he preferred to describe it. His widow, Janice Vogel-Ackles, says:

"His ultimate goal when he was younger was to write, produce, direct, design the sets, do the music, and star in his work. And he could have done it. That's where his heart was."[4]

It was an unusual goal for someone who would soon sign to one of the leading counter-culture rock/folk labels of the 1960s. And Ackles's career ambitions as a singer were non-existent at this point. He said in 1998: "From earliest childhood, one of my ambitions was to be a songwriter. I had others, of course, but songwriting was the dominant goal. But a recording artist? Not on your life!"[5]

One of his early songs was 'Blue River'. It was about the Watts race riots in LA, and had at some point been considered for Cher. In 1967 it came to the attention of Elektra producer David Anderle, an old schoolfriend of Ackles. Anderle was impressed. What exactly happened next has passed into a hazy realm of half-remembered fact – even contemporary accounts differ – but it seems certain that Ackles very quickly followed up this initial interest by playing Anderle a number of other songs. Anderle brought Ackles and his songs to the attention of Elektra president Jac Holzman. Ackles was soon signed to Elektra as a staff songwriter.

Elektra at this time was in a period of transition, moving beyond its folk-based repertoire to sign rock acts like Love and The Doors, while many of the label's roster of singer-songwriters such as Tom Rush were broadening their influences beyond the original folk-blues template. It was the ideal home for Ackles's peculiar brand of musical diversity.

After a few months Holzman told Ackles he should sing his own songs. "My intention was to have lots of other, much better singers record my songs," Ackles said. "Alas, it was not to be. I believe the truth is that Jac Holzman couldn't interest any other singers on his label in recording my stuff, so was forced into offering that chance to me. I had an album released before I had ever performed solo in public."[6] Despite these misgivings about his abilities as a singer, he was delighted to be a part of Elektra's highly regarded stable of singer-songwriters, which at the time included Tom Rush, Tim Buckley and Fred Neil. "I thought myself lucky to be among them, such a truly gifted bunch. It certainly motivated me to want to do my best."[7]

> **"I had an album released before I had ever performed in public."**

After an unproductive and aborted first attempt at recording with an orchestral arranger, singer/pianist Ackles went into the studio with producers David Anderle and Russ Miller, engineer Bruce Botnick, and a group of experienced musicians who were establishing themselves as the Elektra house-band. Michael Fonfara (organ), Danny Weiss (guitar), Douglas Hastings (guitar), Jerry Penrod (bass) and John Keliehor (percussion) were already veterans from the likes of Iron Butterfly (Weiss and Penrod) and Electric Flag (Fonfara), while Hastings surfaced briefly in Buffalo Springfield. They later formed the nucleus of Rhinoceros, making two disappointing albums for Elektra. Fonfara, whose wandering, melodic organ style gave the band's sound much of its distinctive identity, also played later with Lou Reed.

David Ackles appeared in 1968. Its sleeve was one of many classic creations by the Elektra designer William S Harvey, and showed an out-of-focus Ackles gazing through a cracked windowpane – an appropriately obscure image. In 1971 it was re-issued and re-titled as *The Road To Cairo*, after one of its better known songs, and featured a more traditional portrait photograph on the album cover, apparently because the record company thought that potential purchasers needed to see Ackles as a "personality".

This first album was to prove the most immediately accessible and conventional of his records. That said, there are songs here that hint at his later, more challenging style, and could only have been written by him – notably 'His Name Is Andrew', more of which later. The piano, by Ackles, and the drums anchor the band, with Fonfara's organ providing much of the texture and melodic detail, and the bass tending to provide further melodic interest rather than rhythmic underpinning. Hastings's heavily reverb'd and semi-improvised guitar playing is at times reminiscent of Lee Underwood's contributions to Tim Buckley's contemporaneous recordings.

Ackles said of the recording process: "There were some vocals that we went back and added later – it was a combination of both live and overdubbing – but all of the instrumentation you hear from the group was done at the moment."[8] The performances were loose and relaxed, at times to the point of sounding under-rehearsed, as on the out-of-time re-entry after the pause at the end of 'The Road To Cairo'.

The album was an assured songwriting debut, with none of the derivative filler material so prevalent on albums of the era. 'The Road To Cairo', the opener, is one of the record's highlights. A slow blues-based rocker, it tells the tale of an Ackles archetype: the hitchhiking drifter who yearns for home but shies away when given the opportunity to return. It was a near hit for Julie Driscoll and the Brian Auger Trinity (the follow-up to their big UK hit 'This Wheel's On Fire') but their version sounds politely restrained compared to the ravaged original. Nonetheless it did serve to raise Ackles's profile in the UK.

'Down River' is a fine narrative ballad distinguished by a definitive fade-out when the drums and lead guitar join in for the last 50 seconds and Ackles wails rather tunelessly in the background. A momentarily discordant organ resolves into an Al Kooper-style high melodic run, effecting a powerful evocation of the stoical central character, a recently released prisoner who discovers his ex-love has married his friend.

This, like most of Ackles's songs, should be understood primarily as the work of a dramatist, despite being written in the first person. "The songs are autobiographical to the extent that any writer has to draw on the experience of his or her own life," said Ackles. "Certainly emotionally they are, in the particulars. But I draw the line at that. There are some things that I could tell you are true, and some are not, and I don't care to make the distinction."[9] On another occasion he said: "I think anyone who writes has the privilege of translating their feelings into a different framework."[10] This tendency to avoid directly autobiographical or confessional songs only serves to emphasise his elusiveness.

'His Name Is Andrew' has divided Ackles aficionados and critics. For some the six-minute torrent of swirling organ and profoundly pessimistic lyrics concerning "Andrew's" loss of faith and stoic endurance is all rather heavy handed. For others it represents Ackles in all his unique, grandiose splendour. Certainly it is an unusual theme for a "rock" record. Only Scott Walker's 'Seventh Seal' springs to mind as a roughly contemporary comparison, tackling so intensely the themes of faith, doubt and mortality. It's an early example of how willing Ackles was to tackle serious, adult subjects in pop songs.

Themes of spirituality and religion recur throughout his work. "I come from a very strong, almost doctrinaire Christian background," he said, "having been raised – God help me – a Presbyterian. It has resulted in a lot of questioning of values as interpreted by those who think themselves in the know, in positions of power within the church. I'm still fascinated by it."[11]

Notwithstanding the tendency to question and doubt, Ackles remained a regular churchgoer throughout his life. "David was a very spiritual person," says Vogel-Ackles, "but going to church, thinking of things spiritually and having a close relationship with God was very important to him. He was always a religious person, but not fanatically; he didn't have a religious conversion. Because of all this, when he was in the recording business he didn't really get into the lifestyle, and I think it made him suspect to some degree."[12]

The album closes with the plaintive ballad 'Be My Friend', organist Fonfara contributing a magnificently expressive Hammond solo over the fade-out as the piano and guitar tumble in and out of time.

Elektra made significant efforts to promote the album, rewarded with a positive critical response but modest sales. This combination became a hallmark of Ackles's career. Two singles were pulled from the album for release in the UK, the first of which, 'Down River', had a French-language version of 'The Road To Cairo', retitled 'La Route A Chicago', as the b-side. Kenny Everett, reviewing the single in *Disc & Music Echo*, presciently wrote: "This will probably only sell seven copies in the whole country."[13] The second single paired the Brechtian 'Laissez Faire' with 'Blue Ribbons'. Neither release troubled the charts.

"Elektra Records were kind enough to put together a promotional tour to various radio stations," Ackles said later, "and out of that came some additional airplay and exposure. Of course, all of that helps – it all adds up. But I was so green and new to the business I just thought, well, that's standard, that's the way it's done. I had no idea that Elektra really was putting itself out in order to make this possible. Now, in retrospect, I think what an ungrateful little asshole I must have been at the time!

"The album was pretty well received. I got a lot of attention that I was not expecting at all, having never performed in public. I was stunned by the fact that people were actually going out and spending their money on this. Not that I thought it wasn't a product worth spending money on. But I felt that they didn't know who I was from anyone, and I was quite gratified that they were willing to go out and buy it based on very little airplay and, mostly, word of mouth."[14]

Although the debut album failed to achieve a hoped-for commercial breakthrough, it had succeeded in gaining the respect of other artists. Some of the early songs by Ackles were covered by contemporaries: 'Down River' by Spooky Tooth; 'The Road To Cairo' by Julie Driscoll and the Brian Auger Trinity; 'His Name Is Andrew' by Martin Carthy. None of these cover versions sold particularly well. Nonetheless, there was a widely held view that Elektra had found themselves a notable new talent. A late developer, maybe, and someone who would need time to win over a large audience, but a significant new voice all the same.

> "I had no idea Elektra put itself out to make this possible."

Ackles was musically ambitious. For his second album, released a year after the first, he was given a much bigger budget. An initial attempt to record the songs with producer/organist Al Kooper in a stripped-back country-rock style had failed. For the second attempt Fred Myrow, another old college friend of Ackles, was drafted in to do arrangements. Russ Miller alone got the production credits, although Ackles recalled that David Anderle was certainly present as well. Some 22 musicians appeared in the list of credits, guitarist Lonnie Mack being the best known, though only Hastings survived from the first album.

Subway To The Country was released in 1969. The sound was lush and Myrow's arrangements inventive and sophisticated. This musical finesse was to become typical of Ackles's later work. Compared to the first album there are fewer standout tracks to immediately grip the listener, but the songwriting is mature, literate and consistently excellent throughout. It provided further confirmation of his ability – hinted at on the first album – of throwing in an unexpected chord or tempo change to take a hitherto apparently conventional song into a wholly different direction. Lyrically, Ackles was broadening his range, dealing with such unfashionable and difficult themes as mental illness ('Inmates Of The Institution') and child abuse ('Candy Man').

Myrow's arrangements were the perfect foil for the unusual songs, containing elements of film-soundtrack music and moody orchestral experimentation. The introduction of 'Inmates Of The Institution', for example, is reminiscent of a Bernard Herrmann score for a Hitchcock movie. Indeed, Myrow was later to forge a career as a soundtrack composer.

'The Mainline Saloon' is a worthy addition to the inglorious canon of addiction songs in popular music. Ackles barks out the twisted poetry over the backing of a shambling bar band, with tapes of background conversation and clinking glasses thrown into the mix for extra effect. As the song ends, a smattering of unenthusiastic applause ripples from the speakers – unfortunately all too often the singer's real experience when he played live.

'Out On The Road', a gospel-styled epic, is one of the most conventional songs that Ackles wrote – but features his most unhinged recorded vocal performance. The dense arrangement teeters on the verge of chaos, sounding like all 22 musicians credited on the album were joining in. Ackles's voice was mixed quite low throughout the record, and here he roars to be heard above the mêlée through a series of false crescendos before managing to move up a gear for the final repeated chorus. It is a performance of searing dynamic intensity.

The title track of *Subway To The Country* was released as a single. It's a touching tale of a father wanting to take his son away from the grime of the city; melodically and structurally it bears comparison with the orchestral pop compositions of Jimmy Webb. As a song it would have sat comfortably in the charts, yet with Ackles's rough, ragged and guttural vocal it lacked commercial gloss, and no radio-friendly pop artist picked it up.

Again Elektra put some effort into pushing the record. A free promotional single was included with copies of the album featuring Ackles talking about the genesis of the title track, backed by the song itself. Ackles went on the road in the US to good reviews, although he was never happy touring and struggled to translate his songs effectively into a live setting. Having no band of his own he either played solo or, as during his visits to the UK, with a pick-up band of session players. Neither option provided the means for him to recreate the arrangements that gave so much dynamic variance to his recordings. Nonetheless, he supported Joni Mitchell and in August 1970 played at The Troubadour in Los Angeles with Elton John on the occasion of the British singer's first appearance in the States.

Speaking a few years later, John said: "I was topping the bill, but that seemed unbelievable to me. There was no way that anyone could have convinced me that I should be above David Ackles, but they explained to me that he was almost unknown there. I was flabbergasted, but during that week I discovered that people like Ackles and David Blue are disregarded in LA. They're much better known in England. David Ackles was brilliant. I made a point of watching him every night. To see the audience just chatting away while he was singing these lovely songs just tore me apart."[15] This connection with the British singer songwriter was to play an important part in the next phase in Ackles's career.

Despite Elektra's best efforts *Subway To The Country*, like its predecessor, failed to sell in significant quantities. But Holzman kept faith. Ackles was now at the peak of his confidence as a songwriter. In no hurry to record a follow-up to *Subway*, he spent a full two years conceiving a sweepingly ambitious song-cycle about contemporary American life, and this would become his third album. For part of that period, between September 1971 and July 1972, Ackles relocated to the village of Wargrave in Berkshire, England. Ackles said later that the geographical distance from his subject matter gave him a unique clarity of perspective.

As would be expected of a man who had spent most of his adult life on the West Coast of America, Ackles struggled with the British winter, but otherwise he enjoyed living in the UK. His soon-to-be wife, Janice Vogel, joined him in January 1972 and she too was excited by the prospect of living in England. Reflecting on this period in 1998, he said, "I was fortunate enough to do a couple of live concerts, and I did a club date. I did several television shows, including *The Old Grey Whistle Test* [on January 4th 1972], and had a lot of fun doing them: I got to meet some terrific people. As a matter of fact my wife and I wished that I had been able to secure jobs in England so that we could have stayed there."[16]

American Gothic was his best-selling album, and briefly entered the lower reaches of the American charts. On release in 1972 it was greeted with ecstatic reviews on both sides of the Atlantic. Derek Jewell, writing in *The Sunday Times* in Britain, described it as heralding a new direction in popular music. *Rolling Stone* in its review described Ackles as "an important artist whose work eludes categorisation".[17] *Melody Maker* said the record was a classic. Chris Van Hess writing in *The Los Angeles Free Press* thought it a work on a par with *Sgt Pepper*, commenting: "My only real fear is that I may have built it up too much and caused too much expectation."[18] Ackles was to complain later that the review, along with Jewell's and others, had done exactly that.

American Gothic was produced by Elton John's lyricist Bernie Taupin, and was recorded at IBC studios in London. The immensely complex orchestral arrangements were written by Ackles himself, the orchestra conducted by Robert Kirby, also known for his string arrangements for Nick Drake. It was largely recorded and mixed in just two weeks, although preparations, particularly the writing of arrangements, were drawn out.

Lyrically, the album is a state-of-the-Union message from Ackles. Although never a protest singer, he was unafraid of tackling social and political issues. What set him apart from many other writers of the era who tackled similar subjects was his ability to approach the material with the questioning, non-judgemental mind of the dramatist rather than the sloganeering, banner-waving indignation of the protestor. Prostitution and alcoholism ('American Gothic'), divorce ('Waiting For The Moving Van'), Vietnam ('Ballad Of The Ship Of State') and racism ('Blues For Billie Whitecloud') all come under his perceptive, cynical and sensitive scrutiny. Scattered between these "issue" songs are a few wistful ballads populated by his usual cast of rootless drifters and dreamers, balancing between hope and regret.

"To see them chatting away while he sang just tore me apart."

'Family Band', a brief hymnal singalong that starts side two of the original vinyl issue of the album, was one of the few obviously autobiographical songs Ackles wrote. It has been mistaken as a parody, but the story of singing hymns in church on a Sunday evening, "when my dad played bass, and mom played the drums, and I played piano, and Jesus sang the song," was just how it was for the young Ackles.

The defining moment of *American Gothic* is the epic ten-minute 'Montana Song'. A poetic monologue about a man's mythic journey to the Montana of his forbears, it is also a step back in time to a lost rural idyll. As he does throughout the album, Ackles sings these lyrics in the carefully enunciated, almost "announced" style of the stage musical, but in a smoker's baritone that is more blues than Broadway. The song borrows musical themes from Aaron Copland's *Appalachian Spring*. It was a strikingly unusual clash of styles, and *Rolling Stone* said: "It has almost no relation to rock'n'roll and a lot more to do with musical theatre."[19] This comment defined what would become Ackles's dilemma.

American Gothic defied categorisation and easy comparisons. Although traces of soul, rock, folk, gospel, blues and country can be found throughout, the songs go well beyond the normally accepted boundaries of "pop music". Avant-garde and classical influences pervade Ackles's elaborate arrangements, and his background in musical theatre casts its shadow over everything.

Echoes of Gershwin, Brecht & Weill, even Gilbert & Sullivan, are as present as those of Dylan, Leonard Cohen and the other obvious singer-songwriters. Many of the songs sound like they could have been written with some dark Broadway show in mind. Yet despite all the disparate elements, Ackles achieved a unity as well as a strong sense of identity on *American Gothic*. But he didn't find a big audience.

Most considered *American Gothic* his masterpiece, and yet it is also the most inaccessible of his records. It's an album easier to admire than to like. The songs, singing, arranging and playing mark the apotheosis of the musical theatre style that Ackles had been nurturing for so long. It is a tradition that has rarely found its way into the mainstream of pop/rock music, before or since, and while Ackles continued to incorporate more conventional influences, it came to dominate much of his work. It was not widely understood, and so his songs, as they became more rooted in musical theatre, became less attractive to other performers. It is certainly hard to imagine anyone covering 'Montana Song'.

Deprived of the exposure and earning potential of cover versions, at least after the initial flurry from the first album, and with his own records garnering the usual response of puzzled admiration, Ackles was at a dead end. Although *American Gothic* was his biggest seller, in a sense it marked the beginning of the end of his recording career.

After *American Gothic* Ackles left Elektra by mutual consent – and while "mutual consent" is often a euphemism, in this case it appears to be genuine. Elektra had funded three significant albums, including the very costly *American Gothic*, and their artist, although highly regarded, was still only a modest seller. Ackles was considerably in debt to Elektra, having gone over budget on all three records, so the company was clearly unable in the circumstances to fund and adequately promote a fourth album.

When Ackles went to the Elektra office to announce that he thought it was time to move on, he got the sense that they had been thinking the same for some time. There were no hard feelings. Ackles commented in 1998, "I remain enormously grateful to Jac Holzman for everything he did personally on my behalf. I don't believe anything more could have been done to make me a commercial success. It just wasn't on the cards."[20]

Clive Davis, head of Columbia at the time, had admired Ackles for some years. When he made an offer to the newly out-of-contract Ackles, a deal was quickly agreed. Despite having recorded three albums with no real commercial success, he was granted a new start at a major label.

The spectacular reviews for *American Gothic* placed Ackles under considerable pressure. Having been credited with discovering a new direction in popular music, he felt that the burden of living up to those expectations was more than he could reasonably be expected to bear. He talked in interviews in the mid 1970s of experiencing something like writer's block – every idea he came up with he discarded, thinking "this is not as good as *American Gothic*". In the end he resolved to ignore the pressure, side-stepping the issue by going off at a tangent and scaling down his sound. The resulting album, released in 1973, was *Five And Dime*.

Made largely at Ackles's home on a four-track recorder, it is, for him, a modest and simple record. As well as writing and arranging the album, he produced it, gathering together a large group of friends and associates to assist. The relaxed atmosphere and freedom from the constraints of time contributed to the warmth of the record. It was the first of his albums to come in on time and under budget. *Five And Dime* is, artistically and commercially, the least significant of his albums. It lacks the doomy intensity of *David Ackles* and *Subway To The Country* or the daring musical scope of *American Gothic*. Even so, it is another work of consistently high standards.

It is a softer, gentler, more personal and often happier collection of songs, perhaps reflecting a new-found contentment following his marriage to Vogel in December 1972. The most obvious manifestation of this new mood is the light-hearted, ironic 'Surf's Down', featuring the inimitable Dean Torrance from Jan & Dean on falsetto backing vocals. It was a gentle poke at the surfers of the previous decade – who surprisingly had included Ackles in their number – and who had grown up but not moved on. Musically, the song is a plausible pastiche of early Beach Boys and Jan & Dean records, with Ackles impressively transforming his seasoned, throaty and theatrical voice into a suitably nasal adolescent whine.

'Aberfan', the story of the Welsh mining disaster when a slag-heap collapsed on a school, is the album's most complex and challenging piece. It harks back to the mood of *American Gothic* and so appears out of place in these more humble surroundings. The lyrical sentiments, although worthy, sound clumsy, but the song is distinguished by a sinister, suspenseful arrangement. It had originally been a much longer song, in excess of ten minutes, and included a whole section about the My Lai atrocities in Vietnam. Ackles had perceived a common thread of official indifference to human suffering in the two episodes, but decided that the song worked better in its edited form.

The closing track, 'Postcard', is a typically wistful ballad apparently inspired by the time Ackles stayed in England while working on *American Gothic*. It conjures up the image of a man at a piano in a club, in the small hours, and foreshadows Tom Waits in his more sentimental mode.

Before the release of *Five And Dime* Clive Davis, the singer's champion and ally at Columbia, moved on from the company. Nobody stepped forward to support Ackles. This was a catastrophic blow for his career. He was stranded in an environment where he was either misunderstood or ignored. The contract was honoured and the record released in 1973, but only in the US. It received virtually no promotion, and the few copies that did surface were pressed on wafer-thin vinyl. Not surprisingly, *Five And Dime* sank without trace. Ackles spoke at the time about his frustration at Columbia: they were unwilling to finance a tour because the record wasn't selling, yet failed to acknowledge their responsibility to promote it to make it sell. Sadly this is now a forgotten record, and even many Ackles fans are unaware of its existence.

> **"I took the negativity as more of a criticism than I should have."**

Five And Dime was to be his final album. Columbia did not take up his option. "I just found it hard to get a deal," he said. "Part of that, I would have to say, was my own doing. There was so little support that I thought to myself, 'Maybe this isn't what you're intended to do.' Of course I should have been more aggressive, but in retrospect I took the negativity as more of a criticism than I should have."[21]

He continued as a staff songwriter for Warner Brothers with whom he had a publishing contract. He was paid a retainer to attend weekly songwriters' meetings where he was instructed to write to order for artists as diverse as Bette Midler and Three Dog Night. Many of these songs were recorded in the Warner studios, sometimes with then demo-singer Kim Carnes. None was ever recorded by the artist it was intended for, and these songs remain unheard.

Although it wasn't until the end of the 1970s that Ackles finally backed out of the music business, there were indications even before *Five And Dime* that his enthusiasm for the life was wearing thin. Way back in 1968, at the very start of his career, when most people would be brimming with enthusiasm, he was sounding a note of caution. "I don't want to get tied down to doing things that don't bring me pleasure. I don't want to do the endless round of one-nighters," he said back then. "It's the same with recording. I don't want the situation where it's a case of having to have something out by such-and-such a date – I simply can't work that way."[22] As well as being clear that he was in no way inclined to compromise artistically, he didn't really need to make a career out of making records. He certainly had plenty of other skills. Although continuing to write songs for his own amusement, he would move into other areas of work.

In the early 1980s a drunk driver hit his car. Ackles was badly injured and in a wheelchair for six months. His left arm was almost severed, his left thigh-bone virtually pushed out through his back. For 18 months he could not play the piano at all, and the nerves in his arm never recovered enough for him to play for very long. He was in considerable pain, probably for the rest of his life. He recalled his wife, after the accident, standing outside the operating theatre shouting, "Don't cut off his arm! He's a piano player!"

Throughout the 1980s Ackles moved into a number of professional fields beyond music. For four years he worked for the University of Southern California as Dean of Business Programs in the College of Continuing Education. He wrote speculative TV scripts with a writing partner, some of which were sold, though most were not filmed. One that did reach the screen was *Word Of Honor*, a TV movie starring Karl Malden and featuring a young John Malkovich. Ackles was also Executive Director of a fund-raising body for seven years, a position he held alongside his teaching commitments. He was an especially good teacher, popular with students for his verve and energy.

Ackles was diagnosed with lung cancer in the early 1990s and a part of his left lung was removed. Throughout the pain of this illness and his earlier accident he rarely complained. "David was very optimistic about everything," says Vogel-Ackles. "He almost never revealed if he was in the depths of depression, although I'm not really sure if he didn't have those depths. He was always looking forward. There were times when he was angry about physical limitations, but that would last literally for a few hours at most." Martin Aston, writing for *Q* magazine in 1994, was typical of the journalists who tracked Ackles down to his California ranch in these later years and were struck by the dissonance between the man and his music. How could Ackles, whose records were so intense, introspective and grandiose, be such a modest, cheerful and affable man?

"Stuff in the vaults? You bet!"

The reissue of the first three Ackles albums in 1993 had prompted a modest upsurge of interest in his brief but impeccable recording career. As well as Aston's piece in *Q*, articles appeared for several years afterward in *Mojo*, *Folk Roots*, *Ptolemaic Terrascope* and the *NME*. Ackles mentioned that he was talking to Warners about a possible new album. It seemed as if he might be acquiring the belated cult status enjoyed by so many of his contemporaries. Yet this flurry of interest soon blew itself out. The three albums were deleted again, and no new Warners album materialised. In 2000, three Elektra albums were reissued once more, although the Columbia album is yet to make it to CD.

Ackles was delighted that there was a modest resurgence of interest in his records, but at the same time gave the impression that he would not be overly bothered if they continued to languish in obscurity. Although he was proud of the records, they were not the defining features of his life, and his sense of identity wasn't tied up in them. He retained, though, a palpable love of music and the creative process, for which he had found other outlets. In an interview in 1997 about directing Brecht & Weill's *Threepenny Opera* at the University of Southern California, he talked about "the pure joy of creating in this wonderful playpen". His last major project as a writer was a musical called *Sister Aimee*, based on the life of Aimee Semple McPherson, a notorious evangelist of the 1920s. It has yet to be publicly performed.

In late 1997 the cancer returned. Ackles, much diminished physically by the illness, survived for 18 months, remaining optimistic and uncomplaining. He died on March 2nd 1999, shortly after his 62nd birthday. He had not released a record for a quarter of a century and his profile had always been low even when he was active. Yet his death did attract some attention in the UK.

Obituaries appeared in *The Times*, *The Guardian* and *The Independent* newspapers as well as the music press. He was hailed as a unique chronicler-in-song of America, a writer who forged musical poetry out of the mythology of everyday American life.

Shortly before he died, Ackles was enthused by the signs of interest in his work in Britain and began to plan a release of previously unavailable songs. He referred to an extensive archive of such material from which he was able to draw. "Stuff in the vaults? You bet! A lot of it is with demo singers, some with just me and the piano, a few with full orchestra. As with any performer, there are cuts which just didn't fit the concept when the album was put together. These few still don't make up a coherent collection of songs, but maybe one day… ."[23] This project was cut short by his death, although his family plans to release the material in some form in the future.

Of all the stories of disappointment over nearly half a century of pop music, that of David Ackles is one of the most frustrating. His commercial failure can't be put down to self-destructive behaviour or unfulfilled potential, and if anyone deserved commercial success by virtue of talent alone it was Ackles. Yet his career as a singer-songwriter was shortlived and prematurely curtailed. Among the artists covered in this book, Ackles's recorded output is uniquely satisfying. There were no collections of cover versions dressed up as sophisticated interpretations, no tired blues-rock work-outs, no retreading of the same old themes, no terminal lapses in quality control.

The limitations of the term "singer-songwriter" are rarely more obvious than when applied to David Ackles. Like his one-time Elektra colleague Tim Buckley, Ackles quickly transcended the usual parameters associated with the métier. Both were too gifted for the narrow confines of pop/rock music, and when they pursued their respective artistic visions they each created work too esoteric for popular tastes. Both thrived on musical complexity – unlike, say, Tim Hardin, whose best work was a distillation down to bare essentials. And more than is usual on singer-songwriter records, and pop records in general, each made recordings where the arrangements are an integral part of the artistic package and worthy of attention in themselves.

Ackles may never acquire the widespread cult status afforded to Buckley. A happy marriage and a balanced, optimistic personality with widespread achievements in other lines of work aren't the stuff of which romantic myths are formed. Likewise, Buckley's experimental music was dominated by characteristics that appeal to a rock audience – it was wild, blissed-out, despairing, frenzied and apparently intuitive and unplanned. Ackles, on the other hand, as he reached artistic maturity increasingly tended toward music that was formal, controlled and intellectual. But it was no less radical.

[1] Author's interview April 24th 1998
[2] *Beat Instrumental* November 1968
[3] *Folk Roots* December 1996
[4] Author's interview July 1st 2000
[5] Author's interview April 24th 1998
[6] Author's interview April 24th 1998
[7] Author's interview April 24th 1998
[8] Author's interview April 24th 1998
[9] Author's interview April 24th 1998
[10] *Fat Angel* date unknown
[11] Author's interview April 24th 1998
[12] Author's interview July 1st 2000
[13] *Disc & Music Echo* September 14th 1968
[14] Author's interview April 24th 1998
[15] Gerald Newman & Joe Bivona *Elton John* (NEL1976)
[16] Author's interview April 24th 1998
[17] *Rolling Stone* September 14th 1972
[18] *Los Angeles Free Press* volume 9 number 20, May 19th 1972
[19] *Rolling Stone* September 14th 1972
[20] Author's interview April 24th 1998
[21] *Ptolemaic Terrascope* September 1994
[22] *Beat Instrumental* November 1968
[23] Author's interview April 24th 1998

DAVID BLUE

CHAPTER 2

I am the poet who sings of love,
I am the man who cries "never enough",
My bed is broken,
My god forsaken,
I dream of the angels I have cleverly taken.

FROM 'TROUBADOUR SONG' BY DAVID BLUE, *Warner Brothers Music 1973*

David Blue had been writing songs for a decade when The Eagles covered his 'Outlaw Man' in 1973, but was unable to build on this success and remained a minor figure for the rest of his career. After his death in 1982 Blue was all but forgotten, his music strangely overlooked by the otherwise diligent record-reissue industry.

David Blue is remembered, if at all, as a man in Bob Dylan's shadow, clinging to his coat tails, a second-rate copy. Tim Rose recalls Blue coming into Greenwich Village "an angry guy ... he would never be Dylan, and that really pissed him off."[1] This persistent reputation is largely built on the foundation of Blue's first album, released in 1966. "I sounded like [Dylan]," Blue admitted later, "and didn't have any idea what I was doing."[2]

Superficially, the idea of Blue as a Dylan clone seems accurate enough. He did admire Dylan. He was influenced by Dylan. He even looked like Dylan. But as Blue's career unfolded, he revealed more of his own identity. He shed the derivative stylistic trappings that dominate his first recordings and began to make music of sufficient interest to merit reappraisal as more than a mere copyist.

Of all the artists featured here, Blue is the most obscure, the most forgotten. He warrants only a few paragraphs in even the most comprehensive of rock encyclopedias. His back catalogue is unavailable at the time of writing. No luminary of modern song – a Nick Cave or an Elvis Costello – has come forward to champion his cause. He seems destined forever to remain a footnote, an also-ran from Greenwich Village, a bit-player in The Rolling Thunder Revue.

Even when his career reached its modest heights in the early 1970s, Blue was still an elusive figure on both sides of the Atlantic, rarely warranting more than the most cursory press coverage. Tracing the course of his life and career often requires piecing together fragments gleaned from the biographies of Dylan and Phil Ochs, with both of whom Blue maintained close friendships from the early 1960s.

Yet Blue released seven albums between 1966 and 1976, all of which featured collaborators of the calibre of Dylan, Joni Mitchell, Graham Nash, Ry Cooder and various members of The Eagles. He was a well-known and well-liked figure in the Greenwich Village of the early 1960s and the West Coast country-rock scene of the 1970s. He was also one of very few rock musicians to make a decent effort at an acting career, an occupation that for him would supersede music altogether in the late 1970s.

David Blue was born Stuart David Cohen in Providence, Rhode Island, on February 18th 1941. He called himself David Cohen, or S. David Cohen, until the early 1960s, and occasionally thereafter. (We will use the name David Blue throughout this chapter, and the rest of the book, except when referring to circumstances and events when he reverted to his real name.) Little is known about his early years, but around 1958 he joined the Navy for a brief spell, and he apparently spent much of his late adolescence and early adulthood travelling around the US. At some point near the turn of the decade he briefly appeared on the Boston/Cambridge folk circuit as a member of the shortlived Unicorn Jook Band, along with folk artist Eric Andersen.

In 1960 Blue gravitated to New York City's Greenwich Village, then a magnet for the disaffected bohemian youth of America. Like Tim Hardin, Blue arrived in New York nurturing ambitions to act but was quickly distracted by the creative energy surrounding the folk musicians playing in a small group of coffee shops on Bleecker and MacDougal streets. In 1982 Blue reminisced: "When I came to the Village as a young guy about 20, the first place I went was Washington Square park, and I remember seeing Lightnin' Hopkins sitting by the fountain wearing sunglasses and a pork-pie hat, drinking a little gin and playing some blues. It was really exciting."[3]

In one of those coffee shops, The Gaslight, Blue found employment and a place to stay, washing dishes through the evenings and sleeping there at night. He got a guitar and started to make tunes for the poems he had been scribbling for some time. He met Dylan, Phil Ochs and others, and was encouraged by Dylan as he started writing songs. The relationship between Ochs and Dylan was to become tense at times. Some say Blue was present when Dylan humiliated Ochs by calling him a journalist, not a songwriter, after Ochs had dared to criticise the master's new single. But the friendship between Dylan and Blue remained firm.

And Blue was to play a supporting role in an epochal moment in Dylan's story. "I remember one afternoon we were sitting in the Black Fat Pussycat drinking coffee, and Dylan started writing a song," recalled Blue. "He had his guitar, and he was scribbling away, writing on a piece of paper, and he gave me his guitar and asked me to play various chords while he worked on the words. When he'd finished it we went over to Folk City and Bob played it for Gil Turner, who thought it was fantastic. Then Gil got up on stage and played it for the audience while Bob stood in the shadows at the bar. That song was 'Blowin' In The Wind'."[4]

It is not clear exactly when David Cohen became David Blue, but in 1963 he was using the new name episodically. He said later that the name was Dylan's idea, although Eric Andersen has also been credited with dreaming it up. Whether it was a comment on the morose, doleful characteristics of his music isn't known. But he was David Cohen, not Blue, when his first recordings became available on Elektra's *Singer Songwriter Project* collection in 1965.

Blue believed Elektra had approached him because they were looking for "another Dylan". Alongside contributions from Patrick Sky, Richard Fariña and Bruce Murdoch he had three songs, all original compositions. The best is the good-humoured prototype slacker anthem, 'I Like To Sleep Late In The Morning'. All three betrayed an obvious debt to pre-electric Dylan – as did those of Sky and indeed many others then emerging from Greenwich Village.

Jac Holzman, head of Elektra, thought Cohen showed enough promise to warrant an album of his own, and in 1966 *David Blue* was released – his first recording to appear under the "new" name. It immediately preceded Tim Buckley's first album in the Elektra release schedule. Produced by Arthur Gorson, manager of Tom Rush, Phil Ochs, Eric Andersen as well as Blue, the album was clearly the work of a man in thrall to Dylan's controversial new electric music. As we've already heard, Blue's own analysis is that he didn't know what he was doing when he made the record. And Gorson, while certainly a gifted organiser, had no real experience of recording studios. The album was a disaster, and deserves attention now only as a period curio.

> "Dylan asked me to play chords while he worked on the words to 'Blowin' In The Wind'."

Blue stares from the cover with tousled hair, wearing a corduroy jacket, an archetype of the period's singer-songwriter look. He's backed by guitar, bass, drums and organ, an electric band that tries to reproduce the tumbling, chaotic fluidity of *Highway 61* on the 12 self-penned songs. They do not succeed, more often sounding like garage-band copyists working to a second-generation facsimile of the Dylan blueprint. The organ was a Farfisa or a Vox, not a Hammond, the fuzz guitars sound like The Kingsmen or The Seeds, and Blue's flat drawl has none of Dylan's mesmerising invective. Dylan himself was apparently present at some of the recordings, but the magic didn't rub off.

"Mr Blue is a pretty fair lyricist," said *Broadside* magazine's reviewer. "However, he sets his lyrics to music, and with regard to that talent he is impoverished."[5] This opinion is understandable following a casual listen to the record, but isn't fully justified. Closer attention reveals that some of the songs, such as 'Grand Hotel', were the work of an artist with a latent talent for a confessional style of songwriting, somewhere between Dylan's allusive, post-protest period and Tim Hardin's autobiographical mythology. What was missing from the songs, however, was the spark of genius that ignites the best of Dylan and Hardin. A further problem was that Blue's singing was so flat that the simple but perfectly adequate melodies were often obscured – and this was only exacerbated by the out-of-tune electric guitars.

Blue later hinted darkly at a poor relationship with Elektra, speaking of "trouble in the past" without ever being more specific. A planned follow-up with a band called The American Patrol was recorded but never issued, Blue disowning it almost immediately, and the singer's relationship with Elektra ended.

Blue went to Reprise for his second album, *These 23 Days In September*, released in March 1968. Reprise had extracted Blue from his contract with Elektra by buying up the rights to the American Patrol album, on the condition – insisted on by Blue – that it would not be released. Blue later credited Phil

Ochs with getting him signed to Reprise: apparently Ochs's friend Andy Wickham, an A&R man at Reprise, had been persuaded to put in a good word. Produced by Gabriel Mekler, who also played piano on the record, *These 23 Days In September* was the first released Blue album to feature guitarist/musical-director Bob Rafkin. Rafkin, who had served in the ranks of The American Patrol, became a long-time Blue collaborator.

The album marked a substantial leap forward from Blue's shoddy first LP. Sophisticated interlocking acoustic-guitar-based arrangements prevail. This is particularly evident on the title track, which is one of Blue's best songs. He captures perfectly a mood of helpless despair as he sings about the mental collapse of a wife or girlfriend. There is also a much improved re-working of 'Grand Hotel'. In its general feel and some of the details, *23 Days* is an album close to the bedsit classics that Leonard Cohen produced during the same period. While an improvement, the record did little to establish Blue in the US (and was not released in the UK). Its intense introspection was perhaps out of time with the euphoric cultural mood of the hippie era.

Blue retreated for a while, re-emerging in 1970 as S. David Cohen with an album *Me, S. David Cohen*, again on Reprise, and again only released in the US. It was recorded in Nashville in a three-day session and shared its country influences with roughly contemporaneous work by Dylan, The Byrds and The Flying Burrito Brothers. No backing musicians were credited on this very obscure album, but the sound and feel indicates that the Nashville-based session-group Area Code 615 were contributors.

If *David Blue* was his *Highway 61*, then *Me, S. David Cohen* was *Nashville Skyline*. Aspects of the style matched the Dylan album, though the gap between master and pupil was still apparent. But *Me, S. David Cohen* was certainly a much better album than Blue's debut. Leading with Merle Haggard's 'Mama Tried', many of the songs on this relaxed collection lock into an easy country-rock swing that The Eagles were soon to exploit with great commercial success.

The slower and simpler the song, the better Blue's voice sounded. The more upbeat songs, like 'Me And Patty On The Moon', tend to be suffocated by Blue's tuneless efforts to inject some urgency into the proceedings. The ambitious closing track, 'Sara', merges a lengthy spoken-word introduction with a slow Mexican-influenced country ballad section. It was a more successful attempt to blend poetry with song than Tim Hardin's *Susan Moore* album from the same period.

At some point during 1970 Blue had moved to Los Angeles. He was to stay there for the next decade, and became a regular feature on the party circuit with the country-rock elite. Various members of The Byrds, the Burritos, The Eagles and Crosby Stills & Nash would play on his subsequent recordings. Blue also flirted with heroin. It was a brief liaison which never became the addiction that destroyed Tim Hardin, but it nevertheless dominated Blue's life for a short while.

The *Me* album was virtually ignored, leaving Blue at a low ebb professionally and personally. For the best part of two years he did little apart from lose his contract with Reprise. "Yeah … I was into heroin," he said at the time. "Not a lot, but enough to know how fast it can take you down. One of the songs on the *Stories* album is about a friend who's into the stuff, and another's about my own experiences."[6]

Stories was recorded in 1971 and released on Asylum in 1972. Blue reverted to his adopted name, the use of his real name on *Me* having done nothing for his commercial fortunes. *Stories* was produced by Blue and guitarist Rafkin, with help from Henry Lewy who had engineered sessions for the classic first Flying Burrito Brothers album. Former Burrito Chris Ethridge played bass, and Ry Cooder and Rita Coolidge guested. Most of the eight songs on *Stories* were based on economical acoustic-guitar arrangements. This enabled Blue to softly speak-sing the usual confessional lyrics, an approach that best suited his limited voice. Of these acoustic songs 'Sister Rose' and 'Another One Like Me' are particularly successful, with Blue capturing a mellow groove typical of many singer-songwriter records of the time and bearing comparison with Tom Rush's contemporary work. The drawn-out 'House Of Changing Faces' was Blue's heroin confession song, where he tells of still having "tracks to remind me what life was like, high and wasted, when I wanted to die".[7]

The accordion-based 'Marianne' appears to be a song about the same woman immortalised in the Leonard Cohen classic 'So Long, Marianne', with Blue singing: "I knew her from another song her older poet wrote before."[8] The piano ballad 'Fire In The Morning' benefited from a string arrangement by Jack Nitzsche, but only 'Come On, John', the song about an addict friend, disrupts the mood of what is a fine if unremittingly bleak album. Tellingly, 'Come On, John' is the only full rock-band arrangement on the record, underlining the problem Blue had with singing in such a setting.

Despite the despairing tone of the album, Blue said he wrote and recorded it in a positive frame of mind. The depression of his heroin-taking period was in the past, and the distance allowed him to capture it effectively in song. It was the first time he had made a record with a real sense of commitment and purpose. "If you listen to that record and say 'God, what a downer!' then I've succeeded in doing exactly what I wanted to do," he said. "I realised my effectiveness at communicating emotion through that record, because I could put it on and bring everyone down."[9]

Blue made his first visit to the UK in June 1972, to promote *Stories*. Although still a very minor name with precious little evidence of public interest in his work, he was committed to his career for the first time. He was scheduled to make his debut at a big open-air concert at the Crystal Palace Bowl in south London, but his performance was cancelled just hours before he was due on stage. Poor organisation by the promoters meant that there was simply not room on the schedule for the still virtually unknown Blue. But he was able to complete a small college tour, which he enjoyed. He found British audiences more inclined to sit and pay attention than he was used to. A more common experience for Blue had been struggling to get his laments heard above the bar-room chatter while performing as support to some band in a small American rock club.

Returning from his UK visit in an optimistic mood and wanting to record an "up" album, Blue decided it was time to try working with an electric band again, his first attempt since the American Patrol debacle. So in autumn 1972 Blue went to the San Francisco home-studio of Graham Nash, with Nash producing and a band that included Rafkin, Ethridge, ex-Traffic guitarist Dave Mason and ex-Kaleidoscope multi-instrumentalist David Lindley. *Nice Baby And The Angel* was released by Asylum in June 1973. Blue turned again to the country influences that prevailed on *Me*, although the new record featured more dominant lead electric guitar, by Mason, and a far rockier sound than before. It was the one predominantly electric album that Blue recorded where he manages to sustain consistently high standards. Alongside *Stories* it is his most satisfactory work.

> "I could put my record on and bring everyone down..."

This success was achieved in part by careful use of harmonies to sweeten Blue's voice, no doubt at the instigation of producer Nash. Also, Blue introduced simple, repetitive choruses into some of the songs – a device often absent from his earlier lengthy narratives – which gave them greater pop appeal. One of the more commercial songs, 'Outlaw Man', caught the attention of The Eagles, and they recorded a version with slightly altered lyrics on their *Desperado* album. It became Blue's best-known and biggest earning song. Blue himself released 'Outlaw Man' as a single coupled with one of the two acoustic songs on the album, 'Troubadour Song', written about Leonard Cohen.

Reviews for *Nice Baby* were mixed. Allan Jones wrote in *Melody Maker*: "Presumably there must be something about David Blue that makes all these guys give up their time to play on his album, but after several plays I must say it's eluded me."[10] Jones concluded that the album would have been better if it had been made exclusively by Nash, Ethridge and the rest, with Blue playing no part. Conversely, *Rolling Stone* described it as "a great leap forward, impressive in virtually every aspect".[11]

Although hardly qualifying as a commercial breakthrough, the period that encompassed the emergence of *Nice Baby* and The Eagles' cover of 'Outlaw Man' saw Blue at his best known. The artistically successful *Stories* had been a commercial disaster, selling only 2,000 copies. *Nice Baby And The Angel*, on the other hand, sold 15,000 copies in its first week of release.

Blue was encouraged by the response and immediately planned a follow-up in a similar vein, also to be produced by Nash. He toured with a band that included guitarist Don Felder, who later joined The Eagles. Blue appeared well placed to make further progress. But he seems to have hit a creative block – he was never specific about what caused it – and a second Nash-produced album did not materialise. It was two years before another LP finally appeared, by which time the momentum had gone. Those struggles with the creative process and his career-long efforts to get the recognition enjoyed by many of his peers became the subject for the title track of this much-delayed album, *Com'n Back For More*.

The record was made in Los Angeles in 1975 with drummer John Guerin producing, and was released toward the end of that year. Guerin was a member of the jazz-rock band LA Express which had played with Joni Mitchell. (It was widely held that the title song of Mitchell's 1971 album, *Blue*, was written about David Blue, but he said: "The song was written a long time ago, you know, and I hadn't seen Joni for years. It's very flattering, but it wasn't about me."[12]) Various other LA Express musicians appeared on *Com'n Back For More*, and there were cameo appearances from Mitchell and Dylan.

Blue talked up *Com'n Back For More* in interviews at the time, pronouncing it a new, more aggressive style of record. "Compared to my earlier albums this is very direct," he told one paper. "On this album I wanted to play machine gun instead of guitar."[13] He also said that his singing had improved. There is little evidence on *Com'n Back For More* to back up these claims. Rather, it comes across as a laboured, jazz-influenced rock record with poor songs, and with singing no better or worse than most of Blue's previous recordings. It was a bad attempt at a change of direction, and a creative nadir. The only song of merit was a reworking of 'These 23 Days In September', retitled '23 Days #2' and based on a picked acoustic guitar motif with a hovering Moog synthesiser.

It would not have been surprising if Blue's career had collapsed after *Com'n Back For More* but, ever-resilient, he did come back for one more try a year later with what proved to be his last album, *Cupid's Arrow*. Again released on Asylum, this time produced by Barry Goldberg, it marked a return to the country-influenced rock of the *Me* and *Nice Baby* albums. Despite collaborators of the stature of bassist Donald "Duck" Dunn and Band drummer Levon Helm, it was another poor album, distinguished only by the title track, a musical relative to Dylan's 'Knockin' On Heaven's Door'.

The song 'Cupid's Arrow' was Blue's tribute to Phil Ochs – the two had remained friends from the Greenwich Village days. For a spell during the early 1970s they had breakfast together most days: two East Coast migrants, recently beached in LA, talking about music and what they were up to – just as they used to do ten years earlier. Blue was stricken by Ochs's suicide in 1976. In Marc Eliot's book about Ochs, *Death Of A Rebel*, the author tells of an occasion some years after Ochs's death when he and Blue were watching a video of the tortured singer performing in the 1960s. "I put the tape on and neither of us said a word as Phil sang 'The Highwayman' and followed with a particularly haunting version of 'Changes'," wrote Eliot. "When it was over I turned to David to hear what he had to say and saw one of the original self-trained Village iconoclasts unable to hold back the tears. 'Poor Phil,' he said as he buried his head in his hands and wept like a baby."[14]

Blue performed 'Cupid's Arrow' at the Phil Ochs memorial concert on May 28th 1976 in New York, although typically his contribution went unnoticed by the *Rolling Stone* reviewer covering the event. As the last chords of his song died away, Blue called into the microphone, his voice thick with emotion, "I loved Phil Ochs." With 'Cupid's Arrow' he also dedicated to Ochs one of his best songs.

After *Cupid's Arrow*, Blue recorded one more album, which remains unissued. He then returned to acting, his first love. Although Blue's acting career was all too brief, there were signs that he could have excelled in a way that he never did in music. Appearances in Wim Wenders's *American Friend* (1978) and Neil Young's *Human Highway* (1979) were well received, and his recollections of Greenwich Village life were among the more watchable moments of Dylan's *Renaldo And Clara* (1978). As an actor, at least, he was able to eclipse Dylan. There were also various TV films, one of which, *Uncertain Futures*, directed by his wife Nesya Blue, featured a score by Blue. His stage appearances included the lead role in *The Leonard Cohen Show,* which ran in Montreal in 1980.

In 1981 Blue returned to live in Greenwich Village, and found a resurgent folk scene catering for a new generation of acoustic singer-songwriters. Casting himself as an elder statesman, he began writing and performing again. He relished the role of survivor. One of his last songs, 'I Grew Up On the Rolling Stones', was featured in a 1982 TV documentary called *Village Voices*, with Blue narrating. The programme mixed Blue's recollections of the first Greenwich Village folk boom with interviews and songs from some of the contemporary crop of singer-songwriters. When Blue sang 'I Grew Up On the Rolling Stones' there was a hitherto unheard strength and authority to his voice. It is the last known recording of David Blue.

On December 2nd 1982 Blue went jogging in Washington Square park, the very place where he had experienced an epiphany listening to Lightnin' Hopkins all those years before. The now health-conscious and teetotal Blue, with the indulgences of his earlier years long behind him, suffered a fatal heart attack. He was not carrying any ID, so his body lay anonymously in St Vincent's hospital morgue for three days, until somebody thought to look there for the missing singer. Leonard Cohen delivered the eulogy at Blue's funeral. For those who cared, David Blue's life – and death – seemed like a microcosm of his generation. An identikit singer-songwriter would have looked a lot like David Blue: the beginnings in Dylan's wake in Greenwich Village; the definitive suede/denim and curly-haired look; the attempts to forge an identity; a spell on Elektra; drug addiction; moving to the West Coast in the 1970s; hitching up with The Rolling Thunder Review; surviving, cleaning up… and dying on a health kick. Blue had it all – except the flash of genius that set apart Dylan, Hardin, Buckley and others.

Blue's singing voice was a wobbly baritone that at its very best hinted at Johnny Cash, but it was his prime weakness. It was probably the main factor that kept him from rising above the status of minor supporting player. A singer-songwriter who can't sing might seem like a contradiction in terms. Yet many of the great songwriters from the 1960s whose careers still flourish could not sing in the sense that Tim Buckley or Tim Hardin could sing. Leonard Cohen (whom Blue also admired), Dylan himself, Lou Reed – all successfully used technically limited voices to forge a distinctive style that serves their songs, and much better singers were often unable to improve on the original recorded versions. Blue was never able to transcend his limitations in this way, and too often he simply sounds like a bad singer missing so many notes that his tunes, which were sometimes very pretty, were obscured.

In one of the few obituaries, John Bauldie wrote in a Dylan fanzine: "[David Blue] may not have been a genius but he did have a very special gift. He was a singer and a songwriter of considerable and, it now seems, ever-to-be-unrecognised talent … . I can't say for sure but I'll bet he never got his photograph on the cover of any magazine. Until now."[15]

David Blue wasn't a singer of "considerable talent", but he did write some good songs. Of the 70 or so that were released there are enough – maybe ten – that prove his worth as a confessional songwriter. But he frequently fell into the confessional writer's trap of failing to turn the personal into the universal.

Blue did not set trends, but he was always one of the first to spot them and follow them. He was historically important for the people he knew, and for being in the right place at the right time on more than one occasion. In our story he was never a central figure, but a persistently intriguing one.

[1] Author's interview February 2nd 2000
[2] *Melody Maker* November 22nd 1975
[3] *Village Voices* television documentary 1982
[4] *Village Voices* television documentary 1982
[5] *The Broadside* 1966
[6] *Disc* July 1st 1972
[7] 'House Of Changing Faces' by David Blue, Good Friends/Companion Music 1971
[8] 'Marianne' by David Blue, Good Friends/Companion Music 1971
[9] *ZigZag* 41 1974
[10] *Melody Maker* July 7th 1973
[11] *Rolling Stone* July 7th 1973
[12] *ZigZag* 41 1974
[13] *Melody Maker* November 22nd 1975
[14] Marc Eliot *Phil Ochs – Death Of A Rebel* (Omnibus 1990)
[15] *The Telegraph* "Wanted Man" February 1983

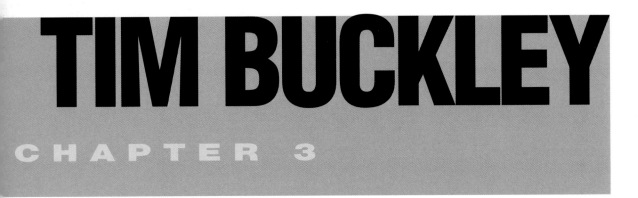

TIM BUCKLEY

CHAPTER 3

And though you have forgotten
All of our rubbish dreams,
I find myself searching
Through the ashes of our ruins
For the days when we smiled.

FROM 'ONCE I WAS' BY TIM BUCKLEY, *Third Story Music 1967*

The strange musical journey of Tim Buckley ranges from folk tenor purity to free jazz freak-out to bar-band R&B – and all in a nine-year career that ended with an apparently accidental death at just 28. Buckley's peak came between 1968 and 1970 with four glorious LPs that pitch his remarkable voice against versatile teams of musicians able to explore the limits of his challenging compositions.

At concerts in 1974 Tim Buckley was in the habit of marshalling his band into a rhythmic funk-rock groove, over which he would then introduce each member to the audience. They in turn would respond with a brief solo flourish, as Buckley exhorted the audience with phrases such as: "I'd like to hear a little respect for my people…" When the band had all been introduced the groove would morph into a rolling R&B finale, with Buckley swaggering at the microphone: "Remember one damn thing – Tim Buckley's in town!"

There was nothing remarkable about a white rock performer of the time adopting the mannerisms of a soul-revue MC. In fact it was common practice. But it was remarkable that Buckley of all people should engage in such traditional showbusiness behaviour. Three years earlier he had been testing the patience of his audience with some of the most radical avant-garde "rock" music recorded. Three years before that he had stood on the brink of pop stardom, an angelic boy-folkie with a soaring tenor voice.

Timothy Charles Buckley III spent the first ten years of his life living in Amsterdam, New York, before moving with his family to Bell Gardens in Los Angeles and then later a few miles away to Anaheim. He had been born on Valentine's Day, February 14th 1947.

At an early age he became interested in country and folk music, and taught himself to play banjo and guitar. He started performing in local bands in his early teens. "The only one that toured was Princess Ramona and The Cherokee Riders," he claimed later. "I got to dress in a yellow hummingbird shirt and a turquoise hat and play lead guitar. I was about 15. I'd get $60 a week plus gas money and a room."[1] He went on to say that it was on the advice of Princess Ramona that he turned to folk music. Whether Princess Ramona actually existed or was a figment of Buckley's ever-fertile imagination is open to question, but regardless of this he did take up folk music and was soon attracting attention in clubs around Los Angeles. He formed a friendship with two other young hopefuls, Steve Noonhan and Jackson Browne, and they were christened The Orange County Three by *Cheetah* magazine.

By now Buckley's musical interests had widened to encompass jazz – particularly that of saxophonist John Coltrane – and the rock'n'roll of Chuck Berry and Little Richard. It is rumoured that he played guitar, uncredited, on the first Byrds album during this period, although this is probably a myth that Buckley allowed to gain credence.

It was while he was playing in a new band, The Bohemians, that he attracted the attention of Mothers Of Invention drummer Jimmy Carl Black, who introduced him to Herb Cohen, the Mothers' manager. Cohen was impressed and booked the 19-year-old Buckley to play at The Night Owl Café in New York. He also approached Elektra's Jac Holzman with a Bohemians demo acetate. "Herb called to tell me that he had a new artist," said Holzman, "and that he was sending us, and no-one else, a demo disc. I didn't have to play the demo more than once … . I asked Herb to arrange a meeting, but I had my mind made up already."[2] Buckley duly signed to Elektra.

The Bohemians, who backed Buckley on that first demo, included musicians who would loom large in Buckley's story. Their drummer was Larry Beckett, a poet who wrote lyrics for Buckley through most of the singer's ensuing career. Bassist Jim Fielder later went on to join Blood Sweat & Tears and Buffalo Springfield, and played on several of Buckley's albums. Van Dyke Parks played keyboards with the band from time to time, and also on Buckley's first album. But it was Buckley solo, not The Bohemians, who released a debut album on Elektra in October 1966. Fielder said later: "I can't remember it ever being spoken about, but it was always understood that, ultimately, it was about Tim. He was the one, and there were no hard feelings whatsoever when it turned into a solo situation."[3]

At about the time he signed with Elektra, Buckley married his high school sweetheart, Mary Guibert. She fell pregnant just as Buckley was about to embark on a tour. When he returned some months later he had a new girlfriend, and the marriage was over. He first saw his son, Jeffery Scott Buckley, eight months after the child was born, and only very irregularly thereafter, although he did provide financial support. There was an aura surrounding Buckley at this time, a sense of impending stardom recognised by all who worked with him. "He was poised all the time to become a major pop artist,"[4] said Elektra producer David Anderle. There is no doubt that Buckley could have been a star – he had the bone structure, the hair, the voice, the talent and the intangible charisma of a man set apart. The photograph on the sleeve of that first album shows Buckley casually dressed, whippet-thin, leaning against a wall. Here, it is clear, is someone with the lingering, mildly androgynous physical characteristics of adolescence and the haughty, arrogant charisma of one assured of his own greatness, one who knew exactly what he was doing.

No doubt sensing his commercial potential, Elektra asked Buckley to record a single in advance of the first album. The now lost brace of songs 'Once Upon A Time' and 'Lady Give Me Your Key' (or 'Lady Give Me Your Heart' according to some reports) was written by Buckley and Beckett after they had listened to the radio for 24 hours straight in an attempt to assimilate the necessary commercial formula. The single was given an American catalogue number by Elektra (it was to have been released after The Doors' 'Light My Fire'), but never appeared.

Tim Buckley was a folk-rock album with spiritual links to contemporary recordings by The Byrds, Love, and The Mamas & The Papas. Of its 12 songs, seven were written by the Buckley/Beckett partnership, five by Buckley alone. Production credits were shared between Paul Rothchild and Jac Holzman. Buckley's singing and predominantly electric rhythm guitar playing were supported by a band including Parks, Fielder and, on lead guitar, Lee Underwood. Underwood became a close friend of Buckley's, and collaborated with him regularly over the years. He was one of the era's more original guitar stylists, eschewing the usual distortion and blues scales for a pellucid, shimmering, wandering jazz-and-raga style that was the perfect foil for Buckley's other-worldly tenor.

"He was poised all the time to become a major pop artist."

Tim Buckley has been reduced to the status of juvenilia in the light of the daring musical explorations that followed, but even if it had been the only record that Buckley ever made it would still be worthy of attention. Indeed, there are many hints of the later journeys in these early recordings. The drawn-out 'Song Slowly Song' is a sort of prototype of the mood music of the *Happy/Sad* era, and the primitive R&B strut of 'Understand Your Man' prefigures *Greetings From LA*. The soaring orchestral folk-rock of 'Wings', with string arrangements by Jack Nitzsche, and the sustained high notes at the end of 'Aren't You The Girl' hint at the as-yet-unexplored potential of Buckley's four-octave voice. Even at the tender age of 19, when many would have been seduced by the seemingly endless possibilities of fame and fortune, Buckley was displaying a dogged faithfulness to his burgeoning creative instincts.

He spent much of late 1966 and early 1967 in New York, backing The Mothers of Invention and Nico. In June '67 he returned to Los Angeles to record his second album for Elektra. The optimism of the hippie era – the belief that youth culture might really "change things" – was at its height. Buckley's album *Goodbye And Hello* was, of all his works, the most readily identifiable with the era that spawned it. An epic, complex, psychedelic-folk crossover, it was produced by Jerry Yester who employed a ten-piece band and further uncredited orchestral musicians. Buckley himself had by now taken up his trademark 12-string acoustic guitar. Fielder and Underwood survived from the first album, joined by musicians such as conga player Carter "CC" Collins and the guitarist John Forsha, both of whom would go on to work regularly with Buckley. Of the ten songs on *Goodbye And Hello*, five are Buckley compositions and five are credited to Buckley/Beckett. Beckett's elaborate lyrical constructs, rich in alliteration and metaphor, haven't aged well and – along with the use of sound effects, reverb-heavy production and quasi-medieval trappings – are a significant factor in anchoring the album firmly in its period. Yet despite all that, *Goodbye And Hello* contains four classic Buckley moments.

The soaring, epic 'Pleasant Street' and the frenzy of clattering percussion and acoustic guitar that underpins Buckley's pleading shrieks on 'I Never Asked to Be Your Mountain' set new standards of musical intensity and invention. 'Morning Glory' and 'Once I Was', on the other hand, are simple ballads of intense emotion.

The acoustic waltz of 'Once I Was', with its poignant and uncredited harmonica figure, has musical and lyrical similarities to Fred Neil's 'The Dolphins', which Buckley was later to cover. The chorus of Buckley's 'Once I Was' goes: "...and sometimes I wonder, just for a while, will you ever remember me?",[5] while Neil's 'The Dolphins' has: "...and sometimes I wonder, do you ever think of me?".[6] Buckley and Beckett were admirers of Neil (who was also managed by Herb Cohen) and briefly visited the sessions for his classic *Fred Neil* album which they rated as the best record of the 1960s. Beckett later said that seeing Neil at work in the studio alerted Buckley to previously unseen possibilities in his own music.[7]

'Morning Glory' was to become one of Buckley's best-known songs, later recorded by Linda Ronstadt among others. The haunting, lush choir effect that dominates Buckley's version was achieved by repeated multitracking of Buckley's and Yester's voices.

Buckley later expressed reservations about *Goodbye And Hello*, particularly the anti-establishment sentiments of the ten-minute title track and the era it represented. "It was really a very tragic period in San Francisco at that time because of the acid casualties," he commented. "There were a lot of people who had no business doing drugs. In *Goodbye And Hello* it was very adolescent – I took sides, whereas now I can't. I said the establishment was wrong ... OK, it's wrong, but I didn't have an answer."[8]

Goodbye And Hello was a modest commercial success, reaching 171 on the *Billboard* chart. This was the time when, if he'd wanted to, Buckley could have broken through to a wider audience. But his creative instincts prevailed over considerations of commercial appeal and career development.

He spent much of 1968 working with a loose aggregation of musicians based on Underwood and vibes player David Friedman, both of whom played on Buckley's third album, *Happy/Sad*, which appeared in the US in April 1969. With these musicians, augmented by various pick-up bassists, Buckley, still only 21, maintained a high profile, touring Europe and making his UK debut during the spring. There were many radio and television appearances, including a guest spot on the penultimate episode of *The Monkees*. During that show Buckley sang a folkish version of 'Song To The Siren', the piece that would do much to establish his posthumous status among successive generations of listeners.

As they toured, rehearsed and recorded, Buckley and his associates were refining a new fusion of the young singer's emerging interests in jazz, improvisation and avant-garde tonal experimentation. Buckley had also, for the time being, severed his working relationship with Beckett, and claimed sole writing credits for *Happy/Sad*'s six songs. Much evidence of this evolution has since become available with the release of several live recordings and radio sessions from 1968 and 1969. This was the period of Buckley's greatest creativity, which lasted roughly three years, until late in 1970. Amid the adventure, exuberance and creative fire he recorded the four albums on which his pioneering reputation rests: *Happy/Sad*; *Blue Afternoon*; *Lorca*; and *Starsailor*.

From the vibes and acoustic bass in the opening phrase of *Happy/Sad*'s first song, 'Strange Feelin'', it was apparent that Buckley had decisively discarded the somewhat derivative folk-rock style of his earlier releases. The languid, elongated, semi-improvisational style of that first song, and the entire album, could not be classified by reference to then-current genres. The album as a whole is a striking work of moods and dynamics rather than just a collection of songs. It certainly isn't folk music, although elements of folk music remain. It isn't pop either, although there is a catchy pop song to be discovered inside the lazy, summery groove of 'Buzzin' Fly'.

It was the jazz influences of *Happy/Sad* that were most commonly referred to by contemporary reviewers as they attempted to categorise the music. But these were only influences, emphasised by the performances of Friedman and Underwood. *Happy/Sad* is not a jazz record. The album appeared out of a collection of stylistic influences, merged by Buckley's vision and shaped by the intuitive interaction of the players featured on the recording.

It has been held that the period of Buckley's career hailed by the release of *Happy/Sad* was one of unique artistic individualism, during which he produced music without precedent. Although it was the case that he could not be easily fitted into any style of the time, there were other isolated examples of contemporaries working with similar ideas – notably Fred Neil on his *Sessions* album and Van Morrison on *Astral Weeks*. Morrison's classic album was recorded in a 48-hour period, probably a month or two after the Tim Buckley album. It's unlikely that any cross-referencing was going on, but rather that the two arrived at similar points by exploring what was essentially the same set of influences.

That Buckley admired and was influenced by Fred Neil, however, is beyond doubt. Beckett has talked of visiting the studio with Buckley while Neil was working on his eponymously-titled Capitol album, and by 1968 Neil's 'The Dolphins' featured prominently in Buckley's live set. It is on *Happy/Sad* that Buckley first began to explore the lower reaches of his extraordinary vocal range, consciously aping some of Neil's vocal characteristics, although never quite coming to match the effortless quality of the older singer's baritone.

Much was made of the loose, improvised sound of the five-piece band (percussionist Collins and bassist John Miller joining Buckley, Underwood and Friedman), but as live recordings of the period show, these improvisations took place around a solid core of musical motifs and defined song structures. The songs and arrangements were not drawn from the ether for the first time in the studio, but were the result of a degree of planning and refining before the recording took place. Buckley said of this: "The trick is to make it sound like it's all happening for the first time – that's what it's all about … . It took a long time for me to write that album, and then to teach the people in the band."[9]

> "The trick is to make it sound like it's all happening for the first time."

Yester shared production duties on 1969's *Happy/Sad* with Zal Yanovsky from The Lovin' Spoonful. One curious detail about the recording came to light over 30 years later when Yester, interviewed for *Mojo* magazine, explained that the ocean sound-effects that underpin 'Love From Room 109 At The Islander' were added to obscure an unacceptably high level of tape hiss which had resulted from the incorrect engagement of the then embryonic Dolby noise-reduction system. If there were tensions between band and producers, as has been recalled by Underwood, they did not show in what was a beautifully recorded album, the pivotal work in the Buckley canon.

Buckley's next album, *Blue Afternoon*, was the first for his new record label, Herb Cohen's Straight – although another would appear on Elektra. There has been some confusion about the order in which Buckley recorded *Blue Afternoon* and its immediate follow-up, *Lorca*. They both resulted from a few weeks of creative frenzy in the later part of 1969. "I recorded *Blue Afternoon, Lorca* and parts of *Starsailor* in the same month. I was hot,"[10] Buckley said in 1974. "That was a complicated time, between labels. But *Blue Afternoon* was done immediately after *Lorca*."[11]

The move to Straight was seemingly precipitated in part by rumours of Holzman's plans to sell Elektra to Warners. In the circumstances it would be expected that the last, contract-obliging album for Buckley's former label would be a rushed, half-hearted affair. Surprisingly, it was *Blue Afternoon*, released in early 1970, that more closely matched that description. "That album was only half-finished," Buckley said. "[It] got kind of lost when I was changing labels."[12]

With the exception of drummer Jimmy Madison replacing Collins for all but one song, the band on *Blue Afternoon* was the same as on *Happy/Sad*. Broadly speaking, the feel of the new record was similar, but with a slightly greater emphasis on traditional song structure at the expense of improvisation. Most of the eight songs were again penned by Buckley only, and had been around for some time in half-completed form, recorded to close a phase in Buckley's career. "When I did *Blue Afternoon*," he said, "I had just about finished writing set songs."[13] Of these, the opening 'Happy Time' is the most obviously pop-influenced song from this period of Buckley's career (and was released as a single in the UK), while the piano-based 'Blue Melody' is the other stand-out track. Buckley himself was credited as producer.

Lorca was released on Elektra a few months after *Blue Afternoon,* in late 1970. It was produced by Dick Kunc, and featured Collins, Underwood and bassist/organist John Balkin backing Buckley. While the second side of the original vinyl release continues in much the same vein as its two predecessors, the two long songs which occupied the first side demonstrate a giant leap into the uncharted avant-garde territory that Buckley had been skirting for some time.

These first two "songs" (the term must be used loosely) were 'Lorca' and 'Anonymous Proposition'. They put an end to any hopes that Buckley would ever return to the palatable folk-influenced style of his early records. The title track is based on a repeated five-note organ/bass phrase over which Buckley intones in a deep bass voice, greatly exaggerating his vibrato. Underwood's sprawling electric-piano improvisations skate over the top of the piece, slipping in and out of dissonance. It still sounds like challenging music, and marks the point when Buckley, in the apposite words of Underwood, "left the realm of showbusiness".[14]

With his next album, *Starsailor*, some felt that Buckley also left the realm of music. Others saw it as the full flowering of the buds that had emerged on *Lorca*. Critics reviewing *Starsailor* in 1971 struggled to describe and categorise the music. Richard Williams writing in *Melody Maker* described it as "some of the most extraordinarily mutant rock music I've ever heard … . He's providing a new direction in which rock can join the New Music."[15] Steve Peacock wrote in *Sounds* that Buckley was "constantly exploring the possibilities of using his voice as an instrument within the overall sound".[16]

For *Starsailor* Buckley's *Lorca* band was augmented by Mauri Baker on timpani, along with two Mothers Of Invention, brothers Buzz and Bunk Gardner, who shared various brass instruments. Larry Beckett also re-emerged, co-composing four of the nine songs. Together with an often multitracked Buckley they created wild, difficult, atonal free-form music. Only the throwaway 'Moulin Rouge' and an eerie interpretation of 'Song To The Siren' lend some semblance of normality to what sounded then – and sounds now – like a radical record. It is the one Buckley album that has often been out of print over the past 30 years.

Attempts to take the *Starsailor* sound on the road met with widespread audience disbelief and resentment, and the album was a commercial failure. Buckley was depressed. What he believed was a creative peak had become a commercial impasse. Straight Records wouldn't support him to tour, and he was driven to booking occasional small club gigs himself. Without sufficient work, his band dissolved. Underwood later confirmed that it was at this time that Buckley started to take heroin, despite more settled personal circumstances. He had married again, and in doing so became step-father to a seven-year-old son called Taylor. The family bought a house and Buckley took a year off.

Buckley, always willing to allow romantic myths about his life to take root, alluded to working during this period as a taxi-driver, as Sly Stone's chauffeur, and as a member of the ethnomusicology department at the University of California, Los Angeles. His wife Judy, speaking in a 1995 *Mojo* article about Buckley, didn't recall any of these activities. In her account he spent days in the UCLA library reading avidly, and acting in an unreleased film, *Why?*, earning $420 a week co-starring alongside another first-time actor, OJ Simpson. Buckley also started work on a screenplay of his own, *Fully Airconditioned Inside,* a comedy about a struggling musician, which would remain unfinished.

Having baffled audiences with his peculiar journey from folk-rock to the avant-garde, Buckley confounded expectations again when he returned to music with a new album some 18 months after the release of *Starsailor*. *Greetings From LA* was released on Warners in 1972 and is a carnal, physical R&B

album with all the stylistic badges of that genre: horn sections; female backing vocals; funky electric Fenders; and songs about sex.

Jerry Goldstein was the producer, and was best known for his work with War. Made at Far Out studios in Hollywood, *Greetings From LA* did something to restore Buckley's commercial fortunes after the audience-alienating *Starsailor*. Although Larry Beckett again co-wrote some of the selections, Buckley was working now with a largely new set of collaborators. Central to this group of musicians was guitarist Joe Falsia, who became a mainstay of Buckley's touring band – and percussionist Carter "CC" Collins again makes an appearance.

Greetings From LA marked the beginning of the third distinct phase of Buckley's career. Surprisingly for an artist who had carved such a distinctive identity on his four previous albums, he was now turning his attentions to an established form. Nonetheless, he had not abandoned experimental inclinations entirely: the vocal explorations on the "speaking in tongues" sections of 'Get On Top' and 'Devil Eyes' were as extreme as anything on *Starsailor*.

As well as marking a musical departure, *Greetings From LA* was a lyrical reinvention. The yearning, mystical, sometimes obscure inner analysis of the earlier records gave way to a libidinous, lecherous, euphoric celebration of the flesh. Nobody familiar with either of Buckley's two previous artistic phases expected to hear him singing, "We had those bedsprings squeaking all night long."[17]

When touring the UK two years after the release of *Greetings*, Buckley talked about the move (some would say retreat) into a safe space after the uncomfortable extremes of *Starsailor*. "I thought I was writing my ass off [during the *Lorca/Starsailor* period] but record sales proved differently,"[18] he said, adding to another interviewer: "I hadn't touched the guitar in a long time and I thought, well, I have to get up to date. I saw nine black exploitation movies, read four black 'sock-it-to-me-mama' books, and read all the rock criticisms … and finally realised that all of the sex idols in rock'n'roll weren't saying anything sexy."[19]

> "Some of the most extraordinarily mutant rock music ever."

But it is certain that this move in a more commercial direction was as much the result of pressure from manager Cohen as it was the latest flight of fancy of the ever-unpredictable artist. *Greetings From LA* was well received critically and sold better than *Lorca* or *Starsailor*. Its follow-up appeared to be a calculated effort to record something commercial to cash in on this interest.

For an artist previously renowned for dogged pursuit of excellence, innovation and individuality, *Sefronia,* which appeared on manager Cohen's new Discreet imprint two years after *Greetings*, was a curiously unfocused affair. Recorded in three studios with upward of 15 musicians, it seemed more like an inconsistent collection of out-takes rather than a thematically and stylistically unified collection. Consisting of five funk/soul work-outs of lesser quality than the similar material on the previous album and a mismatch of flirtations with other styles, it had all the hallmarks of either failing inspiration or lack of interest on Buckley's part.

On 1974's *Sefronia,* Buckley recorded cover versions of other writers' songs for the first time. Of these, Fred Neil's 'The Dolphins' had appeared in Buckley's live set since 1968. Posthumously-released live recordings of the song are far superior to the over-arranged treatment Buckley delivers on this studio version. The string-quartet interpretation of Tom Waits's maudlin, sentimental 'Martha' is out of keeping with Buckley's previously recorded material, and if one were to take away his readily identifiable voice it could easily be the work of any AOR ballad artist. 'I Know I'd Recognise Your Face', written by producer Denny Randell, is an equally undistinguished effort on which Buckley duets with Marcia Waldorf.

Amid the confusion, only the title track emerges as worthy of comparison with the high standards of

Buckley's earlier work. The Buckley/Beckett composition is a two-part piece subtitled 'Sefronia – After Askipiades, After Kafka' and 'Sefronia – The King's Chain' (and was listed as two separate tracks on some versions of the album). It combines the expansive, languid feel of the *Happy/Sad* era with the more considered, planned arrangements of *Goodbye And Hello*, and while not a radical step forward it at least provided some evidence that Buckley's creative fire had not been entirely extinguished.

The two-year period that started with the release of *Greetings From LA* saw Buckley at his most successful since 1968, particularly in the UK. He was touring regularly, and a visit to Britain in 1974 prompted major profiles in *Sounds*, *New Musical Express*, *Melody Maker* and *Zigzag*. He made an appearance on the respected *Old Grey Whistle Test* TV show on May 21st 1974, and opened the year's Knebworth festival. It was Buckley's first live appearance in the UK since 1968.

He was talking enthusiastically of various projects: a double live album encompassing all the phases of his musical journey to date; a musical based on Joseph Conrad's novel *Out Of The Islands*; and the possibility of playing Woody Guthrie in the film *Bound For Glory* (a role for which Tim Hardin had been considered and which eventually went to David Carradine). But it was significant that none of these were to do with his immediate recording career. A tiredness had settled on his demeanour and over his music. If *Sefronia* was a disappointing album, *Look At The Fool*, which appeared six months later, was a desperately weary nadir.

There is little to say about *Look At The Fool*, a tired third instalment in Buckley's funk phase. It is a poor record by any standards, and for an artist of Buckley's abilities can only be excused by speculation that it was recorded as a contractual obligation. Shortly after its release Buckley's long association with manager Herb Cohen came to an end. There were no further artistic reinventions. Buckley continued to play live throughout 1974 and into 1975. He had just completed a tour of California and Texas with a show in Dallas when he died of a heroin overdose on June 29th 1975. He was 28.

He and his band had been partying to celebrate the end of the tour, and a drunk Buckley had scored some heroin at a friend's house. He was taken home barely conscious and put to bed by his wife, Judy. When she checked on him later he had turned blue. The paramedics were unable to revive him. Lee Underwood, in his sleevenotes to the posthumous *Dream Letter* live album, said that Buckley had not been using heroin for some time prior to the incident, and had made an effort to get in shape for the tour. All the signs point to a drunken miscalculation and a tragic accident rather than a deliberate act of self-destruction. The friend who had supplied the heroin was later tried for Buckley's murder. He pleaded guilty to a lesser charge of involuntary manslaughter.

Buckley's death was marked with respectful and sometimes even reverent obituaries in the music press on both sides of the Atlantic, but his relatively low public profile meant there was no posthumous rush on sales. He remained a connoisseur's choice.

In 1983 a British collective of young musicians from the independent scene, calling themselves This Mortal Coil and centred on the evocative voice of Cocteau Twin Liz Fraser, released a cover version of 'Song To The Siren'. It remained in the UK indie chart for over a year. It was an effective interpretation, retaining something of the yearning despair of Buckley's recorded version, but nonetheless with its own identity. It introduced Buckley to the post-punk audience, most of who would have previously categorised him as a self-indulgent hippie – if they knew him at all. Since then his status as a genuine innovator has become established. His albums have been reissued periodically, and most were readily available throughout the 1990s. Starting with 1990's *Dream Letter* there has also been a steady stream of collections of newly unearthed live recordings and studio out-takes, of varying interest and quality.

When an extravagantly gifted artist dies young and beautiful, a romantic myth invariably grows up that can obscure the truth about the person's work, while perpetuating something of their story and reputation. In Tim Buckley's case the myth tells us that he was a wild, free, intuitive musical innovator operating in a vacuum populated only by a few loyal sidemen. There is much truth in this, but truth that requires qualification. The extent of the creative freedom afforded Buckley by his recording contract with Elektra Records in the early stages of his career cannot be underestimated. It provided the secure base he needed from which to embark on his musical journeys. Elektra at the time was a big enough company to offer most of the benefits of a Columbia or a Capitol. It had its own state-of-the-art studios, good distribution, reasonable recording budgets and, in The Doors, a big-selling act that bankrolled less lucrative artists operating on the margins.

In Jac Holzman, Paul Rothchild, Bruce Botnick, William S Harvey and others Elektra had creatively-minded, sympathetic people in key positions. They were able to combine sound commercial, technical and business skills – providing records that were attractively packaged, well recorded and cunningly marketed – and had a genuine appreciation of the spirit of the music. Buckley, more than many others, reaped the benefits of this combination of artistic freedom and corporate muscle. He would not have prospered in a more traditional corporate environment, where hit singles and consistent albums were always expected.

The value of Buckley's later albums – from 1972's *Greetings From LA* onward – has sometimes been exaggerated. While *Look At The Fool* is rightly considered by most to be a poor record, *Sefronia* is held to have some merits, and *Greetings From LA* itself is afforded almost classic status. But if it was possible to consider this period without reference to the earlier work, all of these albums would appear as derivative R&B/funk work-outs distinguished only by an extraordinary voice. Bootlegs of Buckley's touring band in 1974 and '75 reveal a pedestrian, sometimes leaden rock sound with funk pretensions, over which Buckley performed weird simian vocal gymnastics. There is little doubt that he was treading water. Equally, though, there can be little doubt that an artist of his stature had the gifts to reinvent himself yet again. His premature death means that such a reinvention remains in the realm of tantalising speculation. But it is the reinventions that did take place that mark out Buckley as unique. In a nine-year career that ended when he was 28 years old he recorded nine albums, traversing three distinct musical periods.

Lee Underwood has written about Buckley stretching the boundaries of the human voice in rock music in the way that Hendrix redefined the limits of electric guitar playing. Listening to *Starsailor* you can hear what he means. But while Buckley is now often hailed as a musical innovator, his direct influence is strangely absent from contemporary music. The hallmarks of other trail-blazers from the period – The Velvet Underground, say, or The Byrds – are usually clearly heard in the music of artists citing those bands as influences. Buckley, however, may be widely admired, but aspects of his sound tend to be less obviously audible in music of the last two decades. This is because of his extraordinary and, more to the point, inimitable voice. That voice, more than anything else, is his legacy.

[1] *ZigZag* 44 1974
[2] Elektra press release 1966
[3] *Mojo* June 2000
[4] Jac Holzman & Gavan Daws *Follow The Music* (FirstMedia 1998)
[5] 'Once I Was' by Tim Buckley, Third Story Music 1967
[6] 'The Dolphins' by Fred Neil, Carlin Music Corp 1966
[7] David Browne *Dream Brother* (Fourth Estate 2000)
[8] *ZigZag* 44 1974
[9] *ZigZag* 44 1974
[10] *ZigZag* 44 1974
[11] *Melody Maker* May 25th 1974
[12] *Melody Maker* May 25th 1974
[13] *ZigZag* 48 1974
[14] *Mojo* June 2000
[15] *Melody Maker* February 6th 1971
[16] *Sounds* February 6th 1971
[17] 'Get On Top' by Tim Buckley, Third Story Music
[18] *Sounds* August 3rd 1974
[19] *NME* June 8th 1974

TIM HARDIN

CHAPTER 4

I'm the family's unknown boy,
Golden curls of envied hair,
Pretty girls with faces fair
See the shine in the black sheep boy.

FROM 'BLACK SHEEP BOY' BY TIM HARDIN, *Verve Forecast Records 1967*

'If I Were A Carpenter' is Tim Hardin's best-known composition and one of the most memorable tunes of the 1960s. It was a hit three times in that decade alone, and has been recorded by dozens of artists. Yet Hardin was never able to reap the professional and financial rewards of this success, and his forlorn story is one of a terrible and wasteful decline as he pursued ever-diminishing inspiration.

In the mid 1970s Tim Rose and Tim Hardin played about a dozen dates together across the UK, taking it in turns to headline on alternate nights. One night when Rose opened, Hardin was nowhere to be seen as the time came for him to follow Rose onstage. The promoters approached Rose, asking him if he would consider playing again if he were given Hardin's fee as well as his own for the show.

Rose agreed but, just as he was about to go on stage for the second time that night, Hardin shambled into the venue, walked right on to the stage, sat at his Wurlitzer electric piano and ran his fingers over the mute keyboard. He began to sing what was apparently an a cappella version of 'Reason To Believe'. Halfway through the song, a roadie walked on to the stage and turned on the electric piano. Hardin, who had not realised he was singing unaccompanied, was momentarily startled, but continued the song to the end.

That story says a great deal about Tim Hardin. He was completely lost in his music. But by that stage of his life he was a sad, pale, unreliable shadow of his best years a decade earlier, when during a few short months he had written some of the most memorable songs of the 1960s.

Hardin was an extravagantly gifted man whose chaotic life was completely at odds with the well-ordered beauty of his best songs. He could take a few simple chords and a clutch of everyday words and mould them into personal statements of such universal appeal that they deserve to be called standards. The voice in which he sang those songs – a fragile, rough, tender, weary and desperately pleading instrument – gave more of a clue to the man he was.

Of all the singer-songwriters whose talent took root in the fertile Greenwich Village scene in New York City in the early 1960s, Hardin was one of the best. Whereas many, like David Blue and Patrick Sky, started out virtually as Dylan imitators, Hardin quickly found his own road. But it never ran parallel to that of the music business which avidly fed on his songs, and it proved to be a winding, discursive route to a premature dead end. Almost from the beginning it was clear that he would not and could not comfortably work within the industry to which he made such a memorable but brief contribution.

Any telling of the Tim Hardin story must be prefaced with a comment about his relentlessly self-mythologising nature which serves to obscure and distort many of the biographical details. Throughout the many press interviews he conducted between the mid 1960s and the mid 1970s, different versions of the same story appear, years apart, with key details altered. In some cases apparently important things are mentioned – how records were made, the existence of other children apart from his known son, Damion – that are never mentioned again. What follows is therefore an attempt to see the truth through this mist of bravado, drug-induced forgetfulness, romanticism and self-delusion.

Hardin arrived in New York in 1961 with dreams of becoming an actor, enrolling at the American Academy of Dramatic Arts. By this time he had already seen more of the world than most young men of his age. Hardin was born on December 23rd 1941 in Eugene, Oregon, where he spent his first 18 years. He had a brother and a sister. His family life was unhappy, and later he would habitually make disparaging references to his father, Hal. "My father tried to rule me," Hardin typically told a 1960s interviewer. "I'd wake up in the morning and think, 'Oh God, I've got to go to school and I've got to have a talk with my father,' and I'd really want to die."[1]

Hardin's grandmother, Manner Small, was by most accounts an imposing, matriarchal figure, and was predominantly responsible for his upbringing. His family, though, gave him one precious gift – a love of music. His mother, Molly, once had a career in classical music, and his father had been a jazz bass-player. His boyhood friend, Phil Freeman, recalled him sitting at a piano in 1959, ecstatically repeating the mantra: "I've got the music in me."[2]

When Hardin joined the Marines on leaving school, it probably had more to do with escaping what he saw as the restrictive conventions of family life than a desire to serve his country. Not surprisingly, the discipline of the military didn't suit the mercurial Hardin. He later likened joining up to escaping from one prison – his family – into another. This phase in his life could easily be dismissed as a reckless adolescent aberration were it not for one fact. When he was discharged in 1961 he brought home a souvenir of his postings in the Far East, a heroin habit. He talked later in an interview[3] of having done a deal in Hong Kong that provided sufficient heroin to see him through the bulk of his tour of duty.

At some point after leaving the Marines, and after his first spell at Greenwich Village, Hardin apparently taught at Harvard for a semester in the musicology department.[4] What exactly he taught there isn't clear, although he claims he was an adept guitarist by this time, sharing with his Greenwich Village contemporaries an interest in folk, blues and country music. It was during this brief phase at Harvard that he played the Boston/Cambridge folk circuit where Tom Rush and Joan Baez were leading figures, appearing at the Unicorn club among others.

But even at this early stage Hardin was set apart from the others. First, there was his enthusiasm for jazz. "The knowledge of jazz is the knowledge of God,"[5] as he once put it. Second, there was his indifference to the prevalent liberal-left protest leanings of Bob Dylan, Phil Ochs, Joan Baez and many of the rest.

It would be easy to assume that Hardin never joined the protest movement – apart from one brief dalliance courtesy of a Bobby Darin song years later – because he was a writer uniquely concerned with his own inner life and relationships. Yet he believed that his songs didn't really belong to him at all, claiming on many occasions to be merely a channel for the music which, in some mystical sense, already existed outside of him. "My songs aren't personal. They sound it 'cos it was me who revealed them – it was my head that got the lightning shot through it. They're just love songs, true songs … . They mean what they mean."[6]

"They're just love songs, true songs. They mean what they mean."

Before long Hardin was noticed by Erik Jacobsen, later Chris Isaak's producer but then just starting out in the music business. Hardin was placed with Columbia for a one-year contract, probably in August 1964 (although Hardin sometimes recalled it as a year earlier). Several recording sessions ensued, with Hardin concentrating on traditional blues and folk material and derivative early songs of his own in the same style. He often had an electric backing, favouring a muted electric guitar tone, and thus just predated Dylan's controversial rock'n'roll conversion.

These recordings were not issued at the time, and the Columbia deal proved to be a false start. A little over a year later Jacobsen introduced Hardin to Charles Koppelman and Don Rubin, who were also working with the embryonic Lovin' Spoonful. They were instrumental in getting Hardin signed to MGM's new label, Verve-Forecast, and in 1966 the first Tim Hardin records began to appear.

Today, Hardin is best remembered for a handful of songs, including the oft-covered 'If I Were A Carpenter'. Most of them were written in a golden eight-month period from late 1965 into 1966[7] when Hardin worked at a piano in a room in the Los Angeles home of fellow heroin addict and early counter-culture casualty Lenny Bruce. It was at this time that Hardin found his muse.

He had met Susan Morss when she was an actress working under the name of Susan Yardley and starring in a popular TV series, *The Young Marrieds*. Hardin's classic song 'Lady Came From Baltimore' is a mythologised rather than strictly factual account of their courtship. Morss did not, like the "Susan Moore" of the song, come from Baltimore, although her father did "read the law" as a Prosecutor in New Jersey. Whether Hardin himself really lived "outside the law" apart from his drug habit is not clear, although he revelled in presenting himself as a renegade, claiming (falsely) kinship with the 19th-century outlaw John Wesley Hardin. Accounts of earlier relationships tend to suggest that he might well have been "there" to take advantage of Susan, if not literally in the words of the song to "steal her money".[8]

> "At their best his songs transcend genres, and just sound like Tim Hardin songs."

The song is absolutely accurate about one thing, however. He "fell in love with the lady". The tensions that arose in their ensuing relationship as a result of his drug addiction dominated the rest of his life and career.

The first album, *Tim Hardin 1*, consisted of 12 self-penned songs, the best known of which is 'Reason To Believe', famously covered later by Rod Stewart. 'Hang On To A Dream' became a mainstay for The Nice, as well as providing Hardin himself with his only British hit, making number 50 for one week in January 1967.

The record was produced by Erik Jacobsen and featured musicians of the calibre of John Sebastian on harmonica and Earl Palmer on drums. It was a strong debut, released in July 1966. However, Hardin was infuriated that Jacobsen had added a string quartet to a number of the songs without his permission. "I was like a child," he explained later. "They'd added strings and chimes. My ideas weren't followed. It had been left in the hands of people who didn't understand."[9] Some critics agreed with Hardin, commenting that the strings sounded too obviously as if they had been grafted on. This seems an unfair criticism, although the effect was no doubt heightened by the then popular habit of extreme stereo separation.

The 12 songs represent the full range of Hardin's influences, and reveal something about his changeable nature. The fragile pop sensibilities of the vulnerable 'Don't Make Promises' contrast with the swaggering R&B of 'Ain't Gonna Do Without' in which Hardin adopts his womanising "long tall Timmy" persona. It is The Lovin' Spoonful's John Sebastian who provides the piercing harmonica solo on this song. Likewise the dreamy, lovelorn jazz of the vibes-based 'Misty Roses' contrasts with the country-guitar picking and ambiguous lyrics of 'Reason To Believe'. Hardin later commented that this take of 'Misty Roses' was the one recording of his own compositions that couldn't have been improved.

The songs on *Tim Hardin 1* individually mark Hardin's key musical reference points. By *Tim Hardin 2*, which was released in April 1967, he had successfully blended them into a more personal style. From the blues he took an ability to express anguish; from jazz, a fluid melodic style; and from country, a knack for making musical poetry out of simple chord progressions and everyday words. He also had the pop writer's ear for a hook. But at their best, Hardin's songs transcend these genres. They just sound like Tim Hardin songs.

For its songwriting, *Tim Hardin 2* is one of the highlights of the 1960s. Ten beautifully crafted gems, many of them barely scraping two minutes in length, make for a short but perfectly formed album. 'If I Were A Carpenter', 'Black Sheep Boy' and 'Lady Came From Baltimore' are the equal of anything from the past five decades of popular music. The rest of the album isn't far behind. Songwriting doesn't get much better than this.

Incredibly, the self-lacerating Hardin dismissed the album shortly after its release, although his accounts of what happened are typically confused. "I cried like a child when I heard what they'd done [to it]," he said. "I recorded those tracks alone and the [record company then added] some pretty bad backings."[10] In another interview, he said, "I gave the arranger my tapes of the songs, and he orchestrated them. I went into the studio, and cut the lot in half an hour, singing over the arrangements. I was so ill that it didn't matter then."[11] ("Illness" became a recurring and euphemistic motif for drug-related problems in Hardin's conversations with the press from now on.) Years later, Hardin's feelings about the second album seemed to have mellowed. "It's got a very heavy production," he said in 1974, "but the material is so good."[12]

No personnel was listed on the sleeve, although the sound of the instruments – electric and acoustic guitar, bass, drums, flute, vibes and strings – suggests that many of the musicians who appeared on *Tim Hardin 1* were involved. Production duties were shared between Charles Koppelman and Don Rubin. It was an altogether more integrated album than the first. "Long tall Timmy" had moved aside for Hardin the lovelorn poet and would never really make his presence felt again in Hardin's studio recordings.

Although neither of the first two albums sold in vast numbers, Hardin was soon to become a respected name as other artists covered his songs. Bobby Darin got hold of 'If I Were A Carpenter' in 1966 and scored a massive hit in October and November of that year, much to the annoyance of Hardin who, when he first heard the record on the radio, got out of his car and stamped on the ground in rage.

Darin's recording was more than a cover version, being a virtual facsimile of Hardin's style as well as his song. Darin's following album, released in early 1967, included a further four Hardin songs. Hardin responded bitterly to this "theft", accusing Darin of taking both his songs and his voice.[13] Curiously, many years later Hardin would claim that he had actually assisted Darin. "[Darin] said very truthfully, 'I think it would be best for me to sing the way you sing.' So we spent a lot of time together in the studios just in a rehearsal situation, me trying to teach him the [essence] of what makes my voice sound the way it sounds."[14] This is one of the many stories that changed whenever Hardin told it.

> **"Hardin was seen as a rising star among the new generation of songwriters."**

Early in 1968 The Four Tops applied their own inimitable magic to 'If I Were A Carpenter' with similar commercial consequences. Hardin pronounced their interpretation "terrible". The same song would also provide a hit for husband-and-wife duo Johnny Cash & June Carter.

By this stage in Hardin's career he was seen as a rising star among the new generation of songwriters. A significant breakthrough as a recording artist was anticipated. He was also enjoying an apparently idyllic family life, living in Los Angeles with Susan Morss, whom he had now married, and their son Damion, who was born in February 1967.

But encroaching heroin addiction and heavy drinking were taking their toll. It's impossible to unravel whether it was the sensitive, fragile nature of the man that drove him to addiction, or the addiction itself that created those characteristics – or whether the two were inseparable. But together they combined into a destructive force that rendered him incapable of capitalising on the professional and personal opportunities in front of him.

Chronic stage fright and illness prevented Hardin from touring consistently, and he was gaining a reputation for unreliability. He came to the UK in July 1968 to considerable press interest for a proposed tour with Family, but pulled out after only one date – at London's Albert Hall – because of pleurisy. At this concert Hardin dismissed his pick-up backing band after three songs, and then appeared to fall asleep on stage. Nonetheless, a reviewer of that lone appearance said, "Never before have I seen one man communicate with such pure and colourful tranquillity and untarnished emotion."[15]

In April 1968 he had managed to record a decent live album at Town Hall, New York City. It was released on Verve in September as *Tim Hardin 3* and consisted mainly of jazz-tinged settings of his best known songs. Produced by Gary Klein, writer of 1950s hit 'Bobby's Girl', it featured a number of musicians who worked with Hardin on and off for the next few years. They formed the backbone of Jeremy & The Satyrs, and recorded under their own name as well as backing Richie Havens. Hardin's contract with Verve was terminated at about the time *Tim Hardin 3* was released, but there was to be a confusing postscript.

In September 1967 an album titled *This Is Tim Hardin* had appeared on the Atlantic imprint, Atco. It consisted of material recorded before the release of *Tim Hardin 1,* possibly during Hardin's brief stay at Columbia a few years previously. In February 1969 *Tim Hardin 4* came out on Verve; it was a very similar set of derivative self-penned material and traditional folk and blues covers, also possibly from the Columbia sessions but sometimes credited as being recorded at the same concert that produced *Tim Hardin 3.*

> **"I saw him play four hours and he didn't open his eyes once."**

Hardin, speaking in the 1970s, could not recall which sessions each of the albums drew on, although he dismissed them both as collections of demos not worthy of release. It seems almost certain that both albums consist of early recordings made before Hardin had fully formed his style. As such they are of interest to Hardin collectors, but are hardly essential purchases. What is also clear is that they were calculated attempts by the record companies to cash in on somebody who, for all his idiosyncrasies, was now regarded as a major songwriting force.

One point of interest is the version on *This Is Tim Hardin* of Fred Neil's 'Blues On The Ceiling', which betrays some debt to Neil's own distinctive singing style – particularly the habit of dropping off to a low note at the end of a line.

That Hardin and Neil knew each other well is certain. Michael Ochs recalled: "The old Night Owl café [in Greenwich Village was a place where] everybody used to hang out a lot. It used to be Tim Hardin singing, Freddie Neil playing guitar ... John Sebastian playing harmonica. They would go from a Bo Diddley tune to a Freddie Neil tune, back to some classic rock'n'roll. I saw Hardin play four hours straight one night and he didn't open his eyes once. Talk about heroin ... ."[16]

By the time *Tim Hardin 4* was released, Hardin had signed again with Columbia. This time he was brought to the label by Clive Davis, who later also signed David Ackles. In September 1968 Columbia sent Hardin to Nashville for some recording sessions. They were aborted, and the results would not appear until nearly 30 years later, on the *Simple Songs Of Freedom* compilation.

Hardin's first album for his new label appeared a month after the last Verve release. Listened to consecutively, they illustrate how far Hardin had moved in the space of a few years. The new record was *Suite For Susan Moore And Damion – We Are One, One, All In One*. It was a representative title for an ambitious and, some would say, pretentious musical statement. Consisting of a few conventionally crafted songs, spoken-word passages and some free-flowing semi-improvised blues work-outs, it was a celebration of Hardin's life with his wife and son. It represented significant departures for Hardin the writer, as a thematically linked album to be listened to in its entirety – from a man previously renowned for two-minute classics. Before, Hardin had crafted personal feelings into universal statements. This time the songs remained just deeply personal.

Nobody covered the songs from *Suite For Susan Moore*. It was a brave but flawed attempt by

Hardin to broaden the boundaries of his art. The spoken word passages, although heartfelt, sound mawkish, and the whole project is devalued by a sprawling, pointless blues work-out, 'One, One The Perfect Sum', which is at odds with the careful economy of Hardin's best songs.

Gary Klein had again taken on the production duties, and in doing so accepted Hardin's unconventional working methods. Each room in Hardin's new home in Woodstock, New York, was fitted with a microphone linked to a central recording console. Klein was ensconced in a nearby hotel. Whenever Hardin felt inspired, which was frequently in the small hours, Klein was sent for and the singer was recorded wherever he stood. The inconveniences of this approach were partially mitigated by Hardin's uncanny ability to pick up a rhythm or melody exactly where he had left it days previously, even if the time between had passed in an opiate haze. Much of the instrumentation is sparse. Often only a tremolo'd electric guitar or an electric piano provides a spacious backdrop for Hardin's ever more poised and expressive vocal phrasing, heard to best effect on 'First Love Song' and 'Once Touched By Flame'.

Anyone coming to *Susan Moore* for the first time would be forgiven for thinking it was a work of unparalleled honesty. Whether that was the case is questionable as Hardin's marriage started to fall apart either during or shortly after the recording of the album. In all probability the sentiments expressed are more like anguished wishful thinking than fact. But by this time Hardin the family man was losing out to Hardin the junkie.

In Woodstock Hardin found himself once again in the centre of a thriving musical community, but unlike the days in Greenwich Village he tended not to mix with his illustrious neighbours, who included Dylan and Van Morrison. Hardin did appear at the Woodstock festival, struggling to win the crowd's attention at 3am on Saturday morning, but his contribution made neither the film of the event nor the original commemorative album.

"Hardin the family man was losing out to Hardin the junkie."

Hardin was still a respected force in music, but Columbia wanted a hit single. There were no candidates on *Suite For Susan Moore*, and he was not the man to write to order. It was Bobby Darin who was to solve the dilemma, offering Hardin a song in repayment for 'If I Were A Carpenter'. 'Simple Song Of Freedom' was just that – a catchy little number with a message of peace and tolerance. It was recorded in June 1969 with a respected group of session players, including drummer Bernard Purdie, and was the only "protest" song Hardin ever recorded – as well as being his only US hit, reaching number 50 in autumn 1969.

For the second time Hardin was on the threshold of a breakthrough. Most artists who have just had their first hit single would quickly tour and release follow-ups. Hardin had neither the strength to do the first, nor the material to do the latter.

His second Columbia album, *Bird On A Wire*, finally appeared in August 1971. By this time the optimism of 'Simple Song Of Freedom' already seemed like a distant memory of a past era, and any momentum it had given Hardin's career had dissipated. But *Bird On A Wire* was something of a triumph, and is easily the best of his 1970s albums. It was a more conventional record than its predecessor, distinguished by its title song, a racked, epic, country-soul rendition of Leonard Cohen's signature tune, replete with choir. This was also the last Hardin album to include any new original material of note. A picture of Hardin's son Damion graced the inner sleeve, but next to it the lyrics of the excellent and bitter 'Love Hymn' mourn the departure of Susan "with a new friend to LA".[17] The Tim Hardin staring out from the back sleeve has the haunted look of a broken man.

Ed Freeman, fresh from completing Tom Rush's first Columbia effort, produced *Bird On A*

Wire. He was wise both to Hardin's increasingly improvisational singing style and to his unreliability. The musicians, including on some tracks the rhythm section of the then new Weather Report, recorded their loose and funky takes of Freeman's arrangements in advance. Hardin then turned up when he felt like it to lay down his vocal tracks, spinning endless permutations and variations on the basic theme provided by the song's structure. "His rhythm was like a metronome," said producer Freeman. "The tempo was so perfect you could splice anywhere. Once he went to the bathroom halfway through a song. This was on a Monday. He came back on a Thursday and hit exactly the same tempo."[18]

The album was well received but not a big seller. Hardin himself considered it to be one of his better efforts, and described it a few years later as having "good clean superiority".[19] There were no more hit singles.

The most unusual song on *Bird On A Wire*, 'Andre Johray', was recorded in September 1969, a year before the main sessions for the album. A lyrically oblique and presumably autobiographical parable about somebody who could not handle "even the brink of fame", it was Hardin's most experimental recording. Half-spoken, half-sung over a backing track of vibes, guitar, strings and keyboards, and reprising some of the more ambitious mood-pieces on *Susan Moore*, it hinted at a direction that Hardin could have profitably explored had he been able to maintain any momentum as a writer. Sadly, by this time the songs had all but dried up.

In February 1972 Hardin left Woodstock for England, where as a registered heroin addict he qualified for the National Health Service's programme of methadone treatment. A flurry of articles appeared in the British music press at the time proclaiming that Hardin was newly cleaned-up and full of plans.

It was in England that he recorded his last album for Columbia. Released in 1973, *Painted Head* was produced by ex-Shadows drummer Tony Meehan, and featured guitarist Peter Frampton along with a host of the top British session players of the day. Although Hardin's voice still retained its fragile power, there were no original songs on the new album.

Around this time Hardin had started to talk, somewhat unconvincingly, about how he was primarily a singer – how he wanted to record "important" songs, whether he wrote them or not, and that his songwriting was incidental to his main talent as an interpretative singer. That he was capable of great singing had been recognised by Phil Ochs. "I still think [Tim Hardin] was the best singer of the 1960s," Ochs said in 1971. "In his youth he shamed everybody else on the stage in terms of singing and the geometry of singing, and timing, and tones, and musicianship. He was just not to be believed."[20]

> **"His rhythm was like a metronome, his tempo so perfect."**

Among the "important" songs chosen for *Painted Head* were Pete Ham's 'Midnight Caller' and Randy Newman's 'I'll Be Home'. Both were fine songs that suited Hardin, and he summoned up suitably yearning performances for each. But as a whole the album sounds like the well-played, slick product of a producer and some session men rather than the work of Tim Hardin. It gives the impression, rather like Scott Walker's albums of the same period, that the artist himself was incidental to the project. It did not sell, and Hardin's contract was terminated.

Remaining in England, Hardin quickly signed to GM Records, owned by Rod Stewart's manager of the time, Billy Gaff. The album he recorded for GM, *Nine*, contained six apparently original songs. One of these, the fine 'Shiloh Town', which Hardin had first attempted at the aborted Nashville sessions in 1968, was in fact a traditional song of uncertain origin that had also been recorded in the 1960s by Richie Havens. A new version of Fred Neil's 'Blues On My Ceiling' was also wrongly credited to Hardin. Of the remaining four originals, 'Never Too Far' and 'While You're On Your Way' were reworked from *Tim Hardin 1*, while the other two were painfully ordinary.

The album was an improvement on *Painted Head* but hardly a return to form. Despite efforts to repackage Hardin in the style of the day – he appeared on the sleeve in a white suit, platform shoes and gold jewellery, looking not unlike Steve Harley – it was not a commercial success. *Nine* was the last completed Tim Hardin studio album. It did not appear in the US until 1976, but after its UK release in June 1973 Hardin virtually disappeared from view. Staying in England for a few years, he toured briefly with Tim Rose. Reports of those appearances tell of Rose the trouper carrying an increasingly erratic Hardin.

There was talk of Hardin appearing in the title role of *Bound For Glory*, the film about Woody Guthrie – a role for which Tim Buckley was once briefly considered – but it came to nothing. There were periodic reunions with Susan throughout the decade. In 1976 he returned to the US and settled in Seattle where, briefly out of the music business, he was drug-free for a while.

> "In his youth he shamed everybody else on stage in terms of his singing, and timing, and tones and musicianship."

When he did return to occasional live performances it was the usual story – unreliability, inconsistency and flashes of genius. One report has Hardin coming on stage at The Troubador in Los Angeles, throwing up after a couple of songs, being unable to keep up with the band, then captivating the audience by singing a cappella for two hours. Another has him on stage in Montreal, singing while concentrating on a flickering candle placed on his piano, and seemingly oblivious of the audience.

In a 1980 TV documentary made alongside his live album, *The Homecoming Concert*, Hardin ramblingly talked about why he had taken heroin and, tellingly, why he might take it again. He displayed none of the evangelical zeal of the ex-addict, but rather a regret at having given up the drug. He appeared to believe that his health was better when he was on heroin, citing his rapid weight gain since quitting as evidence.

He also told of selling the rights to his songs for $23million that he never received, his managers somehow reneging on the deal and running off to Brazil with the profits. Different stories about the ownership of Hardin's songwriting catalogue have emerged over the years. Tim Rose, when interviewed for this book, clearly recalled Hardin saying that he sold all the rights to his back catalogue for $12,000 some time in the 1960s. What really happened will probably never be known. What is certain is that Hardin was a man ill equipped to manage his business affairs and vulnerable to being exploited.

A chance meeting with his old friend Phil Freeman led to a performance at Eugene, Oregon, Hardin's hometown, in January 1980. The performance was recorded for *The Homecoming Concert*. Freeman recalled: "I could not get him to sing his songs, so I took my guitar from the case and sang 'If I Were A Carpenter' and 'Reason To Believe'. This infuriated Tim. He took the guitar and said, 'Let me show you how it's done.' What I heard was a richness and maturity in Tim."[21]

Despite the incoherent, slurred performance in the accompanying TV interview, Hardin's *Homecoming Concert* was a triumph. In fine voice, he was clearly delighted to perform his best-known songs to old friends in what was his only hometown gig. On the sleeve of the album (originally released on a UK independent) the prematurely aged Hardin, still a few years short of 40, posed with his grandmother, Manner Small, who had raised him.

Shortly after the Eugene concert Hardin moved to Los Angeles to be near Damion and Susan. Once there he tried to get back into the music business again and fell into his old ways, threatening suicide if Susan did not return to him. Old associates were shocked by his physical decline. Former manager Erik Jacobsen came upon him in a studio. "I asked, 'Who's that?' ... Someone said, 'That's Tim Hardin.' He had bloated up to 200 pounds and had lost his hair. I never would have recognised him."[22]

In September 1980 Susan left LA with Damion to escape Hardin. On December 29th of that year Tim Hardin died, having just turned 39. The coroner's verdict was death from acute heroin-morphine intoxication due to an overdose. Whether this was a deliberate act or a tragic error is not clear, but it was a sad, squalid, lonely end. John Lennon had been shot a few weeks before Hardin's demise, but for Hardin there would be none of the grief-stricken adoration, no posthumous hits, no "spokesman for a generation" obituaries. In fact, his death went almost unnoticed.

For most of the 1980s Hardin remained a lost figure, known only to a few devotees, although cover versions of his songs were regularly played on radio stations around the world.

In the 1990s there was something of an upturn in his reputation. Polydor released *Hang On To A Dream*, a double-CD anthology of the Verve years, in 1994. Two years later Sony followed suit with the single CD *Simple Songs Of Freedom*, documenting the Columbia period. Both albums benefit from illuminating sleevenotes by Colin Escott and feature previously unavailable material. In 1993 Robert Plant returned Hardin to the British charts, scoring a minor hit with yet another version of 'If I Were A Carpenter'.

> **"Why, after every last shot, was there always another?"**

The album Hardin was working on when he died appeared on a tiny American independent label in 1981 and again in 1999. Although not a complete work, *Unforgiven* serves as a fascinating coda to Hardin's career. Two of its eight songs are completed studio recordings, the rest home-recorded sketches or sparsely-arranged, studio-recorded demos. Hardin the singer had lost nothing. All of the old qualities – the break in the voice, the elongated phrasing, the confessional intimacy – are present and undiminished. However, Hardin the writer was still nowhere near matching his best work from the mid 1960s, although there are hints of a partial return of his powers. Joe Cocker took up the country-ish title track of the collection, which was one of the finished pieces. The rest of the songs, with marked jazz influences, seem destined to remain largely unheard.

Even if Tim Hardin had never written his songs, he would still deserve recognition as one of the great singers of his time. His songwriting talent burned brightly for a few short months, but he kept his voice until the end. And of course he did write the songs. Their greatness is confirmed by a roll call of those who recorded them: Johnny Cash, Scott Walker, The Small Faces, Joan Baez, The Everly Brothers, Paul Weller, Ron Sexsmith, and many others.

So the question will always remain: how could a man lose his gift so completely? Perhaps Susan Morss was right when she described him as an introspective writer whose sense of his own feelings was increasingly dulled by drug addiction. When he lost touch with his feelings there was nothing else to write about.

Hardin's later albums were not without flashes of greatness, but at best they served only as tantalising reminders of how good he once was. Take *Tim Hardin 1* and *2* out of the body of work and you are left with a beautiful singer who made some ordinary records which in no way establish him as one of the greats. But listen only to those first two albums and you hear one of the great American poet/songwriters of his or any generation.

Paradoxically, it was in two of his songs about other people that Hardin spoke most accurately and prophetically about himself. "Why, after every last shot, was there always another?"[23] he sings in 'Eulogy To Lenny Bruce'. And then, on the version of 'Tribute To Hank Williams' on the *Homecoming Concert* album, he sings some lines expunged from the earlier recorded version of the song: "Whiskey took the heartbreak from too many broken dreams, and what pain wasn't cured by whiskey was cured by too much morphine."[24]

[1] *Disc & Music Echo* July 20th 1968
[2] Sleevenotes to *The Homecoming Concert* by Phil Freeman
[3] *ZigZag* 43 1974
[4] *ZigZag* 43 1974
[5] *Melody Maker* March 25th 1972
[6] *Melody Maker* March 25th 1972
[7] *Beat Instrumental* August 1968
[8] 'Lady Came From Baltimore' by Tim Hardin, Verve Forecast Records 1967
[9] *Beat Instrumental* August 1968
[10] *Record Mirror* July 27th 1968

[11] *Beat Instrumental* August 1968
[12] *Melody Maker* January 26th 1974
[13] *Disc & Music Echo* October 22nd 1966
[14] *Sounds* January 19th 1974
[15] Lon Goddard in *Record Mirror* July 27th 1968
[16] Jac Holzman & Gavan Daws *Follow The Music* (FirstMedia 1998)
[17] 'Love Hymn' by Tim Hardin, CBS Records 1971
[18] Sleevenotes by Colin Escott to *Simple Songs Of Freedom* compilation.

[19] *Melody Maker* January 26th 1974
[20] *Rolling Stone* May 27th 1971
[21] Sleevenotes to *The Homecoming Concert* by Phil Freeman
[22] Sleevenotes by Colin Escott to *Hang On To A Dream* compilation.
[23] 'Eulogy to Lenny Bruce' by Tim Hardin, Verve Forecast Records
[24] 'Tribute To Hank Williams' by Tim Hardin, Verve Forecast Records

FRED NEIL

Would you like to know a secret

Just between you and me?

I don't know where I'm going next,

Don't know where I'm going to be.

FROM 'THE OTHER SIDE OF THIS LIFE' BY FRED NEIL, *Third Story Music BMI*

Fred Neil had two big breaks in the 1960s. At the start of the decade he co-wrote a Roy Orbison hit; at the end, Nilsson's version of his 'Everybody's Talkin'' became a massive hit through the *Midnight Cowboy* movie. Such breaks would have set up many an aspiring songwriter for a glittering career. Neil, however, not only failed to capitalise on these opportunities, but positively shunned success.

In recent years, in-depth articles about an elusive and shadowy folk-rock pioneer have appeared in the music magazines *Mojo* and *Goldmine*. Richie Unterberger in his book *Urban Spacemen And Wayfaring Strangers* devoted a chapter to this same mysterious figure. Thorough, probing and fascinating though all of these pieces were, they could not avoid one central fact – that their subject was not available for comment. And he never really has been.

Even when he was active in the 1960s, Fred Neil eschewed the traditional promotional treadmill of record/tour/interview, avoiding the glare of press and public scrutiny whenever possible. And any notion that he was trying to create an aura of mystique as a marketing device must be seen in the context of his eventual withdrawal from the music business. He hasn't released a new record since 1971, and his last known public performance was in 1977. All attempts to contact him while researching this book failed. The unavoidable conclusion is that he will never again re-emerge from seclusion. He just doesn't want to be disturbed.

The apparent facts about Fred Neil are few, and most of those that are available are darkened by some shadow of doubt. Most of the usual sources of information reveal little. There is a paucity of press archive material, and even once close colleagues and friends have lost track of him, or say they have to preserve his anonymity. It is thought that he is alive and well, and has spent most of the past 30 years in Florida, periodically involved in work for a dolphin-awareness charity, a cause dear to him.

But he does still speak, through the few albums that he recorded in his brief career that have recently begun to reappear on CD. No doubt he still has friends and family with whom he maintains contact, people who know something of his life, feelings and thoughts. For everyone else, however, the music is all that is left.

Neil was born probably in 1937, and raised in Florida. His father worked for Wurlitzer, the jukebox manufacturer, and would travel around the bars of Florida, Georgia and Tennessee repairing and stocking the machines, often taking his son with him. Various unconfirmed reports have Fred playing the guitar from the age of six, writing songs for a living from 13, and performing at the Grand Ole Opry as a child. By the mid 1950s he may have been active on the nascent rockabilly scene in Memphis.

Later on in that decade Neil arrived in New York. For several years there he was just one of many hopefuls stalking the corridors of the Brill Building, writing songs and cutting a handful of singles. Of these obscure recordings the only one widely available can be heard on the 1999 Capitol double-CD compilation, *The Many Sides Of Fred Neil*. It's a cover of the country standard 'Long Black Veil', but Neil's contribution – whatever it might be – is swamped by the dubious harmonies of The Nashville Street Singers. It must have been one of the last of Neil's pre-folk recordings, and reveals absolutely nothing about what was to come.

Neil struck gold once during this period, co-writing a song called 'Candy Man' that was covered by Roy Orbison, initially as the b-side to his huge hit 'Crying'. Neil's writing partner for this song was Beverly Ross, who had previously penned the novelty hit 'Lollipop Lollipop' for The Velours. Not that 'Candy Man' was another novelty song, both writers being well aware that in the parlance of the Southern States a candy man is a pimp. Neil recorded his own version on his debut solo Elektra album some years later, eliminating the stop-starts that were a feature of Orbison's recording. By that time it would be credited to Neil only, and his bluesy vocal somehow manages to hint at hidden meanings in the seemingly innocuous lines: "Come on baby let me take you by the hand, can't you see I want to be your candy man?"[1]

Whether intentionally or not, Neil did not capitalise on the success of 'Candy Man'. Just as Orbison's version of the song was earning Neil the chance of a breakthrough of which other hopefuls could only dream, Neil was embarking on a parallel career.

In the late 1950s and early 1960s, despite the achievements of a few mavericks like Chuck Berry and Buddy Holly, pop songwriting was still largely the preserve of backroom composers sitting at pianos in booths in places like the Brill Building, writing to order for their publishers. That was soon to change, not only with the arrival of The Beatles, but also as a result of the success of Greenwich Village folkies like

Bob Dylan and Tim Hardin. Neil was their contemporary, but for a while – roughly between 1961 and 1963 – he kept a foot in the enemy's camp. During this time he would play folk music by night in the coffee-houses, while during the day he touted pop tunes around the publishers.

Neil must have seemed a strange figure on the coffee-house circuit: a Southern country boy in an urban environment, a hit pop songwriter among folk purists. There was an aura of mystery and suspicion around him that troubled many of his Village contemporaries. David Blue said: "I remember I wouldn't talk to Fred Neil, because he wasn't traditional. I mean, I didn't know what he did."[2] But Neil established a reputation as a mesmerising performer, and came to be widely admired, particularly by other Village singer-songwriters.

Another factor that set Neil apart was his voice, a natural baritone of rare depth, resonance and casual power. It sounded like the voice of an older man from a different generation, from a different time. Indeed, Neil was a good few years older than most of his contemporaries. If his stated birth date is correct he was already in his mid 20s by the time he took to the tiny stages of Greenwich Village in 1961. Photographs taken later in the decade when he would have been 30 or so could easily be those of someone older, but by then Neil's lifestyle and the Southern sun would have taken a toll on his fair, freckled complexion.

The first recordings of Neil the folkie were released in 1963 on a live compilation album on the FM label, which was releasing Tim Rose's early efforts with The Big Three at about the same time. *Hootenanny Live At The Bitter End* featured three Neil songs, the most notable of which was 'That's The Bag I'm In' (later re-recorded for Neil's final album). Apart from an early chance to hear the voice, these tracks confirm that the blues component of the then prevalent folk-blues hybrid was unusually dominant in Neil's case. It was this, plus the later incorporation of jazz influences, raga inflections and the finely honed song-craft brought from the Brill Building that made Neil's mature songwriting so alluring.

> "A hit pop songwriter among folk purists."

Although Neil quickly became a dominant figure in Greenwich Village, it wasn't long before he became the focus of another smaller scene in Coconut Grove, on the outskirts of Miami, Florida. This scene had been effectively kick-started by Vince Martin, another Greenwich Village performer, in late 1961. In time Coconut Grove became Neil's base, from which he would only periodically venture to the folk clubs of New York and, even more rarely, those of other American cities. It was with Martin that Neil eventually recorded his first full-length album.

Tear Down The Walls was released by Elektra in 1964. It was produced by Paul Rothchild and featured John Sebastian (harmonica) and Felix Pappalardi (bass) backing the strummed guitars and harmonised voices of Neil and Martin. Despite the added instrumentation it is a pretty typical album of the latter stages of the folk revival, roughly split between originals and traditional material. The power and originality of Neil's voice is often hidden beneath Martin's higher harmony parts.

Two songs of interest are Neil's own 'Wild Child In A World Of Trouble', later covered by Tom Rush on his first Columbia album, and a version of Bonnie Dobson's 'Morning Dew'. This latter cut – still very much a folk song – serves to illustrate how radical was Tim Rose's later rock interpretation of the song.

Tear Down The Walls was not a big seller, and a planned follow-up with Martin was aborted. Instead, Neil's next release was his first solo album. The title of *Bleecker And MacDougal* referred to the two Greenwich Village streets where all the folk action took place. Although the album had just about enough by way of traditional ingredients to keep the purists happy, it was clear that Neil was moving away from simply giving his own twist to an established style. There were 13 songs on the album, of which Neil wrote 12. He was accompanied by Sebastian and Pappalardi as well as second guitarist Pete Childs. Paul Rothchild was again the producer.

There are no drums on *Bleecker And MacDougal,* but Neil's fulsome, rhythmic 12-string guitar strumming and Childs's spare electric guitar licks lend the arrangements something of the verve of a rock'n'roll recording. All of Neil's songs are of a high standard, sharing an effortless quality present in all of his best material. They can be divided into three main categories. First, there is the jaunty, casual, pop-influenced material like 'Other Side Of This Life', which became one of his most covered songs without ever being a hit. Then there is the funereal-paced crooning blues, on which Neil stretches out for the lowest of his low notes. This style is best heard on 'Little Bit Of Rain' and the one traditional song, 'Water Is Wide', both decorated with shimmering tremolo'd guitar by Childs. Lastly, there are the abrasive R&B-influenced work-outs like 'Gone Again' on which the band and Rothchild conjure up an impressively dense and powerful sound from limited means.

Bleecker And MacDougal was released in 1965, shortly after Tom Rush's first Elektra album, and well before the debuts of David Blue and Tim Buckley. Although Neil wasn't matching Dylan's epoch-defining conversion to electric rock, he was one of the first of the folk performers to make the break from tradition toward a new, integrated sound. *Bleecker And MacDougal* was an album on the cusp of a new era.

Based on the reminiscences of friends and contemporaries, two distinct pictures of Neil's character emerge. One is of the carefree, impractical, good-natured, unhurried, anti-materialist dreamer concerned only with escaping the pressures of day to day life. The other is of the selfish, manipulative, unreliable junkie always seeking to exploit opportunities to his own narcotic ends. Tellingly, most of the latter comments come from Rothchild and Jac Holzman, the people charged with recording the mercurial, intuitive, unpredictable Neil.

Rothchild in particular condemned Neil with some savagery, saying in Holzman's book *Follow The Music:* "[Neil] was a brilliant songwriter and a total scumbag. The forerunner of the unreliable performer … . This is not a nice man."[3] Like so many aspects of Neil's story, the reason why he aroused such contempt in Rothchild remains unclear. Perhaps the perceptive, experienced Rothchild sensed that Neil was not making the most of his talent? John Sebastian has confirmed that there were obvious tensions between the producer and Neil in the studio, with Sebastian and Pappalardi effectively acting as diplomatic couriers, aiding communications between the two men. It is certain, though, that Neil had a serious heroin problem by this time.

Although heroin addiction was by no means rife on the Greenwich Village circuit, it wasn't uncommon either. Unlike Hardin, Neil hadn't been to the Far East to acquire his habit, but possibly got a taste for the drug from jazz musicians he mixed with. Whatever the roots of his addiction, it was to contribute to his increasing withdrawal over the coming years.

In the period between recording *Bleecker And MacDougal* and his next album, Neil left Greenwich Village. In search of solace from the urban environment that seemed peculiarly unsuited to his sensitive nature, he bought a small house in Coconut Grove, where he lived with his wife, Linda. Thereafter he only returned to New York for sporadic engagements. To fund the purchase of this house, Neil committed to recording another album.

Holzman has said that, despite his doubts about Neil's reliability, Elektra would have continued to record Neil. But for reasons now unknown, Neil decided to sign instead with Capitol. The mid 1960s were boom times for the label. With the financial security afforded by a roster that included The Beatles and The Beach Boys they could afford to take a chance on a risky maverick like Neil.

Nik Venet was known for his work producing early Beach Boys albums and was not the obvious choice for a singer like Neil, who had few credentials as a pop performer. But Neil and Venet had met previously, during Neil's Brill Building days, and Venet seemed able to avoid the tense confrontations that had marred the Elektra sessions. He achieved this partly by accepting the singer's preference for spontaneity in the studio. Both of Neil's studio albums for Capitol were recorded directly to stereo, without any mixing, and with the bare minimum of takes. Rothchild, on the other hand, had always sought to steer Neil toward what he felt were the right performances of each song, which entailed practise and repeated takes. Sebastian holds the view that for this reason the Elektra recordings are superior – more disciplined, and less inclined to pander to Neil's "laziness".

Such a view may well hold true for Neil's second Capitol album, *Sessions,* which we will deal with later. But it cannot apply to the first, which is the peak of Neil's achievements. *Fred Neil* was recorded in Los Angeles in late 1966 and released early the following year. Guitarist Childs was the only survivor from the Elektra period. His electric guitar and the drums of Billy Mundi – the first time drums appear on a Fred Neil album – mark a clear transition into what was by now known as folk-rock. Neil's two most enduring songs, 'Everybody's Talkin'' and 'The Dolphins', are the obvious highlights of the nine conventional songs on the album. The tenth track, 'Cynicrustpetefredjohn Raga', was a pointer to the controversial turn Neil's career would soon take.

Child's tremolo'd electric guitar chords open the album, as Neil – his voice noticeably coloured with reverb for the first time on record – languidly intones the world-weary lament that is 'The Dolphins'. Further electric guitars, Neil's 12-string acoustic and even a bazouki weave a jangling, vaguely Eastern tapestry as the song progresses. The "laziness" of which Sebastian complains surfaces as an agreeable looseness, and serves only to complement Neil's vocal performances and subject matter, on this song and on the rest of the album.

'I've Got a Secret (Didn't We Shake Sugaree)' is unusual in that Neil ventures into the upper reaches of his register, where he is clearly not as comfortable as he is with the low notes. It was another of Neil's easy-going, effortless pop-influenced tunes. There are several others on the album, including his original version of 'Everybody's Talkin''. Compared to Nilsson's later hit, Neil's take is slow, pared-down and casual. The arrangement is based on a few meandering guitars, carefully-placed plucked harmonics, and an underpinning bass, with no drums. Over this sparse backdrop Neil sings the timeless words of escape as insouciantly as if he was busking on a beach.

As with most of Neil's songs, the lyrics of 'Everybody's Talkin'' and 'The Dolphins' are ambivalent and elusive – apparently simple, carefree and casual observations overshadowed by obscure references to lost love and personal despair. One of the few occasions when Neil discards this obfuscation is in the exquisite, sleepy lament to lost love, 'Faretheewell (Fred's Tune)'. "Woke up this morning, it was drizzling rain, all around my heart is an aching pain, Faretheewell oh my honey,"[4] sings Neil, reaching right down for one of his trademark low notes on the second syllable of the word "honey". It is another great moment on an album of excellent songs and vocal performances.

Neil was one of a few of the original generation of Greenwich Village singer-songwriters to take an active interest in jazz. Another was Tim Hardin, who shared Neil's habit of dropping down to low notes at the end of phrases. Both singers employ this tactic on their versions of 'Green Rocky Road', a song that featured on *Fred Neil* and Hardin's first album. Both artists claimed they had written the song.

Despite its many merits, *Fred Neil* did not sell well. Neil was reluctant to perform or give interviews, and would casually disregard requests to appear on television. Yet without any significant public profile, he remained widely admired among contemporaries.

The last track, *Cynicrustpetefredjohn Raga,* was as its title suggests a rambling Eastern-sounding improvisation featuring guitar, harmonica and finger-cymbals. Although too long at over eight minutes, it was an intriguingly experimental avenue for Neil to explore. In the context of a collection of conventionally constructed songs it did not sit easily, but it pointed to the direction Neil was to follow when he returned to the studio in October 1967 to record his second album for Capitol.

If on *Fred Neil* Venet had tried to create a comfortable ambience to suit the temperamental Neil, on *Sessions* he took this principle one step further. Neil and Childs were joined in the studio by, among others, Cyrus Faryar, who recorded solo albums for Elektra, and sometime Dylan guitarist Bruce Langhorne. They were then left to their own devices, playing whatever they felt like in an unstructured, unplanned manner, without any direction or pressure from Venet.

Listening to *Sessions* is like eavesdropping on a group of friends playing – albeit exceptionally gifted friends who happen to be jamming in Capitol studios in Los Angeles. The resulting album was little more than an edited version of an improvised session lasting several days, during which Venet kept two tape machines running at staggered intervals so that he never had to stop the proceedings. When one tape ran out he replaced it as the other machine kept rolling.

Like most jam sessions, *Sessions* has a few moments of intense, unexpected brilliance buried in a mess of indulgent, aimless improvisation. It is most interesting as a forerunner of the jazz/blues/folk crossover style that Tim Buckley developed to a much more satisfactory degree on *Happy/Sad, Blue Afternoon* and *Lorca*. Both performers were operating on the boundary between groundbreaking exploration and self-indulgence. Sadly, Neil too often stepped into the latter territory.

There are only seven tracks on *Sessions*, five of which are half-developed improvisations. But listeners coming to the album for the first time get little indication of this from the first two songs, which although very sparsely arranged do at least have a conventional structure. Neil's own 'Felicity' and his cover of 'Please Send Me Someone To Love' are succinct, arranged, conventionally crafted songs. 'Felicity' is reputed to be a paean to Felicity Johnson, the English folk singer. For the main part of this short song Neil accompanies himself on his 12-string before the addition of a bass and Dobro flesh out the sound for a brief middle section. It would have sat comfortably on his first solo album.

'Please Send Me Someone To Love', a Percy Mayfield song, was given a supper-club jazz treatment. Stand-up bass and bluesy guitar licks frame what was one of Neil's most extreme explorations of his low range. So far – two songs in – *Sessions* sounds like a more introspective effort than its two predecessors. But then Neil is captured on tape giving a spoken instruction to Venet about the next song being "very short" before drifting into the doomy, cheerless 'Merry Go Round' which stretches to almost six minutes and sets the tone for the rest of the album.

Sessions is a beautifully recorded album. Venet's judicious coat of reverb warms the acoustic guitars and emphasises the true depth of Neil's voice. But there is no escaping the fact that the material is half-formed. There are moments of transcendence, though. When Neil addresses his mother in 'Look Over Yonder', saying "Are you sorry that you bore me?" you hear something of the tortured possibilities of his voice, but as the song drifts on for another four or five minutes it is hard to maintain attention. This is the song that bears the closest resemblance to Buckley's explorations on the first side of *Lorca*.

Sessions was an odd release. It was certainly not the album to secure Neil any commercial viability as a performer or writer. Perhaps its prevailing mood of despair, introspection and darkness was an accurate reflection of Neil's troubled state of mind; or perhaps it was just the sound of lazy, indulgent musicians playing around with their blues influences. Either way, it was a disappointment. There is no record of what Neil thought of *Sessions*, but it was the last studio album he released. After its appearance, little was heard of Neil for some years. It was during this hiatus when Neil could so easily have drifted out of sight altogether that his position was unexpectedly boosted by the inclusion of 'Everybody's Talkin'' on the soundtrack of the 1969 film *Midnight Cowboy* that starred Dustin Hoffman and Jon Voight.

Venet said later that he was asked to approach Neil with a view to re-recording the song for the film, because the producers thought that Neil's existing recording was too slow. But there was to be no re-recording, Neil not being the sort of man to jump at a career opportunity. It was left to Harry Nilsson to take up the song, which he recorded at a faster pace and with a fuller arrangement. The new version emphasised the song's carefree escapism at the expense of its parallel vein of inherent sadness. *Midnight Cowboy* became the most acclaimed film of the year, and 'Everybody's Talkin'' was a huge worldwide hit. It remains one of the most frequently played songs on oldies radio stations.

Most songwriters would have immediately sought opportunities to exploit this new-found fame, maybe re-releasing their own version of the song, or pitching other songs at Nilsson, or touring and making TV appearances. Neil did none of these things. Occasionally he was tempted out to perform live – and one of these performances, at the Elephant club in Woodstock, New York (where he lived for a while), was recorded for inclusion on his last album, *Other Side Of This Life*. Released by Capitol in 1971, the album consists of one side of live interpretations of Neil's best-known songs, including 'The Dolphins', 'Everybody's Talkin'' and the title track. The second side is a collection of out-takes from earlier Venet studio sessions, some of which were again re-workings of previously released songs. One song that had not appeared elsewhere was Neil's interpretation of 'Ya Don't Miss Your Water' on which he was accompanied by Gram Parsons on piano and vocal.

Other Side Of This Life was a pleasant enough album, but it had all the hallmarks of a contractual obligation. *Rolling Stone* described Neil as one of Greenwich Village's "also-rans"[5] when they reviewed the album. On this half-hearted note, Neil's career as a recording artist came to a halt. He retreated into a silence that was broken only by a handful of public performances over the next few years. Eventually even these ceased, and Neil went into a seclusion from which he has yet to emerge.

There was one further attempt at recording, when he began work on an album for Columbia in 1973. Neil was joined by long-time collaborator Childs, bassist Harvey Brooks and Sebastian, but the results were some inconclusive sessions that were never issued. This group performed at the Montreux Jazz festival in 1975, and some unfamiliar song titles appear on the set-list of that event which indicate that Neil may have written some fresh material since his late-1960s period of productivity.

By the early 1970s Neil's fascination with dolphins had led to his involvement in the Dolphin Project, a charity that rescues mistreated dolphins from circuses and seeks to educate people about the human cruelty foisted on the aquatic mammals. In 1976 and '77 he performed a few benefit shows for this cause. From these events grew a loose coalition of activists and musicians who in 1977 went to Japan to spread their message. So it was that in April of that year, in Tokyo, on a bill with Jackson Browne, Richie Havens and others, Fred Neil performed his last concert for a paying audience.

It is thought that Neil probably still lives in Florida somewhere. Some reports have him living in motels with only a bicycle and a guitar. Assuming he is alive, he is now well into his 60s. When judging Neil's status among singer-songwriters of the same generation it is hard to avoid the conclusion that his undoubted talents were never fully realised. He was first and foremost a blues singer. At his best he took the spirit of the blues and housed it in a musical architecture of singular identity, constructed from the building blocks of folk, jazz and pop influences. He was able to write personal, confessional songs that transcended their origins to become standards. But he only managed this on a few occasions, and after such vertiginous achievement rapidly fell back into aimless improvisation and pointless retreads of his best moments. It was as if he could never really maintain an enthusiasm for his own music for long.

He is important, though, for the influence he had on his contemporaries, and for that handful of songs that still retain their appeal. There are many parallels in his story with that of Tim Hardin. Both writers learnt their craft so well that their best songs are deceptively simple and seemingly effortless. They both drew on all their influences and made songs that are unique yet familiar, personal yet universal. Then they both threw it all away.

Neil was one of the best singers of the era. He was one of very few white performers in pop history to forge a vocal style based on hitting low notes. "That bass voice Fred had!" marvelled singer-songwriter Hoyt Axton. "He'd hit those low notes very clearly and straightahead. What a great singer."[6] And this he seemingly did without any thought for technique or correct breathing. He could just do it. It is fitting that 'Everybody's Talkin'' became his most famous song. Neil's characteristic lyrical twinning of carefree daydreaming and inconsolable sadness tells his own story so well. He is reputed to have written the words on the spot in the studio when under pressure to come up with a song. Casually, without thinking. The song's success gave him the means to make his escape forever. Eric Andersen perhaps put it best when he commented, "[Fred Neil] was always a cross between a rumour and a legend."[7]

[1] 'Candy Man' by Fred Neil, January Music BMI
[2] *Renaldo And Clara* movie 1978
[3] *Follow The Music* (FirstMedia 1998)

[4] 'Faretheewell (Fred's Tune)' by Fred Neil, Carlin Music Corp
[5] *Rolling Stone* June 10th 1971
[6] Robbie Woliver *Hoot! A 25-year History*

of *The Greenwich Village Music Scene* (1986)
[7] *Mojo* February 2000

PHIL OCHS

CHAPTER 6

Some have chosen to decay
and others chose to die,
But I'm not dying, no I'm not dying,
Tell me I'm not dying.

FROM 'THE SCORPION DEPARTS BUT NEVER RETURNS' BY PHIL OCHS, *A&M Records*

Phil Ochs started out as the archetypal protest singer producing "topical songs" on albums with titles like *All The News That's Fit To Sing*. Later in the 1960s he embarked on a fascinating phase of introspective pop experimentation, but by the early 1970s – just ten years since the start of his career – he had become a washed-up alcoholic on the way to an early death.

" On the first day of summer, 1975, Phil Ochs was murdered in the Chelsea Hotel by John Train, who is now speaking. I killed Phil Ochs. The reason I killed him was he was some kind of genius but he drank too much and was a boring old fart. For the good of societies, public and secret, he needed to be gotten rid of. Although he had good ideas, ie An Evening With Salvador Allende and a couple of songs like 'Crucifixion' and 'Changes', he was no longer needed or useful. He was too embarrassing at parties…"[1]

The paranoid, violent, shambling drunk John Train was a sinister figure staggering through the closing chapter of the Phil Ochs story, brandishing a hammer, threatening friends and strangers, men and women. He had started life as some kind of darkly comic alter-ego – Phil Ochs's last creation – but came to acquire a malign power of his own that his creator could not or would not control. When the real Phil Ochs was depressed, directionless, despairing and vulnerable, Train stepped into his skin, spending his money, decimating his relationships and trampling over the detritus of his career, before leaving him broke and broken.

From childhood to the end of his life Phil Ochs found release, escape and inspiration in the movies, sometimes catching as many as six films during the course of a day. He loved the great screen idols – John Wayne, James Dean, Marlon Brando – not in an ironic, distanced way, but with the adoration of a fan, a dreamer and an enthusiast. He loved them for what their images stood for rather than what they really were. He also loved Elvis Presley, an infatuation that was to become manifest in a pivotal episode in Ochs's decline. "I'm a victim of myths, I love the idea of myths," he said. "I love the idea of Hank Williams, I love the idea of Jesse James, I love the idea of Elvis Presley, I love the idea of John Kennedy, and Robert Kennedy, and Malcolm X."[2]

It was ironic, then, that a man so aware of the power of images became one himself, a symbol of the vacuum left by the evaporating idealism of the 1960s folk generation, an archetype of youthful idealism that burnt itself out.

The Phil Ochs who survives in public consciousness is a guitar-toting revolutionary firing acoustic broadsides at Republicans. It's an accurate enough reflection of his early career, when he was recording "topical songs" for Elektra. But one of the tragedies of this most tragic of stories is that as he moved beyond his folk-protest beginnings to the intriguing, ornate, baroque chamber pop of his later A&M albums, he started to lose his modest audience. That music, his best, is all too often obscured by the enduring picture of the strident protestor who finished up a lowly entry in the list of 1960s casualties, way behind the big figures like Jimi Hendrix, Jim Morrison, Janis Joplin and Brian Jones.

Philip David Ochs was born on December 19th 1940 in El Paso, Texas. He had an older sister, Sonia (known as Sonny), and a younger brother, Michael. His father, Jacob, was a Polish Jew who had emigrated with his parents to the US. Unable to get a place in a medical school in his adopted homeland, Jacob had moved to Edinburgh, Scotland, where he studied at the University. There he struck up a friendship with the brother of the woman who later became his wife, Gertrude Phin.

After marrying, Ochs's parents moved to the States. Almost immediately Jacob Ochs was drafted into the army. After postings in several different States he was sent overseas in early 1945, where he saw frontline action in the bloody closing stages of the war with Germany. When he returned, the balance of his sensitive, imaginative mind had become disturbed and he battled with episodic depression for the rest of his life.

The Ochs children had an unsettled childhood. Their father, too unreliable to sustain his own medical practice, found work in tuberculosis hospitals around the country, one of the lowest ranking jobs for a doctor. The family eventually landed up in Columbus, Ohio. Accounts of Phil Ochs's early years describe him as a solitary daydreamer, prone to staring out the window during classes, and finding solace in photography and cinema. By the time the family arrived in Ohio, Ochs had been persuaded by his mother to take up a musical instrument. He settled on the clarinet because the music shop didn't have in stock either a trumpet or a saxophone, his first choices. Despite being an initially reluctant pupil, Ochs excelled, and soon music was added to his list of consuming passions.

As a teenager Ochs chose to attend a military school in order to pursue his musical interests in the institution's band. Once there he became disillusioned with the formal, restrictive nature of marching-band music. By this time he was listening to the radio and developing infatuations for Johnny Cash, Buddy Holly, Gene Vincent and Elvis, passions that would survive through to adulthood. He had cosmetic surgery to correct what he thought was an ugly nose; he grew his straight dark hair long on top and slicked it back, in an attempt to look like Elvis. He started to talk about being a star.

In 1958 Ochs enrolled at Ohio State University where he studied journalism. In early 1959, when Fidel Castro and Che Guevara first started to appear on American television, Ochs adopted them into his pantheon of idols, initially as much for their romantic, rebel-chic appearance as their politics. Dropping out of college before completing his first year, he re-enrolled at the start of what would have been his second. He met a politically aware guitar-playing Elvis enthusiast called Jim Glover with whom he started to write, to play and to sing songs, and won his first guitar from Glover in a bet. They called themselves The Sundowners after a Robert Mitchum film, but following a falling-out with Glover, Ochs began to perform solo.

By now Ochs was consumed by the manic energy that would carry him through early adulthood and punctuate his later depressions. He was writing for the college newspaper, editing his own more radical publication, bombarding the local town newspaper with letters, and spewing out songs by the dozen. Ignoring the protestations of his parents, Ochs eventually quit his studies shortly before graduating. He became disillusioned when he was passed over for editorship of the college newspaper, apparently because he was too politically radical. This time he didn't re-enrol.

> "I'm a victim of myths. I love the idea of Elvis Presley."

It was 1962. Greenwich Village in New York City was alluring for an American youth with a guitar, a political conscience and a few songs. Ochs made the inevitable pilgrimage. Within months he was as immersed in the burgeoning folk community as anyone. He was publishing articles and songs in the radical magazine *Broadside*, playing at Folk City and other clubs, and scribbling lyrics for songs on whatever scraps of paper he could find.

His early songs were rudimentary in construction, sharing similar chord sequences and melodies, and always about something specific: a current event, an injustice, a message. At this stage there was little to separate Ochs from the many other earnest young strummers – except perhaps an almost overpowering self confidence that manifested itself when he would barge in on conversations to tell people he was going to be a star, and when he played his songs to anybody who would listen.

The energetic, articulate, engaging Ochs – shabbily dressed, stammering, hair falling in a greasy forelock over his eyes – pushed through the massed ranks of contenders with enthusiasm and intelligence until he assumed a position in the upper echelons of the Village hierarchy. For a while he, Dylan and David Blue were close friends, a trinity of fast-talking iconoclasts who spoke, wrote and sang with cynicism, idealism, romanticism and a sharp, scathing wit. Their lives were a whirlwind of songs, singing and drinking, having breakfast together, going to Western double bills together. Dylan was the leader, nobody doubted that, but Ochs was the lieutenant, always ready to assume command.

Ochs's songs at this time were a model of what is now thought of as protest music, earnest diatribes against injustice that were passionate in their support of causes, uncompromising in their declarations of right and wrong. Ochs was a personification of the classic folk movement paradox: a sort of fundamentalist liberal, and a critical patriot; the kind of black-and-white persona that Dylan rejected when he later sang, "I was so much older then, I'm younger than that now." But Ochs was also talking about selling a million records and being a star. This dichotomy – the earnest left-wing activist who wanted to be a pop star – was something that he spent the rest of his career trying to resolve.

Ochs didn't like the term "protest song" – he preferred "topical song". When he wrote in *Broadside* magazine about every newspaper headline being a potential song it was no glib slogan, more a modus operandi that he adhered to at the time.

Although by 1963 Ochs's professional life was burgeoning, personally he was already experiencing the sort of confusion that came to prevail later. His father died at about the time that his girlfriend, Alice Skinner, became pregnant. It was an unwanted pregnancy – at least so far as Ochs was concerned – and he agonised over whether to marry Skinner. Eventually he decided he should, seemingly more out of a sense of duty than anything else.

The couple moved into an apartment on Bleecker Street which served as Ochs's base for his constant efforts to advance his career. Alice was instructed to sit by the phone and take calls for Ochs as he performed whenever and wherever he could. By the end of 1963 he had played at the Newport folk festival, visited the incapacitated Woody Guthrie in hospital, and been signed by manager Albert Grossman. All were steps that Dylan had taken before him on the road to folk stardom. Ochs had also become a father, being absent on tour when his daughter Meegan was born. He was to remain an affectionate though often absent father, even though his relationship with Alice fell apart shortly after the birth, and despite his own later disintegration.

Aside from a few minor idiosyncrasies, Ochs's musical career fits into two distinct categories: the folk albums for Elektra; and his later, more ambitious A&M recordings. His first Elektra album was released in 1964, although he'd made a few appearances on record prior to this on folk compilations on the Broadside label.

All The News That's Fit To Sing distilled the "topical song" idea, with Ochs imagining the record as a musical newspaper. It was produced by Elektra head Jac Holzman with Paul Rothchild credited as "recording director". On the cover Ochs sat on his guitar case reading a newspaper in the middle of a wet city street. It was a typical record of the era. Ochs's clear, plaintive voice, sometimes breaking on the high notes, holds forth over an accompaniment of simple strumming and picking, augmented by second guitarist Danny Kelb. It was a good enough album of its type – a style of music that would, in the wake of The Byrds' electrification of Dylan material, appear obsolete within 18 months.

The record was a modest seller. It certainly got nowhere near the million figure that Ochs confidently predicted, but he was undaunted. Throughout 1964 he continued in an unabated frenzy of songwriting, political activism and touring.

In February 1965 his second Elektra album, *I Ain't Marching Anymore*, was released. The Holzman/Rothchild production team again recorded Ochs singing more of his topical songs, including the title track which became something of a protest anthem. It was a more confident effort than its predecessor, but in essence the same sort of record. Dylan's transitional *Bringing It All Back Home*, with its one electric side, appeared at about the same time. The Ochs record sold

just over 40,000 copies, while Dylan's went gold. Although *I Ain't Marching Anymore* displayed a growing maturity and a more definite sense of identity, it was clear that Ochs was already falling behind the game.

Ochs didn't perform at the Newport festival in 1965 when Dylan's traumatic electric set heralded his painful fall from grace in the eyes of the folk establishment. There was a vacancy now for the position of young saviour, and those same establishment powers made moves to deify Ochs. Dylan had defected, sold out, mortgaged his soul; but Ochs was true to his principles. Dylan wrote indulgent, mysterious, mystical poetry and thrashed a Fender electric guitar; but Ochs still railed against war and injustice and strummed an old Gibson acoustic. However, Ochs, writing in *Broadside*, was quick to shake off the crown so eagerly placed on his head. He condemned the booing of Dylan as "unthinking mob censorship". Nonetheless he continued, for the time being, to do what the ailing folk community wanted of him, singing his political songs at benefits and championing the causes of civil liberties, human rights and peace.

Although Ochs had been willing to support Dylan's right as an artist to explore new directions and to challenge his audience, and despite generally approving of much of Dylan's new material, he wasn't wholly uncritical. And an incident occurred in autumn 1965 that has since passed into legend.

It may have been in September after the two singers participated in a Sing-in For Peace at Carnegie Hall, a protest against the Vietnam war. It may have been during a Dylan photoshoot at about the same time. Reports differ. Dylan played Ochs a song that he had earmarked as a single, keen to get Ochs's opinion.

The song may have been 'Can You Please Crawl Out Your Window', or 'One of Us Must Know (Sooner or Later)'. Most accounts state it was the former, including Robert Shelton's in his Dylan biography *No Direction Home*. Marc Eliot, in his biography of Ochs, says that Ochs told him definitively in 1972 that it was the latter. It's possible that Ochs criticised both songs at different times, and the incidents have been fused into a single event.

Whatever song it was, Ochs thought Dylan's standards were slipping, and told Dylan so. Dylan, then in his arrogant, magisterial pomp, was furious. Later – whether hours or days later again isn't clear – the two singers were sharing a cab. David Blue may have been present. Dylan ordered the driver to pull over, and ejected Ochs from the car saying he wasn't a songwriter at all, "just a journalist". Ochs left quietly.

> "With Dylan's fall from grace there was a vacancy for a young saviour, and the folk establishment made moves to deify Ochs."

The episode confirms the esteem in which Ochs held Dylan. When asked later why he had taken the abuse so meekly he said that if Dylan says something to you, you've got to listen. It shouldn't be overlooked, however, that for Ochs to be called a journalist rather than a writer was less of an insult than it might appear. Ochs said himself that in his songs and on the printed page he kept a quarter of himself "in reserve" to observe and write as a journalist.

Nonetheless, a rift opened between the two men that lasted well into the next decade. Ochs said that after being ejected from the car he didn't see Dylan again for years – although Shelton claimed to be present during a meeting between the two singers in Christmas of that year, several months after the incident.

Around this time Ochs left Albert Grossman's charge in favour of political activist Arthur Gorson, believing that the former overlooked him in favour of Dylan. Gorson, with a background in student politics, was new to management but a gifted organiser. Ochs was the first of a stable of clients that came to include Tom Rush and David Blue.

A few months prior to the "journalist" incident Ochs had experienced his first taste of real commercial success as a songwriter when Joan Baez recorded one of his new songs, 'There But For Fortune', and took it into the UK Top Ten. The b-side to Baez's hit was a Dylan song, 'Daddy, You've Been On My Mind'. Ochs relished the fact that his song had been the hit. It appeared in 1966 on Ochs's next album and his last for Elektra, *Phil Ochs In Concert*.

In Concert was different from most live albums in that it did not include any songs that Ochs had previously recorded. It was also unusual because, while it generally gave the impression of being a recording of a single live concert, it was actually spliced together from tapes of three different performances.

Ochs had played a high-profile concert at Carnegie Hall in January 1966, and the initial plan had been to record the show for the album. As the time for Ochs to go on stage drew near, however, he lost his voice in an attack of nerves. Eventually his voice returned sufficiently, with the help of alcoholic lubrication, enabling him to sing just about adequately enough to get through the concert, but not well enough for the tapes of the performance to be worthy of release. Ochs had to repeat the concert in Boston shortly afterward in an effort to get a better recording of the new songs. It was a superior performance, and much of what finally appeared on the album came from that show. But even so, some of the Boston material was sub-standard, and a third recording – of Ochs singing in New York's Judson Hall without an audience – was deemed necessary. The final release consisted of the Boston show interspersed with recordings from the Carnegie Hall and Judson Hall performances.

In Concert marks a transitional phase in Ochs's development. Although still very much a folk record, complete with "protest" songs, it also included more abstract, lyrical material like 'Changes', a minor UK hit for Crispian St Peters and one of Ochs's most enduring songs.

> "His first taste of songwriting success came when Joan Baez covered one of his songs."

The album was the last appearance of Ochs the topical singer, the singing journalist, the protester. It was his biggest-selling release on Elektra, helped no doubt by the inclusion of Ochs's own version of the Baez hit, and crept into the lower reaches of the *Billboard* Top 150. But compared to Dylan's *Blonde On Blonde* and even David Blue's first album, it was a dated record.

Despite the small-scale commercial successes, Ochs was becoming dissatisfied with Arthur Gorson's management and with Elektra Records. Gorson now had a number of high-profile artists and Ochs was just one among several, rather than the focus of attention. Additionally, little headway had been made in persuading other artists to record his songs in the wake of Baez's hit. Ochs, still harbouring ambitions to be a major international star, made two decisive steps.

He had not spoken to his brother Michael for several years. The younger Ochs had come to

Greenwich Village in the early 1960s in the wake of his brother, and had loyally followed him around until Phil, through a combination of disregard and arrogance, had all but driven him away. Michael was by now living on the West Coast, scraping a living as a photographer, when he got a call from his brother demanding that he stop whatever he was doing and become his manager. Michael, with no management experience, did indeed drop everything and was back in New York in a week. Phil gave his brother a 25 per cent cut of everything – an unheard-of deal at the time.

In January 1967 the Ochs brothers set up an office in Broadway, right in the heart of Tin Pan Alley, and set to work to make Phil Ochs the international star he yearned to be. The first step was to secure a new record deal. Ochs believed that Holzman had betrayed him and other singer-songwriters on the label by telling them there was no money for big recording budgets and advances, and then splashing out on The Doors – an accusation Holzman has always denied. Michael quickly settled into his new role, extracting Ochs from his Elektra contract and negotiating a more favourable deal with West Coast label A&M that crucially included a no-censorship clause.

Ochs's first album for A&M was recorded in August 1967 with producer Larry Marks. The singer came into the studio from a coast-to-coast promotional tour organised by his new label, clutching a batch of new songs that had been accumulating over the past year. The folk revival was over, protest music was passé, it was The Summer Of Love – and Ochs was looking for a new sound.

Liberated from the confines of the topical song, he had been exploring a poetic, abstract direction in his lyric writing. It would be wrong, though, to imply that at this point in his career Ochs abandoned his political principles. Songs like the extraordinary 'Crucifixion', about the assassination of John Kennedy, left the listener in no doubt about his loyalties. Although he was still intent on tackling social and political issues, his writing was characterised by the allusive, multi-layered images of the poet rather than the slogans of the campaigning journalist. Whereas before it often appeared that the song was the servant of its subject matter, now he was starting to emphasise the primacy of the song itself. Speaking in *Melody Maker* he said: "A bad propaganda song I agree with isn't better than a good propaganda song I don't agree with. One is a bad song and the other is a good one, period."[3]

"The allusive, multi-layered images of the poet."

Broadening Ochs's sound hinged musically on successfully expanding the arrangements, as most of his songs were still constructed on the bedrock of simple verse/chorus repetitions. Ochs himself had some ideas about what his new sound should be, but his grasp of formal musical language and studio technology was insufficient to communicate those ideas to Marks. The sound they finally achieved was arrived at through a process of exploration and experiment, using orchestral instrumentation and studio technology. It involved Ochs, Marks, the studio musicians, and several arrangers.

This new style endured, with subtle refinements, through a trilogy of albums on A&M using recordings made during an 18-month period. These albums were Ochs's crowning achievement. The first was *Pleasures Of The Harbor*, recorded in August 1967 for a budget of $40,000.

Abandoning for the most part the strummed acoustic guitar chords that had formed the backdrop of previous Phil Ochs recordings, *Pleasures Of The Harbor* unveiled a unique classical-folk-pop sound built on the elaborate piano playing of Lincoln Mayorga and the orchestrations of Ian Freebairn-Smith and Joseph Byrd. Many of the songs – some five minutes or more in length –

were arranged in such a way that each verse and chorus was different, rather than simply repeating in the conventional manner.

Another departure for Ochs was the way in which he sang. Larry Marks said: "He wanted to make sure … that he sounded like a singer as opposed to someone who was delivering his own material. He worked hard on it."[4] This meant that Ochs had to record many of the songs line by line, a method completely at odds with the way he recorded for Elektra, where he had stood at the microphone singing and playing at the same time, not even wearing headphones.

The new style was best heard on the title track and 'Crucifixion'. 'Pleasures Of The Harbor', with its sweeping orchestrations and undulating piano complementing Ochs's nautical imagery, was the first exploration of the "journeying sailor" theme to which he would return several times over the next few albums.

'Crucifixion' closed the album. It was a disturbing allegorical account of Kennedy's assassination, casting the late President as a Christ-like saviour doomed to be sacrificed. Nearly nine minutes in length, the near-psychedelic concoction of strings, flutes, backward tapes and primitive electronic oscillations gradually overpower Ochs's tremulous vocal. Although at times in danger of collapsing under its own ambition, it was an extraordinarily adventurous musical statement, a quantum leap from the previous year's political folk strumming.

'Outside A Small Circle Of Friends' pitted a disturbing lyric about murder and social irresponsibility against a backing of insanely cheerful banjo and a honky-tonk piano. It was on the way to being a hit when radio stations noticed the reference to marijuana and banned it. That was the last time Ochs came close to a major commercial breakthrough.

Marks and Mayorga, this time assisted by Van Dyke Parks and a guest appearance from Ramblin' Jack Elliot, were working with Ochs again for his next album, *Tape From California*, which appeared in early 1968. Marks had felt that *Pleasures Of The Harbor* was overblown in places, and consequently the arrangements of the new album were an economical refinement of the same baroque-folk sound of the earlier record. The result was a more conventional record. There was even a return to acoustic folk for 'Joe Hill', a seven-minute narrative that would have sat comfortably on his final Elektra album. 'White Boots Marching In A Yellow Land', meanwhile, pitched an old-style, plain-speaking, anti-Vietnam lyric, plus acoustic guitar, against a military snare drum and bugle. The cynical triumphalism of 'The War Is Over' made it perfectly clear that it wasn't. The "new" Ochs sound was best heard on the title track, a nearly seven-minute folk-pop creation of splashing drums, bubbling bass guitar and harpsichord. Over this Ochs plaintively sang of a "sailor from the sea" who "looks a lot like me", who has "lost his mind" and should be "put away".[5]

> "Splashing drums, bubbling bass guitar and harpsichord."

Jerry Rubin had met Ochs on a demonstration in 1965. Rubin, along with Abbie Hoffman, was the driving force behind the Youth International Party, the Yippies. He had drawn Ochs into discussions about the aims, tactics and principles of the group in early 1968.

The Yippies planned an alternative rally in Chicago during August 1968 to coincide with the Democratic Party Convention. It was to be the moment when the burgeoning counter-culture would steal the initiative from the establishment in the full glare of the media. In the words of a Yippie statement: "This youth festival will take place at the same time as the national Death (Democratic) Convention in Chicago. It will be a contrast in lifestyles. Ours will be an affirmation of life; theirs is d-e-a-t-h … . This will be … the first coming together of all the people who have

been involved in the youth revolution which has been taking place in America in the past decade."[6] The proceedings started peacefully enough. Ochs and Rubin attracted the media attention they desired when they were arrested for an infringement of livestock laws after attempting publicly to nominate a pig for president. But when tear gas and baton-wielding riot police broke up a demonstration in Lincoln Park, a tense stand-off ensued. Ochs tried to take control, pleading with the crowds through a megaphone, before approaching the line of police and attempting to persuade them, man by man, to cross over to join "the people". Inevitably his attempts failed and the protests collapsed into violence, with the arrest of Hoffman, Rubin and others. What the world's media eventually captured were images of long-haired, strangely-dressed, wild-eyed young rebels apparently fighting the forces of law and order. It was a portent of the death of the 1960s dream.

Ochs was shattered and depressed by the experience. Friends had warned him that the demonstration would be a trap, and that it was inconceivable that a ragged selection of hippies and Yippies could seize power in any way at all from the establishment forces of Middle America. He had chosen to ignore them, and had seemed to believe that the event really could have been the harbinger of radical social upheaval. Although he continued to involve himself in political protest almost until the end of his life, his idealism died in Chicago. He never lost his principles – he just started to lose the belief that they could ever effect change. If one single event could be said to have precipitated his downfall, it was this.

The sleeve of Ochs's next album, *Rehearsals For Retirement*, featured a picture of a tombstone bearing the inscription: "Phil Ochs (American); Born: El Paso, Texas 1940; Died: Chicago, Illinois 1968; Rehearsals for Retirement."

> "Ochs was overwhelmed by the mature Presley's performance."

The songs on the new record were written in a two-week period after the Chicago demonstrations. Guitarist Bob Rafkin joined the established team of Marks and Mayorga for this, the darkest, most introspective album of the trilogy. It was the second LP that Ochs recorded during 1968, and although by now he was beginning to slide inexorably into depression, his creative star was nonetheless still in the ascendancy.

Ochs's fragile, limited voice was often a weakness of his recordings, unable to find the dynamic expression his more dramatic songs seemed to require. Yet he sang with power, restraint and palpable pain on such elegiac piano ballads as the title track, 'William Butler Yeats Visits Lincoln Park And Escapes Unscathed' and 'The Scorpion Departs But Never Returns', achieving a depth and profundity that can now be viewed as the very pinnacle of his career. Elsewhere, the old fire and scathing irony surfaced defiantly on 'I Kill Therefore I Am', a rumbustious country rocker that takes a swipe at "the masculine American man: I kill therefore I am".[7]

Rehearsals For Retirement was a commercial disaster, deleted within a year. Ochs, now living in Los Angeles and drinking heavily, started to think his career was over. For the best part of a year he did little. During this fallow period he went to see one of Elvis Presley's comeback shows in Las Vegas. Initially anxious that his boyhood idol might not live up to expectations, Ochs was overwhelmed by the power and energy of the mature Presley's performance. A youthful obsession was rekindled.

Ochs formed a band, including guitarist Rafkin and pianist Mayorga, and rehearsed a set combining Presley and Buddy Holly medleys with his own songs. He started to wear a gold suit like Presley had worn in the 1950s. This phase of Ochs's career – the "gold suit era" – which had started as a joke but became a confused and confusing concept, was eventually played out to bizarre and destructive extremes. "It's a parody. It is also a study of American hero worship and American folk worship,"[8] he said as the phase was drawing to a close in late 1970. In April of that year, when the gold-suit tour played Carnegie Hall, he said: "If there's any hope for America, it lies in revolution, and if there's any hope for a revolution in America, it lies in getting Elvis Presley to become Che Guevara."[9]

Ochs's last studio album for A&M was recorded in a two-day session during the gold-suit period, with Van Dyke Parks producing, and released early in 1970. When asked why he had taken on the job, Parks cruelly quipped, "Oh, you know me, no job too small."[10] The ironically titled *Phil Ochs Greatest Hits* was packaged in a sleeve which was a parody of an Elvis Presley greatest hits collection from the late 1950s, and included the legend, "50 Phil Ochs fans can't be wrong." Ochs was, like Elvis, by now carrying a few extra pounds, and was pictured squeezed into the gold suit, brandishing an electric guitar. The suit was a lamé creation made by Los Angeles tailor Nudie Cohen, an exact copy of the one Elvis had worn in the 1950s. It was to become a powerful, poignant symbol of Ochs's decline.

The music on *Greatest Hits* was an eccentric blend of then voguish country-rock and Ochs's by now established chamber-pop style. It was much maligned on release and sold very poorly, but is an unfairly overlooked record. Although it lacks the thematic unity of the previous three albums, it reveals little of the haphazard, hurried way in which it was recorded. Ochs's voice retained something of the depth it had acquired on the previous album, and the occasional missed notes only serve to emphasise the heartfelt vulnerability of the songs' sentiments.

The aching piano ballad 'Jim Dean Of Indiana' is as haunting a tribute to a fallen idol as has ever been written, and Ochs sings it beautifully. 'Boy From Ohio' is a simple country lament for lost innocence, while 'No More Songs' is, with hindsight, a chilling prophecy of the writer's block that would afflict Ochs from then on.

The Carnegie Hall gold-suit concert was Ochs's equivalent of Dylan's electric set at Newport in 1965: the moment when he finally cut the cords binding him to his traditional audience. People were baffled by an overweight 30-year-old folk singer dressed like Elvis, singing 1950s medleys and protest songs, and talking about Che Guevara. Toward the end of the evening Ochs – a master of quickfire on-stage banter and in fine voice – was winning over some sections of the audience, but he was booed and jeered by most. The album was recorded for what should have been Ochs's next album, but Jerry Moss of A&M thought a live record with a booing crowd was a bad idea. It was eventually given a limited release later as *Gunfight At Carnegie Hall*.

Meanwhile the tour quietly ground to a halt shortly afterward, and Ochs's career nosedived. The gold-suit debacle sent the already fragile Ochs spiralling into a depression from which he never really recovered. Surviving on a diet of alcohol, junk food and Valium, he became bloated and unwell. He split up with his long-time girlfriend. The crushing depression smothered his creativity, and in the next five years he wrote only a handful of new songs. Speaking in 1971 he said: "I feel older, I feel slowed-down, I feel constantly like I can't write ... . I think something is there intact, I *think*. But I can't rev it up any more."[11]

Without new material to play he was reluctant to tour, and when he did he found an audience expecting only a 1960s man who would play once vibrantly relevant protest songs that were now period pieces. He became a soft target for the press. Tom Rapp shared the bill with Ochs during this period. "This was in 1971 at the Troubadour in Los Angeles," said Rapp, "and there was somebody from a rock magazine backstage just constantly getting him to drink and drink and drink – and then he put out a big article about what a drunk Phil was. I though that was nasty."[12] Ochs travelled widely in the early part of the decade. In Australia in 1973 he recorded a new song, the unremarkable 'Kansas City Bomber', for the movie of the same name. The song wasn't used in the film but was released by A&M as a single. In September of that year Ochs recorded what was a prototype world-music/pop-crossover single in Kenya, 'Bwatue' backed with 'Niko Mchumba Ngome'.

This single was only released in Africa by A&M, but failed to sell even to its target market. Although much has been made of this apparent innovation, which predated Paul Simon's similarly conceived *Graceland* project by more than a decade, it should be seen more as a curiosity rather than a serious attempt at exploring a new style. Although Ochs was credited with writing both songs, the finished recordings feature more of the Pan-African Ngembo Rumba Band than Ochs himself, who only periodically surfaces from the muddy mix.

While in Africa Ochs travelled to Tanzania, telling people he was on his way to meet Idi Amin. On his first night there he was attacked and robbed by three men as he walked alone on the beach. He was half-strangled and badly beaten. Ochs's vocal chords were damaged during the attack, and as a result he lost the whole of his top register. He returned to the States and went to see Frank Sinatra's throat doctor who told him that if he gave up drinking and did specially prescribed vocal exercises for three hours a day, every day, for two years, then he might get his voice back. It was a cruel blow for a limited singer who relied heavily on his upper register. Ochs ignored the doctor's advice and his voice was never the same again.

Periodically the old Phil Ochs would emerge from the fog. He found a new hero in Salvador Allende, who had grabbed power in Chile in the world's first peaceful Marxist revolution. He travelled to the country and met Victor Jara, the renowned Chilean folk singer. Back in Los Angeles after the Africa trip he heard about the military coup that had left Allende and Jara dead. Outraged and galvanised, he planned a tribute concert to draw the world's attention to the atrocity. Teaming up with old manager and compatriot Arthur Gorson, Ochs's "Evening With Salvador Allende" was his biggest triumph of the 1970s, although it had taken the late addition of Bob Dylan to the bill to sell out the Madison Square Garden Felt Forum.

> **"Jerry Moss of A&M thought that a live record with a booing crowd was a bad idea."**

Dylan's involvement in the evening was the result of a chance meeting with Ochs outside the Chelsea hotel. It marked the final healing of the rift that had opened up nearly ten years before when Ochs had criticised Dylan. The two planned a tour together, a series of shows in small clubs across the country, with proceeds going to charity. The idea germinated as the two old friends and rivals talked, and eventually became The Rolling Thunder Revue – in which Phil Ochs was not involved.

The Watergate scandal fascinated Ochs and prompted his last single, consisting of re-recorded versions of two earlier songs, 'The Power And The Glory' and 'Here's To The State Of Richard Nixon', once again on A&M. The damage to Ochs's vocal chords was only too apparent, despite attempts to disguise the limitations with careful pitching and strategically placed female backing vocals. The record failed to sell, and Ochs's recording career ended.

As the decade wore on Ochs's malaise was punctuated with increasingly bizarre episodes, the strangest of which was when he reinvented himself as John Butler Train. He decided he needed to sign with Presley's manager, Colonel Tom Parker, to relaunch his career. When Parker didn't respond to his calls, he approached Kentucky Fried Chicken's Colonel Sanders, or at least the company that owned the rights to the franchise, and actually succeeded in setting up a meeting with them to discuss his proposals. The corporate representative soon found an excuse to terminate the meeting with the drunken, stammering Ochs.

He opened a bar called Che and planned to invite the Mafia to the launch party. The venture closed within days after Ochs had ploughed in his remaining savings. He planned to move back to the East Coast and hired a truck to move all his possessions – which somehow got lost en route. Ochs turned up at a friend's house early one morning in his last item of clothing, the gold suit, caked in dried vomit. His friends and family made unsuccessful efforts to persuade him to seek help, or in some cases abandoned him.

John Train appeared in the summer of 1975. By this time Ochs was effectively a homeless alcoholic. He was seen back on the streets of Greenwich Village, begging from friends and strangers, threatening them, and sometimes attacking them. He drank himself into oblivion. Friends speculated that Ochs was somehow gaining security by hiding behind the invented persona of John Train. It seems unlikely that he really believed he had become somebody else, but the pain and despair that drove him to such extreme behaviour was real enough. Tom Paxton said: "Phil was one of the most tortured people I have known personally. I think there was real disease there. For one thing, alcoholism, in a rampant stage. And clinical depression."[13]

> **"He thought you have to suffer to create."**

By October of 1975 John Train was retreating and Ochs was returning to something like normality. He went to see his ex-wife Alice and daughter Meegan for a final visit. In November he performed a concert at Folk City in Greenwich Village.

Early in 1976 Ochs went to his sister Sonny's house and asked if he could stay for a few days. A sort of calm seemed to settle. He played cards incessantly with her two sons. He visited a psychiatrist and made an appointment for another consultation. He went to buy a new guitar, but couldn't find one he wanted. He even performed a few songs for friends at a party. But on April 9th 1976, alone in Sonny's house for just ten minutes while her son David went to the shops, Phil Ochs hanged himself from the bathroom door. He was cremated the next day, and his friend Andy Wickham scattered his ashes from Edinburgh Castle, which Ochs had visited as a child.

A Phil Ochs memorial concert in Madison Square Garden's Felt Forum in July 1976 drew 4,500 people, the biggest audience Ochs had attracted for years. Many of his old friends and compatriots – David Blue, Jack Elliott, Dave Van Ronk, Eric Andersen, Jerry Rubin – appeared and sang and spoke their tributes. Allen Ginsberg, wearing the infamous gold suit, appeared on stage with Tim Hardin for an Elvis Presley medley. Hardin also sang a touching version of 'Pleasures Of The Harbor'. Ramsey Clark, a former US attorney general turned anti-war activist, described Ochs as "a driven man … . How many of them do we have? He cared."[14] It was the most famous that Phil Ochs had been for many years.

Ochs's legacy has been well served in the years since his death. Regular reissues, intelligent compilations, two full-length biographies and a TV film drama about his life shown on Britain's Channel 4 have all helped to keep Ochs's name alive. Yet in spite of this his music has failed to catch the imagination of successive generations of music fans. He is rarely mentioned as an influence by contemporary artists, and any cult that surrounds him is minor compared to that of a Tim Buckley or a Nick Drake. Perhaps the level of posthumous exposure he has been afforded actually undermined the chance of a romantic myth developing through word of mouth. Before he died he repeatedly asked his brother, Michael, if the songs would live on. If they do, it is only in the memories of a very small audience.

Yet Ochs remains an important figure. He was the epitome of the Greenwich Village protest singer and, more than any of their contemporaries, his life and career regularly intersected Dylan's. He was also one of the few of those original folkies to become actively involved in the counter-culture of the late 1960s. Musically, he started as a minor, derivative figure before working up to some notable and unusual achievements, primarily heard on his four albums released by A&M between 1967 and 1970.

But ultimately he was destroyed, or destroyed himself. Michael Ochs said: "He was your typical person who can't face their own problems, so wants to live for the problems of others ... . He was very depressed. There was a family history of manic depression, and ... I think Phil egged on the manic-depression thing, because he thought you have to suffer to create."[15]

Ochs crammed a lot into his glory years. Between 1963 and 1970 he recorded seven albums, was almost constantly politically active, wrote occasional perceptive journalism, toured, travelled, drank heavily, maintained a hectic social life and watched thousands of films. His schedule would have taxed the most stable of men, and it proved too much for the fragile, depressive Ochs. He wrote in an obituary of kung fu star Bruce Lee: "Maybe he lived more intensely than any human being can live. Or maybe he died for the same reason James Dean died. He had too much of the fire, and the Gods were jealous."[16] There is surely something of Phil Ochs's own story in these words.

[1] Marc Eliot *Phil Ochs – Death Of A Rebel* (Omnibus 1990)
[2] *Rolling Stone* May 27th 1971
[3] *Melody Maker* July 27th 1968
[4] Marc Eliot *Phil Ochs – Death of a Rebel* (Omnibus 1990)
[5] 'Tape From California' by Phil Ochs, A&M Records
[6] "Yippie Announcement! Yippie!" 1968
[7] 'I Kill Therefore I Am' by Phil Ochs, A&M Records
[8] *Guitar Player* October 1970
[9] Carnegie Hall concert April 3rd 1970
[10] *Rolling Stone* May 27th 1971
[11] *Rolling Stone* May 27th 1971
[12] Unpublished interview for *Strange Things Are Happening* 1988
[13] Jac Holzman & Gavan Daws *Follow The Music* (FirstMedia 1998)
[14] *Rolling Stone* July 15th 1976
[15] Jac Holzman & Gavan Daws *Follow The Music* (FirstMedia 1998)
[16] *Take One* volume 4, number 3

TOM RAPP

He knows the use of ashes,
He worships God with ashes.

FROM 'THE JEWELER' BY TOM RAPP, *Warner Brothers*

Tom Rapp was the leader of Pearls Before Swine, a loose-knit band of psychedelic mavericks who set Auden to music and put Bosch on one of their sleeves. Casting the Pearls aside, Rapp became a solo singer-songwriter in the 1970s, but seemed out of step with the changing times. He quit music before he was 30 to become a lawyer, but a cult following encouraged Rapp to make a limited return in the late 1990s.

Before Tom Rapp's story crossed that of any of the other artists in this book he was known as the leader of a studio-bound psychedelic underground folk group, Pearls Before Swine. They had a penchant for writing songs about big issues – war, space, love – and for putting the poetry of Shakespeare and Auden to music. Compared to other artists in this book, this first career phase may have been untypical, but Rapp's formative influences were relatively conventional.

A Reprise press release from 1970 charts the points in Rapp's early musical development: "His first influences were Presley, The Everly Brothers and the pop tunes of the 1950s. At age 12 he stopped singing and playing because he found pop material sterile, but he was reinspired to play and sing by 'Blowin' In The Wind'." It was a well-trodden path: a love of the first generation of rockers, followed by disillusionment, then an attraction to folk music and an encounter with the all-pervading influence of Dylan. It was, in other words, the same route travelled by Phil Ochs, Tom Rush and so many others.

Tom Rapp was born in 1947 in Bottineau, North Dakota, close to the Canadian border. His parents, Dale and Eileen Rapp, were both teachers. He has two sisters, Kathy and Patty. When he was still a young child his family moved to Minnesota where at the age of six he was given a guitar. A country & western player living next door taught the young Rapp some chords, and a few years later he learned to play the ukulele.

Although he did finally get to share the stage with Dylan in 1975 – at The Bitter End in Greenwich Village, with Ramblin' Jack Elliott – there is an intriguing possibility that the two men had been on the same bill nearly two decades earlier. By the age of ten Rapp was entering talent competitions singing Elvis Presley songs. "Looking back at a scrapbook my parents used to keep," he says, "I saw that one of the other contestants on a show was a Bobby Zimmerman, who sang and played guitar. I have no first-hand memory of that, or indeed if it was the same Zimmerman who went on to some sort of fame."[1] Rapp came second, losing to a woman who twirled batons. Zimmerman apparently came fifth.

The Rapp family moved from Minnesota to Pennsylvania before settling in Eau Gallie, Florida, in 1963. Whether or not Rapp did encounter the young Bob Dylan at the talent contest, he did come across him indirectly in Florida in 1963. "I heard 'Blowin' In The Wind'," Rapp says. "I remember calling into the radio stations [asking them] to play Peter, Paul & Mary's version again and again until I finally bought the single and saw the song was written by someone named Dylan."[2] It was an unfamiliar name, but Rapp had his local record store send away for a copy of *The Freewheelin' Bob Dylan* album. Inspired by what he heard, and later by albums by Joan Baez and The Byrds, he became a folk singer and started to perform with his schoolfriends Wayne Harley (banjo), Lane Lederer (bass) and Roger Crissinger (tambourine and organ). Together they formed the first line-up of Pearls Before Swine.

Over the years Rapp has given different accounts of writing his first song. Sometimes he refers to an unrecorded tune called 'Be A Man, Join The Klan' – a liberal protest effort with a title of which Phil Ochs would have been proud. Rapp had the pleasure of seeing this song adopted by the Florida folk scene that centred on Fred Neil (although there is no suggestion that Neil performed it). Different artists added their own verses and customised the melody, just as they did with the traditional songs prevalent in the folk revival.

On other occasions Rapp has said that his first song was 'Another Time', a philosophical treatise about the indifference of the universe. He wrote this after surviving a serious car crash unscathed. This became the first song on the first Pearls Before Swine album. Rapp and his fellow nascent avant-folk experimenters had taped on a home reel-to-reel recorder a few of his early songs, including 'Another Time', as well as some Dylan covers. They had eight demo discs cut, packaged in a hand-drawn sleeve with a blown-up band snapshot taped to the front. One of these homespun demos was sent to ESP Records, home of anti-establishment rock-theatre poets The Fugs.

Rapp had bought some Fugs albums from the same store that had supplied his copy of *The Freewheelin' Bob Dylan*. The group's primitive experimentation struck a chord, and Rapp thought that

ESP were just waiting for some teenagers from Florida to provide twisted, amateurish folk-rock songs that shared something of the same spirit. ESP wrote back saying that the Pearls Before Swine demo, despite being so badly pressed as to be virtually inaudible, was probably the sort of thing they were looking for.

It was ESP's habit to pay for their artists to record using the cheapest local facilities available, so the group were booked into a primitive two-track studio set up in a garage owned by a country & western musician. There the youngsters awkwardly and anxiously recorded their anti-Vietnam songs as the studio owner's redneck friends looked on suspiciously. Inevitably the results were unsatisfactory, and the band were invited to New York City for a second effort. They spent four days and nights recording their first album with engineer Richard Alderson at the tiny Impact four-track studio. The entire album was recorded for $1,500. It was May 1967.

At the time ESP was a small independent label, expecting to sell no more than 10,000 copies of each release. "They hired people that they thought had something interesting to say. They had simple one-page contracts and put you in the studio and said, 'Do what you want; don't spend too much money doing it,'"[3] says Rapp. The ethos of low budgets and artistic freedom suited Rapp and his cohorts, giving them space to explore their fertile ideas unhindered by conventions of musical and technical correctness, or requests for hit singles. It was this spirit of naive musical adventure that has done much to endear Rapp to subsequent generations of underground musicians.

The ESP label was the focal point for a loose-knit scene. "Most of those I knew were the other groups who recorded at Impact Sound behind what is now called Lincoln Center: The Fugs and Ed Sanders; Pete Stampfel and the Holy Modal Rounders,"[4] says Rapp. Although each of these groups had its own agenda, there were similarities between them. They combined literary, hippie and anti-establishment aspirations in often folk-influenced music. But where Sanders and Stampfel were almost old enough to be beatniks, Pearls Before Swine were the new kids on the block, a bunch of fresh-faced enthusiasts barely out of their teens.

> "Do what you want; don't spend too much money doing it."

By 1967, when Pearls Before Swine first arrived in New York, the Greenwich Village folk circuit was past its heyday. Many of the prime movers had drifted to the West Coast where attention was focused on the burgeoning psychedelic scene. Culturally, the ESP bands had more in common with this West Coast underground than with their near-contemporaries in Greenwich Village. They were resolutely experimental and self-consciously part of the counter-culture. Their hair was long and their politics confrontational.

Sanders, who had connections with the Yippies (the Youth International Party), was a prime mover. "He took a group of hippies on a bus tour of the suburbs," says Rapp. "All the hippies were gawking and pointing at the suburbanites with their backyard grills and swimming pools. A very political time ... lots of anti-war songs."[5] Musically, the ESP groups had a closer link with the Village writers, sharing with them roots in folk, bluegrass, jug-band and country music, though with less of an obvious debt to Dylan.

In the absence of formal musical expertise, and with a low budget, Rapp and his colleagues were forced to rely on innovations and ideas when recording their debut, *One Nation Underground*. They had both in abundance. On the record, released in 1967, psychedelic folk reminiscent of Donovan collides with Farfisa-driven punk and hard-to-categorise repetitive minimalism, all thrown together with the undisciplined, creative exuberance of youth. A children's song, 'Playmate', gets a garage-band treatment; 'Morning Song' is a mantra-like organ-based drone; and 'Another Time' is cast as a gentle acoustic folk song. 'I Shall Not Care', one of the album's most unusual and complex pieces, moves through successive phases of all three styles.

One Nation Underground introduced all the characteristics that would appear in Rapp's later recordings. The songwriting was consistently interesting though rarely exceptional, and the themes explored were more literary and intellectual than was common in pop music of the era. Unexpected details often crop up in the arrangements. Despite the eccentric, unconventional nature of the album, it became the most commercially successful ESP release ever. Different estimates have it selling between 100,000 and 250,000 copies. Even the lowest of those would make it one of the bestselling albums featured in this book.

Pearls Before Swine's status as psychedelic mavericks was confirmed by their decision to use a reproduction of the then obscure Hieronymus Bosch painting *The Garden Of Earthly Delights* on the front cover of their debut. No photographs of the band themselves appeared for some time, which gave rise to many rumours concerning their identity – rumours which the ever-mischievous Rapp was happy to let go unchecked.

The second Pearls Before Swine album was recorded a year later, again with engineer Richard Alderson at Impact studio. It appeared in 1968. This time a reproduction of a Breughel painting adorned the front cover. *Balaklava*, released when protests over American involvement in Vietnam were at a peak, had an overt anti-war message. Rapp says: "It was consciously about Vietnam. We chose the Battle of Balaklava as the theme because it was really the last time war was considered glorious."[6]

The album opens with a scratchy recording of Trumpeter Landfrey, a soldier who had survived the Charge of the Light Brigade. It was taken from a record Rapp had acquired which compiled early recordings of 19th century figures. A recording of Florence Nightingale, taken from the same source, is also used on the album.

Musically, *Balaklava* marks an emerging confidence, and is a development of many of the ideas that were first sketched on *One Nation Underground*. In the studio the band had been augmented by Joe Farrell and Lee Crabtree on various instruments, and together they added new layers to an already complex and intriguing sound. Sound effects, whispered vocals, flutes, acoustic guitars and generous amounts of reverb float in and out of the mix, both on Rapp's own compositions and a successful cover of Leonard Cohen's 'Suzanne'. Against the odds, with limited resources and no previous experience, Pearls Before Swine had recorded two of the most adventurous and complete recordings to emerge from the psychedelic period, which was otherwise littered with interesting but half-formed musical ideas.

'Guardian Angels' on *Balaklava* was a nostalgic little song based on a chamber string section and with a vocal performance that sounds like it was sung through an old radio microphone. One of the album's sleevenotes explains that it was recorded in Mexico in 1928 on 78rpm equipment. This was entirely false, of course, although plausible given the sound of the song. It gave rise to the rumour that the members of Pearls Before Swine were all in their 60s, one of the suitably arcane myths that shrouded the group until pictures of later line-ups appeared on subsequent albums. It was also believed that the band had a dwarf drummer and, later, that Rapp had become a gravedigger in Italy. It wasn't until their fifth album, *City Of Gold*, that Rapp consented to photographs of band members on the sleeve. Fans could see that Rapp was in fact an earnest, bespectacled, bearded young man with long corkscrew hair.

During 1968 two events occurred that had a bearing on the future of the group. By the time *Balaklava* was recorded, Jim Bohannon had replaced Roger Crissinger, the first of the original four members to leave the band. From that time, Rapp would be the one fixed point in a constantly changing line-up. Although other musicians played a significant role in later Pearls Before Swine recordings, it became a loose collective rather than a band in the traditional sense, and increasingly a vehicle for Rapp's idiosyncratic vision. On September 11th 1968 Rapp married a Dutch woman, Elisabeth Joosten. She became the second longest-serving member in the ever-fluctuating band personnel, singing and occasionally contributing to songwriting on four subsequent albums.

By the third Pearls Before Swine LP, *These Things Too*, Rapp's manager Peter Edmiston (formerly involved with The Fugs) had moved the group to the Reprise label. Rapp had by now fashioned a more mature interpretation of the same basic set of ideas that had served him so well on the first two albums. For the first time the music was beginning to share some resemblance to the contemporary work of other singer-songwriters, perhaps because Rapp alone was now the dominant creative force.

Despite the shift to Reprise and bigger recording budgets, the album was again recorded partly at the small four-track Impact studio. Rapp, always experimenting, was happy to work in modest surroundings. "It required all kinds of manoeuvres to get the extra tracks on there, mixing down constantly, but [co-producer Richard Alderson] was a genius at that," says Rapp. "We did some of the songs at RKO, the motion picture studio, and we recorded directly on to 35mm film, just to see if there wasn't some clarity in that."[7]

For *These Things Too*, released in 1969, Elisabeth Rapp and Jim Fairs joined original members Tom Rapp and Wayne Harley. Fairs was a multi-instrumentalist who had previously been a member of 1960s group The Cryan Shames. He was also credited as co-producer, with Alderson. The band was augmented by several studio musicians, establishing a trend that would continue throughout Rapp's subsequent recordings.

Opening with an Auden poem set to music, *These Things Too* is less dominated by the psychedelic experimentation of the first two albums; much of the overt quirkiness is replaced by more subtle and sophisticated musical ideas. Lyrically, Rapp's writing remained unsettling and often obscure, and although always ambitious it was not entirely successful. He had a tendency to shape his words into mysterious fables scattered with some memorably odd images, but tarnished with an over-reliance on mock medieval phrases. 'Man In The Tree', from the later *Use Of Ashes*, for example, opens with the arresting statement: "The man in the tree is staring at me, all of the blood dripping down".[8] It then meanders into talk of "my lady ... weaving a robe of silk and moonlight".

Rapp had by now established his political and confessional styles, the two most common themes among contemporary singer-songwriters. But his strange, individual perspective marked him out as a maverick in a category of his own. It was the strangeness of his material that appealed – and indeed continues to appeal – to underground audiences and musicians. However, this very strangeness meant that his otherwise imaginative and well-crafted songs were not widely covered by commercial artists.

> **"Two of the most adventurous recordings to emerge from psychedelia."**

Throughout their late-1960s career, Pearls Before Swine were primarily a studio-bound recording collective. Their complex arrangements, often constructed with unusual instrumentation ("swinehorne", celeste, oboe, electric violin, banjo), and Rapp's soft, thin voice did not translate well to a live setting. They had played live in 1968, sharing a weekend bill in New York with Country Joe & The Fish, Electric Flag and Chuck Berry, but they didn't appear on-stage again until 1971. In the early 1970s the core of a stable Pearls Before Swine line-up endured for several years, though augmented live and on record with many other musicians. Rapp has said he considers this the best performing version of the group – from around 1972 to 1974 – including Art Ellis on flute and Billy Rowlands on cello. After that, he says, "I was solo with just a harmonica and guitar."[9]

Tom and Elisabeth Rapp moved to Holland in 1969 with the strange and unrealised idea of recording in England with Mickie Most. There they stayed for about a year, in an idyllic riverside cottage, and Rapp wrote a set of songs that would appear on the next Pearls Before Swine album. The couple then returned to the US to live for a while in Woodstock, New York, at a time when Fred Neil and Tim Hardin were also based there.

The Use Of Ashes was released by Reprise in 1970. It had been recorded in a three-day period in

March of that year in a studio in Nashville with the nucleus of Area Code 615 supporting Rapp, now the sole remaining original member, and Elisabeth. Edmiston was credited as producer. The album includes one of Rapp's best-known songs, 'Rocket Man', which Bernie Taupin said partly inspired his song of the same name written with Elton John. Rapp's was written on the day of the first moon landing, in 1969, when he was living in Holland. It was based on a Ray Bradbury short story called *The Rocket Man* that had made an impression on the teenage Rapp.

Another of the songs, 'Reigal', was inspired by the story of a German ship that had been sunk during World War Two by the US, even though it was known that Allied prisoners of war were aboard. Rapp had read about the Reigal in *The International Herald Tribune* and, greatly affected, found that when he sat down to write about the story the song virtually wrote itself, with lyrics and tune coming fully formed at the first attempt.

In 1971 the ever-prolific Rapp followed *The Use Of Ashes* with *City Of Gold*, also recorded partly in Nashville. It was the first album to list Rapp by name as the artist, the full credit being "Thos. Rapp – Pearls Before Swine". He is also noted as producer.

City Of Gold is in all respects the most conventional recording to appear by Rapp or Pearls Before Swine. Only the brief opening song, a musical rendition of a Shakespeare sonnet, is in keeping with his usual approach. Otherwise it is a conventional collection of country- and folk-influenced material. Its minimal acoustic-rock arrangements bear a strong stylistic resemblance to Dylan's *John Wesley Harding* album, the LP that had first inspired Rapp to call in the Area Code 615 musicians.

Although a pleasant record, its sparse instrumentation and the presence of three cover versions leave the impression that it was less considered than previous albums. Indeed, Rapp later referred to it as a "lighter" collection of songs. There is an obvious debt to Dylan: the final song, 'Did You Dream Of', borrows the chord progression from 'Lay Lady Lay'. Of the cover versions, Rapp's interpretation of Leonard Cohen's 'Nancy' suitably evokes its poignant and desolate mood, while his melodious, upbeat, folk-rock version of Jacques Brel's 'Seasons In The Sun' is effectively at odds with the bitter sentiment of Rod McKuen's translation of the lyric.

The next album appeared in 1971, titled *…beautiful lies you could live in*, this time credited to Tom Rapp/Pearls Before Swine, with Edmiston again listed as producer. It had been partly recorded in Woodstock. This may account for the obvious steal of The Band's ascending harmony vocal part from their song 'The Weight' that appears on Rapp's poppy, uptempo 'A Life'.

After the parenthesis of *City Of Gold*, the new album was a return to the ornate, intricate psychedelic-folk of *These Things Too* and *The Use of Ashes*. It includes another Cohen cover, 'Bird On A Wire', which Rapp gives an epic country-influenced treatment similar to the version recorded by Tim Hardin on his album of that title released the same year. Apart from those two songs – 'A Life' and 'Bird On A Wire' – the album was dominated by Rapp's now established mystical introspection and musing. The plaintive 'Butterflies' is one of his best songs, but there was a sense that the formula was starting to wear thin.

The last Tom Rapp album to be released by Reprise, *Familiar Songs*, appeared in 1972. As the title suggests it is made up of several previously recorded Pearls Before Swine songs, this time appearing in incomplete new versions rather than as a best-of compilation of existing recordings. Rapp says, "I was working on an album, re-recording a number of old songs, and it just wasn't going well. We gave up on it for a while, but one day I went into a record store and there was a new album, *Familiar Songs*, with my face on it. It was a complete surprise to me."[10] It was a half-finished experiment and a substandard record that doesn't deserve consideration alongside Rapp's main body of work.

After leaving Reprise, Rapp, now formally a solo artist, recorded two albums for Blue Thumb in quick succession. Both were released in 1973. The first of these, *Stardancer*, was later described by Rapp as one of his favourites from his own body of work, and was the first record since *One Nation Underground* over which he exercised sufficient creative control to determine how it should be played and recorded.

With songs like 'Stardancer', 'For The Dead In Space' and the earlier 'Rocket Man', Rapp had acquired something of a reputation as a writer of "space songs". Since childhood an enthusiastic reader of science fiction, he had been further alerted to the imaginative possibilities of space travel when living in Florida near Cape Canaveral between 1963 and 1967, witnessing early Apollo rocket launches. This reputation persisted even as late as the Challenger explosion in 1986, when 'Stardancer' was used by National Public Radio in news bulletins about the disaster. Rapp had in fact written the song as a tribute to his father, who coincidentally died a week before the Challenger disaster.

The final album Rapp recorded before leaving the music business for a protracted period was *Sunforest* which appeared late in 1973. Stylistically there is little to separate it from much of his early work, and at the time of release his wistful, erudite folk-rock seemed like a distant echo from another time. The album was marred by inconsistency in sound quality, with several of the songs suffering from distortion. "The whole record was put through a process called Aphex," says Rapp, "which was supposed to do wonderful things for the sound. It didn't."[11] It seemed a shame that the work of an artist so concerned with detail as Rapp should be afforded such shabby treatment. This all too obvious technical fault was picked up by reviewers, and Rapp's recording career ground inauspiciously to a halt.

Both of Rapp's solo albums as well as the Pearls Before Swine LPs sanctioned by him were of consistently high standards. But if one criticism could be made of Rapp's music it is that it failed to develop. The first two albums had a naive, primitive enthusiasm and a surplus of ideas. Rapp then created a more sophisticated version, using many of the same ingredients – and persisted with it. The records had detailed, meandering instrumentation, often mystical lyrics, and sweet pop-folk melodies, but by the 1970s this was starting to appear dated. A review of 1972's *...beautiful lies you could live in* described Rapp's sound as "1967-vintage folk-rock".[12] *Sunforest,* which appeared 18 months later, was described as "soft psychedelic folk-rock that fuses politics and mysticism in a manner reminiscent of Donovan".[13]

> "Melody, mix-and-match instrumentation and lo-fi inventiveness."

The first of those reviews, by Richard Cromelin, identified a number of other "serious obstacles littering [Rapp's] path to musical/poetic fulfilment".[14] Although Cromelin's tone was often scathing and his comments sometimes contradictory, he did put his finger on a number of the characteristics that dominate Rapp's music, and his criticism can serve as the framework for an analysis of Rapp's recording career.

One of Cromelin's targets was Rapp's voice, which he described as "an ugly instrument". Although "ugly" is unfair, the records do reveal Rapp as a limited singer. He was unable to push his voice beyond a certain point, and this in turn hampered his ability to draw from styles that required more dynamic expression than his lisping, soft, half-spoken whisper allowed. When he did attempt something different, like the aggressive punk snarl of the first album's 'Dear John', the effect was original and entertaining but not entirely convincing.

Cromelin believed that the constantly shifting line-up of backing musicians hindered Rapp's development. It is true that by the early 1970s Rapp's recordings were increasingly out of step with the times. Perhaps, having defined his original style, he would have benefited from the security of working with a regular band and been more able to explore new ideas? Taking into account comments Rapp has made about instructing the Area Code 615 musicians to play in particular styles, it seems likely that he retained some control over how the many musicians he worked with would play. The decision to persist with one style was primarily his. The irony is that after an early career marked by inspiration, experimentation and the fluid interchange of ideas, Rapp's later work seemed almost formulaic in comparison. It's not that these later albums are in themselves of a poor standard or lacking in imagination. *Stardancer* is one of his best. It's just that they are more or less interchangeable with much of his earlier work. There was little sense of progression after *These Things Too*.

What Cromelin was willing to grant was that Rapp had an "ability to write melodies that sound simple and ordinary, but that twist about to become … satisfyingly original."[15] This was certainly the case, with most of Rapp's best songs combining naggingly familiar melodic phrases with unexpected chord, key or time-signature changes. Cromelin also considered that Rapp's lyrics deserved the status of poetry, although with hindsight this aspect of Rapp's songwriting – with too-obvious "big" statements and sometimes self-consciously archaic phrases – has dated more than the "1967-vintage folk-rock".

Rapp continued to perform until 1976. For most of the three-year period since the release of his last album he played as a solo artist, accompanying himself on guitar and harmonica. It marked a return to his folk roots – and in this respect Rapp's career was conducted in reverse compared to many of the other artists featured in this book. The experimentation came first; then there was a retreat into something more conventional. It was a retrograde step that was never going to take Rapp anywhere, and by 1976 his career had lost all momentum. "I just wanted to get out because I had been doing it for about ten years," Rapp said. "We finally ended the [Vietnam] war, you know, so I figured it was time to go on and do something else. At that point I felt I had met everybody, played with everybody."[16]

Another phase of Rapp's life drew to a close in 1976 when he split from Elisabeth. They had had one son, David. Having released nine albums in six years, Rapp disappeared from the music scene before he was 30 years old, still young enough to embark on a more conventional career.

By the mid 1980s, despite low-profile reissues of the first two albums, the names of Tom Rapp and Pearls Before Swine were all but forgotten, surviving as the most obscure of cults in the collective memory of a tiny coterie of underground enthusiasts. Rumours circulated among the few who were interested that he was dead (based on a false report of his demise run by *NME* in 1974) or, as we've already seen, that he was working as a grave-digger in Italy.

In 1988 the independent British music magazine *Strange Things Are Happening* traced Rapp, alive and well and working as a lawyer, and interviewed him at length. Sadly the magazine folded before the interview was published. Rapp's story remained untold until another small British publication, *Ptolemaic Terrascope*, traced him in 1993. Editor Phil McMullen published a long interview and career overview across two issues, and this stands as the most detailed press coverage ever afforded Rapp and Pearls Before Swine. Shortly afterward American magazine *Dirty Linen* published their version of Rapp's story.

Ptolemaic Terrascope is an independently-produced, occasional magazine published by Nick Saloman, also known as underground guitarist-singer-songwriter Bevis Frond. His magazine offers wide-ranging coverage of underground and experimental music from the 1960s onwards, with a strong emphasis on psychedelia and contemporary low-budget independent music. Pearls Before Swine could have been tailor-made for the magazine to unearth at a later date: they were obscure, folky, experimental, interesting. Indeed, Rapp had become something of a hero to the crop of mainly American artists who often feature in the pages of the magazine. It was a short step from writing about Rapp to persuading him to perform and record.

In 1997, at the age of 50 and after a hiatus of 21 years, Rapp appeared on stage again. *Ptolemaic Terrascope* promoted the first of its Terrastock festivals of alternative music in Providence, Rhode Island, where Rapp performed with his son, David. Further gigs followed in Boston and New York, and in 1999 he played the third Terrastock festival, this time held in London. The music of Tom Rapp and Pearls Before Swine, with its convergence of melody, mix-and-match instrumentation and lo-fi inventiveness, seemed strangely contemporary in the company of the young 1960s-influenced underground experimentalists with whom he shared the bill.

A new Tom Rapp album was released in 1999 to coincide with the UK visit, recorded with collaborators from the independent underground, including Damon & Naomi, and Nick Saloman. *Journals From The Plague Year* did little to remind the listener of the quarter of a century gap between the last Rapp recordings, being broadly similar in approach to his earlier work. It was released to respectful reviews on the small Woronzow label, owned by Saloman.

Rapp was pleased and mildly bemused by his "rediscovery". He says: "I really thought that all the body of work was now in the 'dead language of vinyl' and would never be heard by anyone again." He had not realised that any of his recordings were available on CD until *Terrascope* editor McMullen had contacted him.

The *Ptolemaic Terrascope* interview replaced all the intrigue about Rapp's post-music life with a story of success in another field – and success achieved without compromising the ideals that had energised him during the 1960s. In 1976 he had become a cinema projectionist, and then started to study at Harvard, from where he graduated with an economics degree in 1981. He then studied law at the University of Pennsylvania, qualifying in 1984, since when he has specialised in civil-rights and discrimination cases. His conversation reflects a continuing commitment to his youthful principles. "Whenever I get the chance I recite the lessons of the sixties: Love is real / Justice is real / Countries have no morals – you have to force them to do the right thing / Honesty is possible and necessary / Everything is not for sale."[17]

In 1995 Rapp married his long-time girlfriend, Lynn Madison. They live in New Jersey. He has no plans to give up his legal work, but hopes to continue performing and recording.

By the time his two Blue Thumb albums appeared back in the early 1970s, it already appeared as if Rapp might be forgotten, a minor figure of unrealised potential. His audiences had dwindled and there was an unavoidable sense that his inspiration, although still active, had somehow been preserved from another era, untouched and undisturbed.

But earlier in his career, after the vibrant experimentation of the first two Pearls Before Swine albums, on *These Things Too* and *The Use Of Ashes*, his creative vision was fully realised. These are individual and unique records, packed with detail and revealing something new on every listen. But that vision was always personal, and Rapp was unable or unwilling to communicate it in a way that struck a universal chord, in the way that Tim Hardin or Fred Neil did in their best songs. For that reason Rapp's songs were not widely covered in the mainstream and were not considered classics, and his records, though consistently good, have never risen above cult status.

There were no hit singles, and although his songs did come to be covered – and still are – it is by artists as eccentric and curious as Psychic TV, This Mortal Coil and Flying Saucer Attack. He is the definition of a cult albums artist. Rather than the individual songs, it is his records as an entire body of work that deserve respect and hold the attention, both for their unorthodox arrangements and their absorbing, melodic inventiveness.

[1] Unpublished interview for *Strange Things Are Happening* 1988
[2] Unpublished interview for *Strange Things Are Happening* 1988
[3] Unpublished interview for *Strange Things Are Happening* 1988
[4] Author's interview August 1st 2000
[5] Author's interview August 1st 2000
[6] Unpublished interview for *Strange Things Are Happening* 1988
[7] Unpublished interview for *Strange Things Are Happening* 1988
[8] 'Man In The Tree' by Tom Rapp, House Of Mysteries Inc 1969
[9] Sleevenotes from the Edsel reissue of *Sunforest*
[10] Unpublished interview for *Strange Things Are Happening* 1988
[11] Author's interview September 9th 2000
[12] *Rolling Stone* February 17th 1972
[13] *Rolling Stone* October 25th 1973.
[14] *Rolling Stone* February 17th 1972
[15] *Rolling Stone* February 17th 1972
[16] Sleevenotes from the Edsel reissue of *Sunforest*
[17] Author's interview August 1st 2000

TIM ROSE

CHAPTER 8

My mama often told me
Tim you've got to bend to get along,
But if you bend you're bound to break,
So I don't bend at all...
I gotta do things my way.

FROM 'I GOTTA DO THINGS MY WAY' BY TIM ROSE & RICHIE HUSSAN, *Screen Gems-Columbia Ltd 1966*

One of the most powerful singers to record in the 1960s, Tim Rose seemed close to breaking through to mainstream success several times, not least with his brooding version of 'Hey Joe' and a blistering rock re-write of 'Morning Dew'. Somehow success eluded him, and for a while in the 1980s he recorded TV jingles and worked as a stockbroker, before coming back to music in the 1990s for a second try.

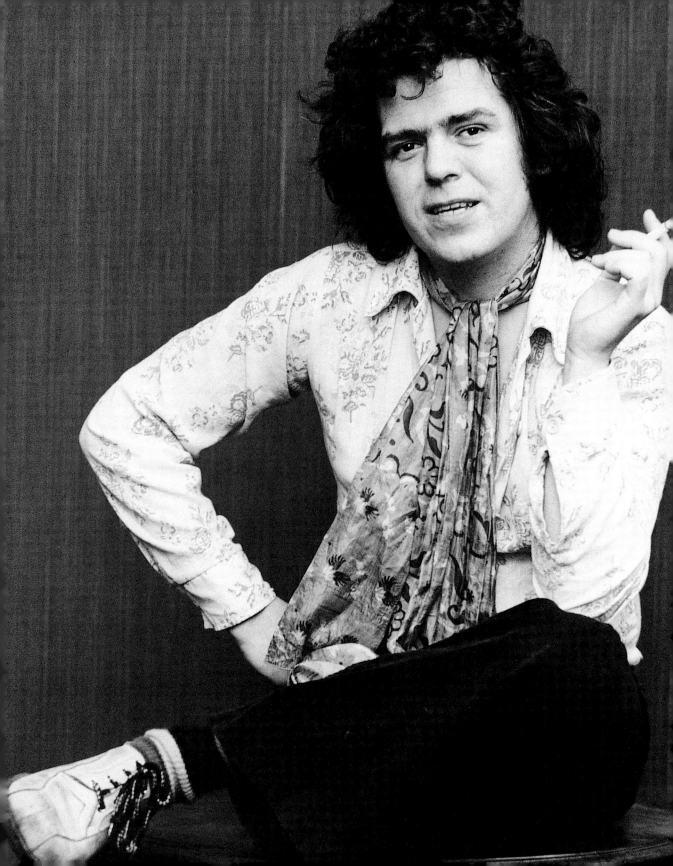

n autumn 1996 Tim Rose stepped on to the stage at the Half Moon pub in Putney, London, which had been the site nearly 20 years ago of his last British performance. It had taken some persuasion by promoter George McFall before Rose took the gig, because he was concerned that after two decades away no one would turn up to see him.

Rose was visibly overwhelmed by the response from the 200-plus people who packed into the pub's smoky back room. After performing with menacing intensity a selection from his considerable back catalogue – songs about murder, defiant independence and impending apocalypse – and offering good-natured reminiscences about his stop-start musical career of 35 years, Rose stood at the door and warmly shook the hand of every single member of the audience as they left.

Rose will not reveal his age, "just to keep it interesting". But a late-1960s Columbia press release suggests that he was born on September 23rd 1940. That would seem about right for a man who first arrived on the Greenwich Village folk scene in the early 1960s, having served as a navigator in the US Air Force. He also has a tendency toward vagueness when discussing the details of his early life – probably connected to his desire to conceal his age rather than to failing memory. In all other respects he is alert and articulate.

Although accounts differ, Rose was probably born and raised in Washington. He recalls at eight years old listening to DJ Wolfman Jack play blues on the radio.[1] Musical aptitude was in the family – Rose's grandmother had been a pianist in silent movie houses, and his aunt, who raised him, had studied opera. The first instrument he learned was the five-string banjo, followed by the guitar. He became accomplished enough on both to win a high school prize as the best musician in the school.

> **"Tim Rose's name appears many times in the labyrinthine family tree that links the careers of The Lovin' Spoonful and The Mamas & The Papas."**

At 13 Rose was studying for the priesthood in a seminary. "I was thrown out for smoking," he says. "I realised I wasn't going to be the Pope. If you can't be the boss why join the company?"[2] Yet despite these nascent rebellious tendencies, Rose like many of his generation submitted to the discipline of the armed forces, becoming a Bomber-Navigator in Strategic Air Command.

Returning to civilian life, Rose lived at various times in Washington, New York and Chicago. In each city he took steps to develop a musical career, initially as a singer, guitarist and banjo player in a confusing array of prototype folk-rock groups. Rose's name appears many times in the labyrinthine family tree that links the careers of The Lovin' Spoonful and The Mamas & The Papas, among others. The most notable of his early groups was The Big Three, but others included The Triumvirate, Michael & Timothy, and The Smoothies.

The Smoothies were a vocal group that included in its ranks John Phillips, later of The Mamas & The Papas, and Scott Mackenzie, of 'San Francisco' fame. Rose was their guitarist for a while and played on a single. After he left, they became The Journeymen, recording several albums – by which point Rose was in the US Air Force. Afterward Rose formed a shortlived folk duet, Michael & Timothy, with another ex-Smoothie, Michael Boran. When that project faltered Rose met Mama Cass Elliot and moved to Chicago to form The Triumvirate, with John Brown.

Rose remembers this as being late 1962; Brown thinks it was a year later. The Triumvirate never recorded, and was another shortlived aggregate with apparent tensions in its ranks. The Big Three grew out of The Triumvirate when Brown was replaced by James Hendricks (not Jimi Hendrix, but a white singer-guitarist who later recorded as a solo artist). The Big Three recorded two albums of harmony-based folk and gospel-influenced material on the FM label in the early 1960s. They split in 1964 primarily because of musical tensions between the two dominant partners, Rose and Elliot. "Cass was very difficult to work with," Rose said recently. "She was always right. I was not easy to work with either, because I was very, very singular about what I thought we should be doing. [I was a] little intense and probably needed to lighten up a bit in those days."[3]

What Rose wanted to do was to go electric, whereas Elliot preferred a more traditional folk sound. These tensions can be heard in the often uncomfortable compromises that surface in Big Three recordings. Drums and electric guitars – unusual for folk at the time – are used sparingly, but always in the context of otherwise traditional folk interpretations of their material. There were also tensions between Elliot and Rose because of what Rose describes as her unrequited love for him, apparently dating back to their days in The Triumvirate – a contention supported by Brown.

After The Big Three disintegrated Rose briefly joined a group called The Feldmans who played the same club circuit as The Big Three, ending up at the Night Owl in Greenwich Village. Rose recalls that his friend Lenny Maxwell brought in David Rubinson from Columbia records. "David said he was not interested in the group, but was interested in me and would I like a deal with Columbia? I said yes, of course. The other guys were a little upset … ."[4]

Initially Columbia paired Rose with producer Bob Johnston, renowned for his work with Bob Dylan and Leonard Cohen. Together with the Nashville musicians who formed Area Code 615 – Charlie McCoy, Kenny Buttrey and others – Rose and Johnston recorded a song by Chip Taylor (writer of 'Wild Thing') as a single. It attracted little attention. Rose was then paired with Rubinson to make what became his eponymously titled debut album, released in 1967. It is this record, an intense, forceful folk-rock milestone, on which Rose's reputation stands.

> "Would I like a deal with Columbia? I said yes, of course."

Rubinson contributed rather risible sleevenotes to the album, all about Rose's "raw, tough, brutishly simple sexuality". The picture on the front cover appeared to reinforce this view, the thickset Rose dressed in a tight black T-shirt and smoking a cigar, staring belligerently at the camera in a seemingly unconscious parody of a macho stereotype. The music, however, communicated something deeper, with the rasping, abrasive power of Rose's voice tempered by a pained vulnerability.

Rose, Rubinson and probably Johnston assembled between them a stellar cast of session players to perform on the record, including the legendary soul drummer Bernard Purdie, fresh from a stint with Aretha Franklin, and Richie Hussan, former bass player from The Feldmans. Completing the nucleus of the line-up were Felix Pappalardi (Cream producer and later Mountain bassist) and guitarists Jay Berliner and Hugh McCracken. This core group was augmented at various times by pianists, string players and backing vocalists. Although these musicians were in no sense a band, having not played together before the sessions, they achieved what so few groups of individually talented session-players manage: they gelled as a group, and created an identifiable sound.

Purdie's characteristically aggressive contribution is a highlight of the recording, although Rose himself was less than complimentary. "Bernard is Bernard – he does Bernard. If it happens to fit what you're doing it's brilliant, but if it doesn't, he doesn't know how to change."[5] Rose's recollections of his career are full of top-flight musicians who failed to understand what he wanted. His later albums would provide plenty of examples, but even Rose admits that Purdie and the others got it right for 'Hey Joe', one of three stand-out songs on *Tim Rose*, alongside 'Morning Dew' and 'Come Away, Melinda'.

Paradoxically for an artist normally described as a singer-songwriter, none of these songs was a Rose composition. The origins of 'Hey Joe', the famous murder ballad also known as 'Blue Steel .44', are uncertain. Telling the story of a man who catches his wife with another man and shoots her before escaping to Mexico where "a man can be free", it is generally credited to an obscure folk-blues singer named Billy Roberts (William M. Roberts). He seems to have vanished from the scene by the time the song became a garage-band standard in the mid 1960s (although there are reports that Roberts was present in the studio for the recording of a subsequently unreleased Fred Neil album in the 1970s).

Many think it unlikely that Roberts wrote the song, and figure that the original writer must be lost in the murky history of American blues. Rose says it is an old Appalachian song that he first heard performed in Florida when he was a child. By the time Rose made his 'Hey Joe' it had already been recorded by The Leaves, who released a version in 1965 entitled 'Hey Joe Where You Gonna Go' credited to Chester Powers, a pseudonym for another Greenwich Village songwriter, Dino Valenti. The group released a second attempt a year later with the abbreviated title, and this version was an American hit. It was also recorded by The Byrds and Love.

> "Rose delivered 'Hey Joe' with a suitable sense of restrained malevolence."

All of these interpretations took the song at a frantic pace. Rose rearranged it to something probably closer to the spirit in which it was originally written, slowing it down and delivering the lyrics with a suitable sense of restrained malevolence, gradually building to a wailing crescendo before fading.

Rose's take of the song was recorded live in the studio, with no overdubs, and in its unedited form it stretched to over six minutes. When it was finished producer Rubinson played it down the telephone to Columbia executive Clive Davis, who announced that he wanted it in the shops the next morning. The record did not appear quite so quickly, but it was out within a few days. It was late 1966, a few months before the release of his debut album, and for the first time Rose began to get noticed.

'Hey Joe' was attracting considerable interest, becoming a regional hit in San Francisco, when its progress was stalled after a ban in the Southern States for supposedly glorifying violence. In January 1967 a young black guitar virtuoso named Jimi Hendrix broke into the UK charts with a version of the song that bore a striking similarity to the Rose recording.

Rose claims that Chas Chandler, Hendrix's manager, had heard Rose's version in a club in Los Angeles. Impressed with the record, Chandler had taken a copy to Hendrix, who had just moved to the UK, demanding that Hendrix record it as his first single. Hendrix obliged, and cut his version in London on October 23rd 1966. Hendrix biographers Harry Shapiro and Caesar Glebbeek give some credence to this story in their 1990 biography, though they also say that Chandler had earlier seen Hendrix perform the song at the Café Wha, and was pleased as he had already decided it was the song he would use to launch his business career in the UK.

In the absence of information about exactly when the two performers started playing their slow arrangements of the song, it must remain a point of dispute whether Hendrix copied Rose's interpretation. Did Hendrix and Rose each find the inspiration for their versions from a common source, an early blues interpretation? It is after all likely that the song was first a slow blues and that the adolescent, punkish Leaves/Byrds/Love interpretations were a mutation of this original template. Or did Hendrix pick up the song from Love's Arthur Lee when the two had worked together in 1963/64?

Whatever the truth, Rose didn't profit directly from the Hendrix version as he failed to copyright his arrangement in the way that Paul Simon copyrighted the interpretation of 'Scarborough Fair' (which he had reputedly learned from Martin Carthy). But the story that Hendrix's version was a copy of Rose's was common currency for a while in the late 1960s, and Rose did benefit from the exposure that this debate afforded him.

'Come Away, Melinda' and 'Morning Dew' were both folk songs warning of coming nuclear apocalypse – and were given similar interpretations by Rose. He would start subdued and restrained before moving up through increments to a peak of fevered intensity, a style that suited the gravel-throated singer. 'Morning Dew' in particular is a classic recording, driven by Purdie's propulsive drumming. Inexplicably, despite extensive airplay on both sides of the Atlantic, the song was not a hit.

On Rose's version of 'Morning Dew', and others thereafter, Rose was given a co-writing credit with the song's original composer, Bonnie Dobson. Dobson was a Canadian folk singer who had written the song around 1960. Her original was a mournful dirge based on a central refrain of "take me for a walk in the morning dew". It was recorded by Fred Neil and Vince Martin in 1962, and it is in their version, still very much in a traditional folk style, that the phrase "walk me out in the morning dew" first appeared.

When the Neil/Martin version was released the naive Dobson was persuaded to sign a publishing deal with Elektra for the previously unpublished song. Somehow, when Rose came to record the song he was cut in on the credits. How this happened isn't clear, although speaking in 1993 Dobson gave the impression that it was against her will, and that she had been told that it was linked to the song being "in the public domain" but unpublished for some time before the Neil/Martin version appeared.

Whether Rose deserved a co-writing credit for 'Morning Dew' is a moot point. That Dobson originally wrote the song is not in dispute. That Rose's radical reinterpretation served as the inspiration for covers by artists as diverse as Lulu, The Jeff Beck Group and Episode 6 – and in doing so greatly enhanced the earning power of the song – is also not in dispute. Furthermore, the quantum leap from the Neil/Martin interpretation to Rose's cut cannot be denied. Rose energised 'Morning Dew', but he didn't write it. However, it's unlikely that the song would have become a standard, with more than 60 known recorded versions to date, without Rose's blueprint rock version.

> "It's unlikely that 'Morning Dew' would have become a standard without Rose's blueprint rock version."

'Come Away Melinda' appeared on the *Rock Machine Turns You On* album, one of the first budget "sampler" compilations. Because of this, it is one of Rose's best-known recordings among a particular generation of record buyers. Co-written by Weavers guitarist Fred Hellerman, the song had featured in The Big Three's repertoire a few years earlier. Their version was sung by Cass Elliot, with Rose and Hendricks politely harmonising behind her. Rose's portentous, ominous interpretation remains the definitive version of the song.

Alongside the cover versions on Rose's debut album were five of his own songs, the best of which were the folk-pop 'You're Slipping Away From Me' and 'Long Time Man', a close relative of 'Hey Joe' in which the murdering protagonist languishes for the rest of his life in jail rather than escaping to Mexico.

Rose's apparently contradictory vocal characteristics of macho posturing and vulnerable pleading seem an accurate representation of his personality. Reflecting today on his career in the 1960s, he says, "I had an ego the size of a donkey's dick, but my self-respect was this high,"[6] and makes a small space between his index finger and thumb.

> ## "Blunt and insulting... also kind and gentle, intelligent and generous."

The contradictions were apparent to critics at the time. "He's not the easiest person in the world to like or understand," said one. "He's blunt, argumentative, insulting and opinionated. All true. He's also kind and gentle, intelligent and generous. Also true."[7] The signs are that this tension remains, with his conversation still veering between bold assertions of unique qualities and disarmingly frank admissions of insecurity.

Despite excellent reviews and considerable radio airplay, *Tim Rose* the debut album did not sell. Crucially, it did not spawn any hit singles, still the benchmark of rock success in 1967. Rose believes that Columbia were uncertain about how to promote him – a folk singer with a rock band, and an album with a cover of Gene Pitney's hit 'I'm Gonna Be Strong'.

Although the widely expected commercial breakthrough hadn't materialised, there remained a sense that Rose was still poised to become a major star. His voice had the same rasping, throaty, abrasive, soulful characteristics that Rod Stewart and Joe Cocker would soon use to forge lucrative careers. He was a scorching live performer. He could pen a decent enough tune. Perhaps most importantly, he had widespread support among DJs, the press and his contemporaries, particularly during his first visits to the UK in 1967 and 1968. But somehow it didn't happen.

By 1968 Rose was spending much of his time in Britain. In 1967 he had played a few dates backed by The Aynsley Dunbar Retaliation, quickly establishing a reputation as a live performer of rare intensity and charisma. When he toured again in 1968 it was with a trio that included a pre-Led Zeppelin John Bonham. There were TV appearances and radio sessions. A non-album single was released, 'Long Haired Boy', a self-penned, cynical folk-rock song about groupie culture, produced by Al Kooper, with an accompanying black-and-white promo film. It was one of the best songs Rose ever wrote, but despite acclaim and airplay it didn't chart in the UK or the US, and in fact by this time Rose was spending so much time in the UK that his impact in his home country was waning.

Most observers considered Rose's second album a disappointment. *Through Rose Colored Glasses* was recorded in New York and produced by one Jack Tracy, not a well-known name. It lacked the immediate, visceral impact of its predecessor, and when it was finally released in 1969 much of the initial momentum gained by 'Morning Dew' and 'Hey Joe' had subsided. Furthermore, if it had been difficult to categorise Rose before, now it was even harder.

Generally, *Through Rose Colored Glasses* is a slicker, more pop-influenced album than its predecessor. Instrumentation is often complex and sophisticated, featuring horns, strings, woodwind and banjo at various points, from an uncredited but apparently long list of session players. Rose was not satisfied, and says that while he's worked with some great musicians "they just have not been particularly good on my stuff".[8] Eight of the 12 songs were Rose originals, the pick of the crop being the moody organ-based ballad 'Angela'.

With hindsight, *Through Rose Colored Glasses* suffered unfairly in comparison with Rose's earlier album. But it certainly provided evidence of the problem that became increasingly apparent throughout Rose's subsequent recording career.

It was clear that Rose's musical interests and abilities were eclectic and far-reaching. He was capable of moving effortlessly from a bluegrass banjo tour de force through a pretty folk-rock pop song to a blasting rock work-out – and frequently did. But therein lay the problem. Whereas contemporaries like Tim Hardin, David Ackles and Tim Buckley at their best were able to fuse a variety of influences into something uniquely their own, Rose's recordings too often demonstrated a lack of identity that manifested itself as simply dabbling in a range of styles. "I tried to do too much with each album," Rose admits now. "I dispersed my energies. You can do whatever you want as a writer and singer ... and you won't sell."[9]

Through Rose Colored Glasses wasn't a bad record, hinting at interesting directions that were to remain sadly unexplored, notably on the drums-and-vocals-only 'Maman', another anti-war song of genuine power. But it just wasn't what Rose needed to capitalise on a promising start. The record sold poorly, establishing a pattern which repeated itself for the rest of the first phase of his career, patchy albums recorded at some expense with big name contributors offering only sporadic glimpses of the talent so extensively revealed on the debut LP.

Rose moved back to the States where he continued to perform with a new sidekick, guitarist Andy Summers, later of The Police. By this time Rose had become a qualified pilot (he still holds a commercial license) and supplemented his income by working as a charter pilot, as well as recording voiceovers for TV commercials. He met up with a Welshman, Jonathon Rowlands, who set up a one-album deal with Capitol. In spring 1970 Rose returned to the UK to make what became the cumbersomely titled *Love – A Kind Of Hate Story*. It was recorded at Island studios in London.

> "You can do whatever you want as a writer and singer ... and you won't sell."

Taking control of the project was famed producer Shel Talmy (Kinks, Who, Manfred Mann), and he assembled a backing band of top UK session players, including drummer Clem Cattini and bassist Herbie Flowers. The resulting album is uneven, with plenty of tantalising glimpses of Rose's potential, but lacking in overall cohesiveness. Talmy must shoulder much of the responsibility for this. His mix of the basic band's guitar, keyboards, bass and drums – sometimes augmented by horns and backing vocals – was chaotic, with Rose's vocal often all but lost in the mêlée. The musicians, particularly bassist Flowers, too often muddle inventiveness with indulgent displays of technique for its own sake.

Five of the ten songs are Rose originals, the best of which is the harpsichord-based 'I Know Two People', about a failing marriage. Of the cover versions, the take of The Bee Gees' 'I Gotta Get A Message To You' almost gave Rose a UK hit single: the desperate, yearning sentiments of the song matched the best qualities of Rose's singing. He appeared on British TV's *Top Of The Pops* to promote this single, meeting and sharing mutual respect with The Bee Gees themselves who were appearing on the same episode. In contrast, the boozy, bar-band unsubtlety of Peter Sarstedt's 'Where Do You Go To My Lovely' provided an illustration of Rose's tendency sometimes to rely merely on the power of his voice to overwhelm the listener. Despite yet more favourable press coverage and airplay in the UK, the album was ignored in the States, and by the end of 1970 Rose was once again a part-time musician, pilot and voiceover artist.

He reappeared in 1972 as the first signing to Playboy Records, a new company attached to Hugh Heffner's girlie magazine empire. For his album for Playboy, again entitled simply *Tim Rose*, he was teamed at his own request with former Spooky Tooth frontman Gary Wright. Wright produced the record at Olympic studios in London, contributed three songs, and used his then backing band, including Mick Jones (later of Foreigner) on lead guitar.

Two of Rose's three contributions, 'Going Down To Hollywood' and the solo acoustic 'You Can't Keep Me', were the best of what was yet another inconsistent work. Wright brought to the sessions three songs, best described as failed British attempts at Southern Boogie and which pandered to the worst excesses of Rose's singing – all aggression and bluster, with no finesse. A funereal-paced interpretation of The Beatles' 'You've Got To Hide Your Love Away' in a Joe Cocker style was the most successful of the cover versions.

> **"His lyrics repeatedly centre on independence and self-reliance."**

Another of the covers was a pained, overbearing take of Tim Hardin's standard 'If I Were A Carpenter'. When the two toured together a few years later Rose dropped the song from his set, anxious about how the ever-critical Hardin might respond to the interpretation. In fact, Rose's solo acoustic take on the song – which he performed live but sadly chose not to record for the album – is far superior to his recorded version and may well have been a match for anything the failing Hardin was then capable of.

Rose recognises that as a songwriter he was never a match for somebody like Hardin, believing correctly that his main strengths are in singing and interpretation. His lyrics repeatedly centre on themes of independence and self-reliance, and too often are matter-of-fact and conversational. Hardin was able to use similarly simple, down-to-earth words to create poetry, whereas Rose frequently sounds just blunt and direct.

Similarly Rose's melodies, often closely following the chord progressions, lacked the elusive combination of fluidity and simplicity that mark out a classic song from a merely good one. For these reasons Rose was never able to secure a position of respect as a writer whom other artists would turn to, and his songs were not widely covered. But often it was the appearance of his own material that served as welcome relief amid the morass of mediocre cover versions that formed the bulk of the Wright-produced album and the rest of his output in the 1970s.

Tim Rose was well received in the US, but the fledgling Playboy label lacked the marketing muscle and expertise to capitalise on the interest, and the album quickly and quietly sank. It didn't get released in the UK until 1974 when Pye licensed it from Playboy for their progressive imprint, Dawn.

Rose, encouraged by Jonathon Rowlands, returned to the UK that year to find that he was still held in high regard by the music business establishment. 'Hide Your Love Away' was released as a single and was awarded single of the week in *New Musical Express*. Yet again there was a buzz in the press, some radio airplay, TV appearances and acclaimed live shows. Yet again both the single and the album failed to sell. Undeterred, Rose signed to Atlantic, for whom he made *The Musician* in 1975.

It was recorded at Rockfield Studios in Wales and IBC in London, largely produced by Rowlands, and once again featured a roll-call of session players including Andy Summers and pedal-steel guitarist BJ Cole. But *The Musician* was a weak record. Perhaps discouraged by the repeated failures of earlier efforts dominated by Rose's aggressive, direct style, the new album was a slick soft-rock collection with jazz and country inflections. Whether this change in direction was instigated by Atlantic, Rowlands or Rose himself isn't clear. But it wasn't a success, and contained little of merit. A bizarre fuzz-bass interpretation of Neil Young's 'Old Man', lush synth-strings on the title track, and classical and pedal-steel guitar embellishments couldn't disguise a fundamental lack of direction. It was a commercial and artistic nadir, rightly described by Allan Jones in *Melody Maker* as "a rather poor record".[10] For many years it appeared to mark the end of Rose's career.

The Musician appeared right at the end of 1975. Dr Feelgood were playing in the pubs, and within a year the first wave of punk bands would be sweeping all before them. Rose hung around in London for a few years longer, and still commanded respect when playing live. A tape of a solo concert at The Drury Lane Theatre broadcast on London's Capital Radio in 1976 reveals Rose shorn of unsympathetic backing and delivering mature, powerful interpretations of a selection from his back catalogue. He embarked on the previously mentioned dates with Hardin – and most nights by all accounts Rose played the dishevelled, broken songwriting genius off the stage. But London was by this time becoming a singularly inhospitable place for all but the most obdurate of 1960s survivors. Rose was clinging to the wreckage of a career, and seemed increasingly like a man out of place and out of time.

In 1977 an album that would become *The Gambler* was demoed for Atlantic in a stripped-down guitar-based style. The songs were well received by the label, which funded a £100,000 recording session. The result was an over-arranged, over-produced collection that the company then declined to release. Rose was disillusioned and broke. "Most of us from the 1960s don't have any money," he says now. "We made Faustian bargains, and by the time we wised up it was all gone."[11] It was around this time that Rose humiliatingly had to borrow £10 from John Bonham at a music business party just to get by. He also had to borrow money, this time from his mother, to catch a budget Laker Airways flight home to the US. There ensued two decades of mixed fortunes.

> "London became an inhospitable place for all but the most obdurate of 1960s survivors."

When Rose returned to New York in the late 1970s he found that all his old contacts in the music world had disappeared. Finding it impossible to restart a musical career and having lost touch with his royalties, he was forced to work as a labourer, fitting plasterboard walls.

His fortunes improved after a significant phone call. "A guy sang something to me and asked if I could sing it back. I said yes, so he said, 'Be at the studio tomorrow morning and sing it for me.' It ended up being a Wrangler jeans commercial and it ran for five years."[12] This led to a run of TV jingles which funded Rose's return to college to get a degree in the mid 1980s.

When Rose graduated he found that his TV contacts had dried up, so he worked for a spell as a stockbroker, getting out when the stock market collapsed in 1987. He got married. He started to do voiceovers again. He drank a lot. Throughout this unsettled spell Rose's musical career was in abeyance, and he restricted himself to the occasional low-key club date in New York.

By the turn of the decade his marriage was in ruins and he was drinking heavily. He was reduced to drunkenly trying to impress "20-year-old secretaries from Brooklyn" at parties with tales of how he used to know Paul Simon. His marriage broke up shortly afterward and Rose realised it was time to stop drinking. Yet by this time, and although he was unaware of it, there was a resurgence of interest in Rose in the UK. Nick Cave had recorded one of his songs, 'Long Time

Man', in 1986, and reissues of his classic first album were introducing Tim Rose to a new generation of record-buyers.

In the early 1990s Rose began to think about a return to music. In 1996 he recorded some demos with Pierre Tubbs, the producer of the unreleased *The Gambler*. While in the UK working on these recordings he was persuaded to make that appearance at the Half Moon venue in south London. The success of that performance once again relaunched Rose's meandering career – a surprising re-emergence after two decades away. Rose now cut an avuncular figure: grey-haired, portly, bespectacled, looking something like a hybrid of George Melly and an American college professor. But the ferocity of his performance was undiminished.

In 1997 Rose released his first new album in over 20 years, *Haunted*, on a tiny British independent label, Best Dressed Records. A self-produced collection of live interpretations of old favourites and new demo-like studio recordings, the record appeared to be hurried and ill-conceived, an impression reinforced by the shoddy packaging. Reviews were neither fulsome in their praise nor overly critical. Sales were poor on account of seemingly non-existent distribution. At first glance it seemed like a rather sad postscript, a tired effort to recall former glories.

In fact *Haunted* deserves further attention. The singing is uniformly excellent on both the studio and the live recordings. Crucially, Rose is not relying simply on the power of his voice. Of equal significance, much of the new self-penned or co-written material – notably 'He Never Was A Hero' – was of a high standard.

> "It's not the 1960s any more. A lot of people don't realise that."

Since the release of *Haunted*, Rose has continued to perform live regularly, including a brief tour in 1999 with Robert Plant's Priory Of Brion. At the time of writing Rose is recording a new album in Norway, a Dutch TV documentary about his life and career is in production, and he is planning a one-man show of music and anecdotes about his long and chequered career. As a consummate raconteur, he should excel in that role.

Rose is philosophical about the disappointments that forced the 20-year hiatus in his career. "John Bonham was my drummer – six months later he's in Led Zeppelin. Andy Summers was my guitarist – six months later he's in The Police. If you itemise all of those things there seems to have been a pattern in my life. I was not destined to be a big star. Maybe I would have killed myself. Other people did. I just wish I could have made a little more money."[13]

But destiny apart, it was the lack of a clear vision – or the inability to communicate one – that prevented him from fulfilling that early promise. Too often his records sound like Tim Rose fighting against the ideas and egos of unsympathetic producers and sessionmen who apprehended only the brutal power of his voice. They did not appreciate his capacity for subtlety, innate vulnerability and dynamic range, instead creating backing tracks that did little but underline their lack of understanding.

Rose's best recordings – 'Morning Dew', 'Hey Joe', 'Come Away, Melinda', 'Maman', 'Long Haired Boy' – succeed through his keen sense of dynamics. Unlike many talented live singers, he was able to translate a sense of performance and drama onto record, but only if his backing players were sympathetic. Yet only on his first album – whether by happy accident or design – did he find musicians who were able to play consistently to his unique strengths.

Even now when talking about his musical career Rose is strangely fatalistic for a man so stridently independent and strong-minded. He seems to want control, up to a point, but then relinquishes it. "It's out of my hands – I can handle the recording and the writing, but the rest of it is somebody else's responsibility,"[14] he says of his current work in progress. This combination of fatalism, wilful independence and uncertain direction did not serve him well during his career in the 1960s and 1970s. Throughout his story there emerge episodes where he travelled in one direction for a while, then turned around and did something else when it didn't work out. There was no game plan.

Tim Rose currently lives in central London, near the Portland Place home of the BBC, responsible for so much of his airplay over the years. He is a survivor, and proud of it. He still nurtures ambitions to perform, write and sing, but is aware of the pitfalls a man of his age faces when trying to relaunch himself in a music business more concerned with image and packaging than ever. Although the brash confidence of youth has subsided, it has not entirely disappeared.

Most of all, he is keen not to live in the past. "It's not the 1960s any more – a lot of people don't realise that. I've not made it yet, so I can't be a has-been. I'm the last great underground artist of the 1960s."[15]

Rose is aware that future success depends on being able to reinvent himself – with reference to his past achievements, but without simply retreading former glories. "I don't want to hang out with any other people who made records in the 1960s. I'm through with that. I've always wanted to move on. I'm not doing another new version of 'Hey Joe' or 'Morning Dew' ever again."[16]

[1] Author's interview February 3rd 2000
[2] Author's interview February 3rd 2000
[3] Rose interviewed by Brian Mathieson March 1st 1998
[4] Rose interviewed by Brian Mathieson March 1st 1998
[5] Author's interview February 3rd 2000
[6] Author's interview February 3rd 2000
[7] *Disc & Music Echo* July 19th 1969
[8] Author's interview February 3rd 2000
[9] Author's interview February 3rd 2000
[10] *Melody Maker* December 27th 1975
[11] Author's interview February 3rd 2000
[12] Rose interviewed by Brian Mathieson March 1st 1998
[13] Author's interview February 3rd 2000
[14] Author's interview June 28th 2000
[15] Author's interview February 3rd 2000
[16] Author's interview June 28th 2000

TOM RUSH

CHAPTER 9

The rainbow life from show to show,
The smiling faces come and go,
There's years of roads and highway signs,
And the hours go on for miles and miles.

FROM 'WRONG END OF THE RAINBOW' BY TOM RUSH AND TREVOR VEITCH, *copyright control 1970*

Tom Rush was the first person to bring Joni Mitchell, James Taylor and Jackson Browne to widespread public attention when he recorded their songs on his classic 1968 album *The Circle Game*. Rush often overlooked his own material in favour of that of other writers, but his song 'No Regrets' from *Circle Game* has proved as enduring as many by his better known contemporaries.

I n 1975 Tom Rush summed up a career that had already lasted the best part of 15 years. "I just muddle along looking for songs," he said. "I'm here because I couldn't make a living with an English Literature diploma from Harvard."[1] Peeling away the veneer of laconic interview-speak there remains one central truth in these words. Rush's career was, and still is, all about songs. More often than not other people's songs. Sometimes his own.

He was born in Portsmouth, New Hampshire, in 1941, and is the eldest of three adopted children. Like many children Rush learned to play the piano, in his case for six years, while never really becoming enthusiastic about the instrument. He was more interested in learning the tunes his older cousin, Beau, taught him on the tenor ukulele. Later he picked up a guitar.

Rush's father was a teacher; his mother sometimes volunteered in a psychiatric hospital. "One of the things she volunteered was me," said Rush, "and I formed a band composed of inmates from the criminal wing."[2] So it was that he gave his first performance, at the hospital's annual patient's party.

Rush's route into the folk revival was similar to that of most of his contemporaries. He had an early enthusiasm for rock'n'roll, then an emerging attraction to the direct simplicity of traditional music. He played in a covers band at school, performing the hits of Chuck Berry, Little Richard and Elvis Presley. Then, while travelling with his family through Jackson, Wyoming, Rush was captivated by a Josh White recording he heard on the radio. What appealed was the appearance of something authentic in White's music. This was ironic given that White was a folk singer and guitarist operating at the more commercial end of the market, performing traditional songs and his own compositions on the cabaret circuit. For many folk stalwarts White was not quite the real thing. Rush knew nothing of this, however, and simply loved the sound of White's guitar-playing and voice. He said, "I decided I wanted to be Josh White. I spent a lot of time trying to learn how he played – so he was a major influence."[3]

> **"I decided I wanted to be Josh White, and spent a lot of time trying to learn how he played."**

In 1959 Rush enrolled at Harvard to study English Literature. With his passion already sparked by White he was quickly immersed in the burgeoning Boston and Cambridge folk scene over which Joan Baez presided. He adopted the denim, suede and corduroy uniform, and with his well-defined Ivy League good looks and swept-back thick brown hair he soon became something of a folk scene pin-up. He began to perform at local clubs like The Unicorn, The Golden Vanity and Club 47. He also presented a 30-minute slot every Wednesday night on Harvard's radio station, WHRB, which he would fill with live sessions by local performers, occasionally playing a song himself.

Like Phil Ochs, Rush dropped out of college early in his studies, and actually succeeded in scraping a living as a performer for a while. He returned to his studies a year later, though, and unlike Ochs did eventually graduate. Perhaps this was an early indicator of the pragmatic common sense that allowed him to adapt to changing tastes and circumstances later in his career. During that year off he acquired a taste for the travelling troubadour's life, appearing in New York and Philadelphia. When he performed in Florida on a circuit dominated by Fred Neil, Vince Martin and David Crosby, Rush caused something of a stir because he knew a different set of songs from the overlapping repertoires of the other performers.

In 1962, when he was 21, Rush became one of the first of the new generation of folk performers to cut an album, recording *Live At The Unicorn* over two nights at the Boston club. It was a basic, no-frills production funded by a local promoter, Dan Flickinger. Only distributed locally, it remains a very rare record, despite being reissued in 1986.

Live At The Unicorn is not only a document of Rush's emerging singing and interpretative talents, but an intriguing artefact from the folk revival. Rush says of the album: "Dan Flickinger ... brought down a 'portable' Ampex the size of a washing machine to the Unicorn and taped my sets ... . The finished product was distributed from the back seat of Dan's Studebaker, and several hundred copies were sold before the venture folded."[4] Later he would view the album with some ambivalence. "Listening from the perspective of 25 years of experience, some of these early performances make me wince," he said when the album was reissued in 1986. "Still, it represents a moment in the 1960s folk scene, and a starting point for an artist. I'll stand behind it."[5]

Whatever the merits of this first effort, the young Rush had done enough to come to the attention of Paul Rothchild, then newly appointed at Prestige, a record company competing with Elektra and Vanguard to sign as many up-and-coming folk singers as possible. Rush was duly signed to the label, and the first of his two albums for them was recorded in May 1963. *Got A Mind To Ramble* featured Rush accompanying himself on guitar, sometimes augmented by Fritz Richmond on washtub bass, and singing a range of traditional and contemporary material. Like many folk records of the era it was recorded in very primitive circumstances, in this case in somebody's living room and captured on a portable tape recorder.

It is a typical enough album of its type, distinguished only by the first showings of what would become the two dominant themes in Rush's recording career. First, it demonstrates his unwillingness to be tied down to any one style of music. He prefers simply to choose songs that he likes, regardless of their origin, and calls himself a "generalist". Second, it showcases his emerging abilities as an unusually accomplished guitarist capable of complex fingerpicking and abrasive slide work as well as the usual rigorous strumming. He also experimented with open tunings, and was in the habit of tuning his guitar down a tone from normal pitch.

> **"The first album was distributed from the back seat of a Studebaker."**

The second of Rush's Prestige albums, *Blues, Songs And Ballads*, was recorded in a "proper" studio in New York during a confusing period where he appeared to be recording for two labels simultaneously. Producer Rothchild had moved to Elektra Records and wanted to take Rush with him. Rush was still contracted to Prestige for one more album but said he would only make another record for them if Rothchild could produce it. He then went to Elektra and said he'd like to sign with them, but only if they would release Rothchild to produce a contractual-obligation album for Prestige, thus discharging Rush's obligations to them.

Neither company was happy with the arrangement. Prestige was angry with Rothchild for "deserting"; Elektra did not want their new star producer to work for a competitor. But they both wanted to release new Tom Rush albums. Eventually Rush recorded two albums together: one for Prestige and one for Elektra, both produced by Rothchild. The Elektra album was released shortly before the Prestige, although the latter tends to be listed in discographies as the third Tom Rush album with the Elektra release as the fourth.

Blues, Songs And Ballads, which appeared on Prestige in 1965, is broadly similar to the label's first Rush release, but with a greater emphasis on traditional standards. Richmond again accompanies on washtub bass. Although a well executed set of performances, it leaves the impression of a perfunctory fulfilment of contractual responsibilities. The eponymous Elektra album, on the other hand, marks a development in Rush's style.

Released in January 1965 immediately after Phil Ochs's *I Ain't Marching Anymore* in the Elektra release schedules, *Tom Rush* was the first of his albums to feature a wider range of instrumentation. On bass was Bill Lee (father of film director Spike Lee), and the established team of John Sebastian and Felix Pappalardi played, respectively, harmonica and guitarrón (a Mexican acoustic bass guitar). Ramblin' Jack Elliot or "Daddy Bones" (John Herrald) played second guitar on some songs.

> **"Al Kooper, then just coming to attention for his work with Dylan, played lead guitar on the electric material, wrote the sleevenotes, and seems also to have had the role of bandleader and arranger."**

Rush again drew on traditional material and contemporary composers, and included two Woody Guthrie numbers ('Do-Re-Mi' and 'I'd Like To Know'), plus an old Leiber & Stoller composition that The Coasters had recorded as a b-side, 'When She Wants Good Lovin''. It was still a record with the hallmarks of the folk movement, but contained the first signs that Rush was moving on.

The sleeve of Elektra's *Tom Rush* featured a photograph by William S Harvey, a definitive image of the period's singer-songwriter style. Rush, looking lean and hungry, dressed in corduroys, cowboy boots and a suede jacket, his guitar case at his feet, stands lighting a cigarette against a backdrop of railway tracks and cranes. Themes of travel and solitude were popular in the imagery of the period, and in Rush's case recurred throughout his later recordings.

Although Rush was yet to secure widespread record sales or to start writing his own material, he was respected as a worthy and talented performer. As yet he had not broken out of the folk circuit, but on his next album he took a substantial step toward the pop audience. During 1966 Rush signed with manager Arthur Gorson, who was by now also taking care of Phil Ochs and David Blue. Both were in the process of moving beyond folk-blues, and Rush did the same with his second Elektra album, *Take A Little Walk With Me*.

By the time this record was released in 1966, Dylan had already been cast out of the folk community for going electric, and in the process reached a much wider audience. Rush was one of the first of Dylan's contemporaries to follow suit. *Take A Little Walk With Me* had one electric side (mainly cover versions of 1950s rock'n'roll songs) and one acoustic side, making it Rush's equivalent of Dylan's *Bringing It All Back Home*. Rush, though, punctured any notions that by going electric he was making some decisive artistic statement, saying, "I just like those old songs. I always have. Nothing more. No theories. Just plain enjoyment."[6] *Take A Little Walk With Me* was also significant in marking Rush's debut as a songwriter.

The album was produced by Mark Abramsom. Al Kooper, then just coming to attention for his work with Dylan, played lead guitar on the electric material, wrote the sleevenotes, and seems also to have had the role of bandleader and arranger. Bruce Langhorne, another guitarist who had played with Dylan, was also in the line-up.

The electric side has five of the songs the young Rush had enjoyed as a schoolboy learning the guitar, including Willie Dixon's 'You Can't Tell a Book By The Cover' and Chuck Berry's 'Too

Much Monkey Business'. Rush's own 'On The Road Again', a loping electric blues work-out, sits well in such esteemed company. The best of these tracks, though, is the authentically fierce take of Bo Diddley's 'Who Do You Love'. For this, Rush adopts a low, growling vocal style that he would use periodically on later recordings, and Kooper contributes piercing, highly-distorted lead guitar.

The acoustic side is more in the style of Rush's earlier recordings. It features two songs by Eric Von Schmidt, a friend from the Cambridge/Boston circuit, one of which, 'Joshua Gone Barbados', became a staple of Rush's live set for many years. Rush had already recorded a Von Schmidt song on his first Prestige album. The album closes with an interpretation of 'Galveston Flood' dominated by a slide guitar chord motif that Rush achieved using a knife on the strings.

A myth grew up that Dylan played on *Take A Little Walk With Me*, which Rush admits he did little to discourage. It centres on the contribution of one "Roosevelt Gook" who is credited with playing piano on the electric side of the album. "Gook" was long thought to be a pseudonym for Dylan, probably because he had once performed under a similarly bizarre name, Blind Boy Grunt, on another artist's record. In addition, it was no doubt thought that Kooper's by now well established association with Dylan might have persuaded Dylan to make an appearance. Rush now says that "Gook" was in fact Al Kooper himself, although this does seem odd as Kooper was also credited under his own name as lead guitarist.

In the mid 1960s Rush was performing regularly across the States, also crossing the border to Canada on occasion. It was during a two-week residency at a club called The Chessmate in Detroit, in the winter of 1965/66, that Rush first encountered the Canadian singer-songwriter Joni Mitchell. She played a guest set during one of his performances and impressed Rush with both her singing and songwriting talents. Mitchell was then an unrecorded hopeful who sounded not unlike Judy Collins.

> "It was at The Chessmate club in Detroit that Rush first met Joni Mitchell."

During the two-week engagement Rush suffered a recurrence of a collapsed lung that had first caused him problems at Harvard. He needed surgery, and was unable to complete the residency. Mitchell deputised for him for the second week, and took the opportunity of handing Rush a tape of several of her songs, including 'Urge For Going' and 'The Circle Game'. Rush, not a prolific writer himself and always on the lookout for new material, was sufficiently impressed to start performing the songs live. He also tried to persuade Jac Holzman to sign Mitchell to Elektra, but Holzman declined on the grounds that she sounded too much like Collins, who was already making records for Elektra.

Rush recorded a version of 'Urge For Going' in a demo studio in 1966. It was similar to the take that eventually appeared on Rush's next album, already featuring Bruce Langhorne's descending electric guitar part that survived to the officially released version. A reel-to-reel tape of this first demo version found its way to Jefferson Kaye, a DJ on WBZ radio, a Boston station with a particularly powerful transmitter and therefore a wide audience. Kaye played the song and was inundated with requests to play it again. For a year and a half it was one of the station's most requested songs, and was widely recognised and admired in the Boston area, despite being commercially unavailable. This was almost certainly the first publicly performed recording of a Joni Mitchell song.

As well as discovering Joni Mitchell, while in the process of finding songs for his next record Rush also came across the work of James Taylor and Jackson Browne. He has described the three as "kindred spirits artistically",[7] and they contributed the bulk of the songs to Rush's new album, *The Circle Game*. It was a pivotal work in both Rush's career and the emergence of the singer-songwriter movement. *Rolling Stone* magazine later pinpointed it as the album that ushered in the genre.

In 1967 Rush made the first of what would become regular visits to the UK. In interviews with the British music press he was keen to point out that he was not a folk singer, although he accepted that he was also not really a pop artist and was generally hard to categorise. Certainly he had the looks, smile and easy charm of a pop star, and a number of television appearances bolstered his female following and a reputation as a ladies man. To an extent this has persisted throughout his career.

Rush's previously neat, swept-back hair was spreading into an unruly, curly mop. He grew a drooping moustache – which in time became something of a trademark – although one reviewer thought it "realistic" but "false". The gauche college boy wearing Guthriesque clothes had become what then passed for an elegantly casual man about town. A feature in *Disc & Music Echo* from this period concentrated on these attributes, and consisted almost entirely of reported flirtatious banter between Rush and the female writer.

> **"Here was an unaffected, almost casual vocal delivery and the atmosphere of confessional intimacy, as heard later on records by the likes of Jackson Browne and James Taylor."**

When *The Circle Game* finally appeared in 1968 it had been two years since Rush's previous album, by the standards of the time an unusually long gap between releases. Rush puts the delay down to a difficulty in finding material, although the recording of the album, with its more sophisticated arrangements and production values, took longer than Rush's previous efforts. Gorson is credited as producer, although Rush says, "Today he would probably have been called an executive producer. The musical side of things was taken care of by Paul Harris, and Arthur was co-ordinating the project."[8]

With its sympathetic orchestrations, impeccable musicianship and consistently strong material, *The Circle Game* was a very impressive album. *Rolling Stone*'s assertion that *The Circle Game* marked the beginning of the singer-songwriter movement disregards earlier excellent contenders for that title by Tim Hardin, Fred Neil, Phil Ochs, Tim Buckley and others. But Rush's album was the forerunner of a style popularised by the commercially dominant singer-songwriters of the early 1970s: much of his unaffected, almost casual vocal delivery and the atmosphere of confessional intimacy would be heard on later records by the likes of Jackson Browne and James Taylor.

Rush's influence on the careers of Taylor and Browne cannot be underestimated. He included two of Taylor's and one of Browne's songs on *The Circle Game*, as well as three by the then unknown Mitchell. Rush has always disavowed any special foresight, saying in *Rolling Stone* in 1975: "If I hadn't done it, those people would have gotten recorded anyway. They were just too good to go unnoticed."[9] James Taylor, though, acknowledged his debt to Rush, saying: "I copied and learned a lot of his arrangements, so I guess it's fair to say that Tom was not only one of my early heroes, but also one of my main influences."[10] In the same article, Browne talked of his admiration for Rush and the role Rush had played in bringing him to public prominence.

Browne's contribution to *The Circle Game* was 'Shadow Dream Song', one of the best tracks on the album. Taylor's two songs, the cheery 'Sunshine Sunshine' and the upbeat 'Something In The Way She Moves' haven't worn so well. Of Mitchell's contributions, 'Urge For Going' and 'Tin Angel' share a lonely, introspective, downbeat feel that pervades much of the album, but her title track with its now too-familiar imagery of circus carousels creaks with age.

Rush contributed two songs to *The Circle Game*. The first, the instrumental 'Rockport Sunday', was there to show off his guitar-playing prowess. This piece segues into the album's closing song 'No Regrets' which, thanks to later hit cover versions, would become the most enduring of Rush's compositions.

The sales of *The Circle Game* easily exceeded Rush's previous releases, and it achieved his highest chart placing yet in the US. It was also the last Tom Rush record released on Elektra, apart from a later compilation drawn from his three albums for them.

In 1970 Rush signed with Columbia and his first album with the new label was another eponymously titled collection. It was produced and arranged by Ed Freeman who on completing the project immediately went to work with Tim Hardin on *Bird On A Wire*. Hardin's keyboard player Warren Bernhardt also appeared on Rush's record. The country influences and the use of orchestration alongside rock instrumentation make for some similarities between the two albums, but where Hardin's effort proved to be his last creative gasp of any note, Rush by now looked like he was settling in for a long career.

There were no original songs on the new Columbia album, Rush instead concentrating on interpreting further material by Jackson Browne and James Taylor, alongside songs by other writers both known and unknown. He was assisted throughout by guitarist Trevor Veitch, beginning a working partnership that endured for several years in the early 1970s.

Columbia's *Tom Rush* was a quality record of well played, effortlessly sung and carefully chosen songs. It established a style that persisted throughout Rush's next two albums for the label, with folk, country and orchestral elements punctuated by laidback, funky guitar-rock reminiscent of The Band. While the record lacked intensity and any career-defining moments, it was far better than most collections of cover versions.

The opening song, 'Driving Wheel', written by little-known Canadian singer-songwriter David Wiffen, is one of the best songs and arrangements on the album, a stretched-out, mournful, slow rock ballad that intensifies as a horn section joins in. It peaks with a clattering, train-like percussive effect achieved by looping a snare-drum beat, propelling the song toward an elongated fade-out.

'Drop Down Mama' by Sleepy John Estes had earlier appeared in stripped-back acoustic style on Rush's second Prestige album. Here it is transformed into a driving rocker. A similar treatment is given to Fred Neil's 'Wild Child (World Of Trouble)' which had appeared on the reclusive Neil's early-1960s album with Vince Martin. 'These Days' is one of two Jackson Browne songs featured. Previously recorded by Nico on her 1968 album, *Chelsea Girls*, it is one of Browne's best songs, and Rush sings the lyrics in an understated, almost conversational manner that complements their world-weary resignation.

Tom Rush was well received by critics and lingered in the lower reaches of the US album chart for four months. It was the second and last of his records to reach the Top 100. This was the time

> **"Thanks to later hit cover versions, 'No Regrets' would become Rush's most enduring composition."**

of Rush's greatest prominence. Encouraged by the success of his previous two albums, he recorded his second Columbia album, *Wrong End Of The Rainbow*, shortly after *Tom Rush*. It was released late in 1970, nine months after its predecessor.

Ed Freeman handed over production duties to Area Code 615's keyboard player David Briggs, but retained some involvement in the project, arranging the string and horn parts. The sound and style of the album was broadly similar to *Tom Rush*, although this time Rush himself contributed four songs, three co-written with guitarist Veitch. Two more James Taylor songs were chosen, including his standard 'Sweet Baby James'.

> **"If I sit down every morning and stare at the guitar for a few hours, on a regular basis, I produce a few songs."**

The eccentrically titled 'Came To See Me Yesterday In The Merry Month Of' is the least successful cut on the album, and one of the oddest songs Rush ever recorded. Starting with an Irish-folk-style singalong it moves into a quirky rhythmic shuffle that hints at Caribbean influences, with Rush adopting an indeterminate "ethnic" accent to deliver the cryptic lyrics. It is of interest only in that it was another example of Rush giving a break to a new writer, in this case British singer Gilbert O'Sullivan.

Three of the four self-penned songs ably demonstrate Rush's ability to produce material that is a match for the output of the better-known writers to whom he so often turned. Only the undistinguished blues rocker, 'Rotunda', fails to impress. The title track, 'Wrong End Of The Rainbow', is a country-rock jangle about life on the road, reminiscent of later Byrds material. 'Merrimack County' is an introspective, traditional-sounding folk ballad with a neat harmony part by Veitch, while 'Starlight', the one song Rush composed without the assistance of Veitch, is an affecting, quasi-gospel, piano-based ballad, with Rush crying out to Jesus his "sweet saviour" as the chorus swells on Freeman's lush string arrangements.

Wrong End Of The Rainbow spent two months in the US album chart, although it failed to break into the Top 100. It was a lesser commercial performance compared to its two predecessors, but it did attract good reviews as enjoyed by the earlier albums. *Melody Maker* described it as "masterly".[11] The Rush and Veitch partnership continued for Rush's third Columbia release, 1972's self-produced *Merrimack County*. Although a competent record, it tends toward the formulaic. Sales were down, and while Rush continued to perform regularly, his career was running into difficulties.

There would be a pause of two years after *Merrimack County* before the next album appeared. Tensions with Columbia surfaced, and Rush tried to leave the label, but was held for one more album. His partnership with Veitch was amicably severed. Mark Spector, later the manager of Joan Baez, was hired to take on production duties for the new recordings. What resulted was an attempt at an album with wider appeal, featuring many of the trappings of the commercial country recordings then coming out of Nashville. It was an unsuccessful attempt to capture a larger audience that succeeded only in alienating Rush's existing fans.

Much of what Spector brought to *Ladies Love Outlaws* – notably the lush orchestrations – sounds like commercial blandishments. And Rush's instinct for a good song seemed to be deserting him, with a good deal of the material straying dangerously close to the middle of the road. Only the version of Guy Clark's 'Desperadoes Waiting For A Train' impresses, another example of Rush championing a then little-known writer. James Taylor and Jackson Browne repaid Rush for his earlier favours to them by helping out on backing vocals on the album, although for contractual reasons Browne was not credited. Apart from a later best-of compilation, *Ladies Love Outlaws* was to be Rush's last Columbia album.

The one original composition on 1974's *Ladies Love Outlaws* was an orchestral re-arrangement of 'No Regrets', replete with a searing fuzz solo by Elliott Randall, the Sha Na Na guitarist. In 1975 the recently reformed Walker Brothers recorded a duplicate of this arrangement in a London studio, including an approximation of the guitar solo. Scott Walker's grandiose voice was ideally suited to 'No Regrets', but even the vocal phrasing was copied almost exactly from Rush's second version. The Walkers' near six-minute take was to become the title track of their comeback album released on GTO that year.

When the Walker Brothers version was released in November 1975 it immediately attracted attention and airplay on regional radio stations in the UK. However, BBC Radio One preferred the Tom Rush version, which was released as a single shortly afterward in direct competition to the Walkers release. It was given a place on the station's playlist and for a week or so was widely heard on British radio. The chance of a debut UK hit single for Rush, 13 years after his recording career had begun, seemed briefly to be a very real possibility, although Rush himself was unaware that his recording was attracting such attention.

But the reformed 1960s heart-throbs promoted their version heavily with television appearances and interviews, and eventually proved to have more selling power than a respected but only moderately successful singer-songwriter. Although Rush's version officially remained on the Radio One playlist, DJs began to play the Walker Brothers interpretation, which went on to become a massive hit.

Although Rush had seen not only his song covered but also his arrangement copied, the Walker Brothers effort did make a classic from what before then was just one of many excellent album tracks. "I was delighted, imitation being the sincerest form of flattery," says Rush. "It did occur to me once or twice that it was a shame that my version wasn't a big hit."[12] It seems unlikely, however, that Rush's take would even have been released as a single if The Walker Brothers hadn't recorded the song.

In spite of the publicity created by the Walker Brothers hit, Rush's own career came to a halt shortly afterward, and he did not record again for the rest of the 1970s. "I stopped recording more because I was just burned out," he says. "I'd been on the road too much for too long, and I decided to take some time off to reassess what I wanted to do. I retired for nine months, probably in 1976 or so, then I started playing again, with low-profile, low-stress schedules. I was doing it almost as a hobby."[13]

Unable to secure a satisfactory record deal, and facing dwindling attendance at his live performances, Rush began to wonder where the audience for his type of music had gone. "It didn't seem possible to me that all the people had fallen off the face of the earth at the same time, so I tried different ways of reconnecting with the audience,"[14] he says. One way was to commission some market research in 1979 which defined his audience as predominantly 30-something professionals. Rush figured that such people would happily pay more money to see a concert in a comfortable theatre, rather than pay less to go to the dingy 500-capacity rock clubs where he was performing at the time. He took a chance and booked a 2,500-seat theatre, the Boston Symphony Hall, doubled his normal ticket price – and sold out the venue ten days before the show. Since then he has toured regularly, performing highly professional acoustic shows in places that he believes his audience will find congenial.

In the early 1980s Rush formed his own low-key record company, Night Lights, and began releasing occasional albums, often concentrating on re-worked versions of his best-known material. He also reissued his first album, *Live At The Unicorn*. Midge Ure returned 'No Regrets' to the British charts in 1982 with a synthesiser-based arrangement over which he croons a poor copy of Scott Walker's vocal interpretation.

As well as touring as a solo act, Rush now periodically performs concerts with other artists – normally one of his surviving contemporaries like Tom Paxton, plus a couple of new singer-songwriters. These shows go under the banner of Club 47, a reference to the famous venue where Rush played some of his very first dates as a folk singer.

All the signs are that Rush has succeeded in his attempts to reconnect with his old audience. Apart from that brief nine-month retirement in the late 1970s he has maintained an uninterrupted performing career of high standards for nearly 40 years, a unique achievement among the artists featured in this book. This longevity and consistency has much to do with talent: Rush is, simply, a good singer, guitarist, interpreter and songwriter. But he has also been pragmatic and business-minded enough to pace himself and to adapt. It is hard to imagine Tim Hardin or Phil Ochs, even if they had survived into middle age, undertaking market research to identify their audiences.

After having two children by his first marriage, Rush recently had a daughter with his second wife. When interviewed for this book he was planning a series of shows to celebrate his 60th birthday. He would like to record an album of new material, but hopes to find a record company to release it rather than put it out on his own label. In fact he has been talking about this for years, and there is the sense that the relaxed, unhurried characteristics of his best music find their way into his life and career.

This laidback attitude may explain why Rush has recorded not much more than an album's worth of his own material throughout his career. Of his lack of productivity he says: "It's partly because I'm lazy. Writing is extremely hard work. I should do more songwriting. I've learnt that what I've got to do is sit down every morning and stare at the guitar for a few hours. If I do that on a regular basis I produce a few songs."[15]

Perhaps there is a lack of confidence as well. In interviews coinciding with the release of *The Circle Game* back in the 1960s he reckoned that the contributions of the other writers were superior to his own. But it is his song 'No Regrets' on that album that has gained classic status. Rush is a performer committed to doing what is necessary in the service of his material – regardless of who wrote it. "I really think the song is the most important thing," he said once. "It's [about] getting the song across and letting the song tell its own story, without getting in the way of it."[16]

[1] *Melody Maker* August 9th 1975
[2] *Rolling Stone* January 2nd 1975
[3] Interview by Wally Breeze March 7th 1998 at www.jonimitchell.com
[4] Tom Rush at www.tomrush.com
[5] Sleevenotes from Night Light reissue of *Live At The Unicorn* 1986

[6] *Melody Maker* May 20th 1967
[7] Interview by Wally Breeze March 7th 1998 at www.jonimitchell.com
[8] Author's interview August 30th 2000
[9] *Rolling Stone* January 2nd 1975
[10] *Rolling Stone* January 2nd 1975
[11] *Melody Maker* May 8th 1971

[12] Author's interview August 30th 2000
[13] Author's interview August 30th 2000
[14] Author's interview August 30th 2000
[15] Author's interview August 30th 2000
[16] *Melody Maker* January 8th 1972

ILLUSTRATED
discography

The illustrated discography consists of reproductions of the sleeves of all "official" albums by our nine featured performers, released between 1963 and 1976. Release dates and catalogue numbers are for the original US releases, except where noted. When albums were reissued with different sleeves, both the original and the reissue are illustrated.

DAVID ACKLES
discography

■ ☐ David Ackles
Elektra EKL 4022 mono, EKS 74022 stereo
Released 1968

☐ ■ The Road To Cairo (reissue of David Ackles)
Elektra EKL 4022 mono, EKS 74022 stereo
Released 1971

■ ☐ Subway To The Country
Elektra EKS 74060
Released 1969

☐ ■ American Gothic
Elektra EKS 75032
Released 1972

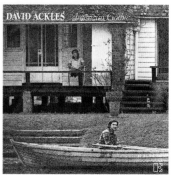

■ ☐ Five And Dime
Columbia KC 32466
Released 1973

DAVID BLUE

discography

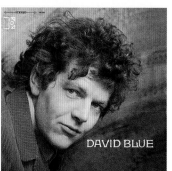

■ ☐ **David Blue**
Elektra EKL 4003 mono, EKS 74003 stereo
Released 1966

☐ ■ **These 23 Days In September**
Reprise R6296 mono, RS 6296 stereo
Released 1968

■ ☐ **Stories**
Asylum SD 5052
Released 1972

☐ ■ **Nice Baby And The Angel**
Asylum SYL 9009
Released June 1973

■ ☐ **Com'n Back For More**
Asylum SYL 9025
Released 1975

☐ ■ **Cupid's Arrow**
Asylum 7E-1077
Released 1976

Me, S. David Cohen
Reprise RS 6375
Released 1970 (not illustrated)

■ □ □ **Tim Buckley**
Elektra EKL 4004 mono, EKS 74004 stereo
Released October 1966

□ ■ □ **Goodbye And Hello**
Elektra EKL 318 mono, EKS 7318 stereo
Released October 1967

□ □ ■ **Happy/Sad**
Elektra EKS 74045
Released April 1969

■ □ □ **Blue Afternoon**
Straight STS 1060
Released February 1970

□ ■ □ **Lorca**
Elektra EKS 74074
Released October 1970

□ □ ■ **Starsailor**
Straight STS 1064
Released 1970

■ □ □ **Greetings From LA**
Warner Bros K46176
Released October 1972

□ ■ □ **Sefronia**
Discreet K49201
Released May 1974

□ □ ■ **Look at the Fool**
Discreet K59204
Released November 1974

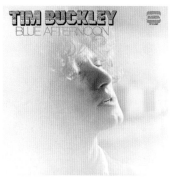
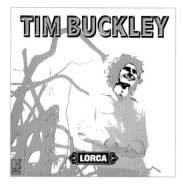

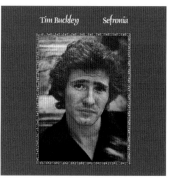

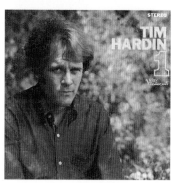

Tim Hardin 1
Verve FTS 3004
Released July 1966

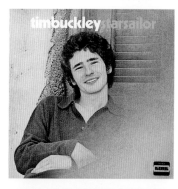

Tim Hardin 2
Verve FTS 3022
Released April 1967

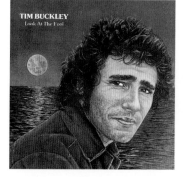

This Is Tim Hardin
Atco SD 33 210
Released September 1967

discography

■ □ Tim Hardin 3 - Live In Concert
Verve FTS 3049
Released September 1968

□ ■ Tim Hardin 4
Verve FTS 3064
Released May 1969

■ □ Suite For Susan Moore And Damion - We Are One, One, All In One
Columbia 9787
Released June 1969

□ ■ Bird On A Wire
Columbia 30551
Released August 1971

■ □ Painted Head
Columbia 31764
Released January 1973

□ ■ Nine
GM Records GM 1004 (UK), Antilles AN 7023 (US)
Released June 1973 (UK), 1976 (US)

FRED NEIL
discography

■ □ **Vince Martin & Fred Neil**
Tear Down The Walls
Elektra EKL 248 mono, EKS 7248 stereo
Released 1964

□ ■ **Bleecker And MacDougal**
Elektra EKL 293 mono, EKS 7293 stereo
Released 1965

■ □ **Little Bit Of Rain (reissue of Bleecker And MacDougal)**
Elektra EKS 74073
Released 1970

□ ■ **Fred Neil**
Capitol ST 2665
Released 1967

■ □ **Sessions**
Capitol ST 2862
Released 1968

□ ■ **Other Side Of This Life**
Capitol SM 657
Released 1971

■ □ □ **All The News That's Fit To Sing**
Elektra EKL 269 mono, EKS 7269 stereo
Released November 1964

□ ■ □ **I Ain't Marching Anymore**
Elektra EKL287 mono, EKS 7287 stereo
Released February 1965

□ □ ■ **Phil Ochs In Concert**
Elektra EKL310 mono, EKS 7310 stereo
Released March 1966

■ □ □ **Pleasures Of The Harbor**
A&M SP4133
Released August 1967

□ ■ □ **Tape From California**
A&M SP-4138
Released July 1968

□ □ ■ **Rehearsals For Retirement**
A&M SP-4181
Released 1968

■ □ **Phil Ochs Greatest Hits**
A&M SP-4253
Released March 1970

□ ■ **Gunfight At Carnegie Hall**
A&M SP-9010
Released 1975

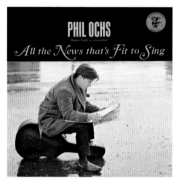

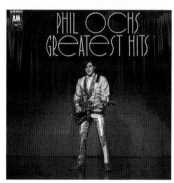

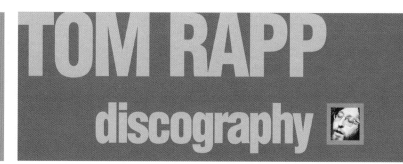

TOM RAPP
discography

Pearls Before Swine
One Nation Underground
ESP DISK 1054
Released 1967

Pearls Before Swine
Balaklava
ESP DISK 1075
Released 1968

Pearls Before Swine
These Things Too
Reprise RSLP 6364
Released 1969

discography

■ ☐ **Pearls Before Swine**
The Use Of Ashes
Reprise RSLP 6405
Released 1970

☐ ■ **Thos. Rapp - Pearls Before**
Swine City Of Gold
Reprise RSLP 6442
Released 1971

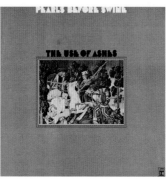

■ ☐ **Tom Rapp/Pearls Before Swine**
…beautiful lies you could live in
Reprise RSLP 6467
Released 1971

☐ ■ **Tom Rapp Familiar Songs**
Reprise MS 2069
Released 1972

■ ☐ **Tom Rapp Stardancer**
Blue Thumb BTS44
Released 1973

☐ ■ **Tom Rapp Sunforest**
Blue Thumb BTS56
Released 1973

■ ☐ **Tim Rose**
Columbia 9577
Released 1967

☐ ■ **Through Rose Colored Glasses**
Columbia 9772
Released July 1969

■ ☐ **Love - A Kind Of Hate Story**
Capitol ST 22673
Released November 1970

☐ ■ **Tim Rose**
Playboy PB101
Released 1972

☐ ■ **The Musician**
Atlantic K50183
Released 1975

 discography

■ □ □ **Got A Mind To Ramble**
Prestige/Folklore 14003
Released 1963 (Fantasy reissue pictured)

□ ■ □ **Blues, Songs And Ballads**
Prestige 7374
Released 1965 (British issue pictured)

□ □ ■ **Tom Rush**
Elektra EKL 288 mono, EKS 7288 stereo
Released 1965

■ □ □ **Take A Little Walk With Me**
Elektra EKL 308 mono, EKS7308 stereo
Released 1966

□ ■ □ **The Circle Game**
Elektra EKL 4018 mono, EKS 74018 stereo
Released 1968

□ □ ■ **Tom Rush**
Columbia 9972
Released 1970

■ □ □ **Wrong End Of The Rainbow**
Columbia 30402
Released 1970

□ ■ □ **Merrimack County**
Columbia 31306
Released 1972

□ □ ■ **Ladies Love Outlaws**
Columbia 33054
Released 1974

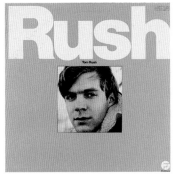

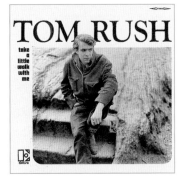

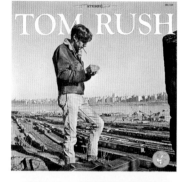

ANNOTATED
discography

The annotated discography includes all of the albums listed in the illustrated discography, plus selected singles, posthumous releases and compilations that include otherwise unavailable or rare material. Track listings, names of producers and musicians involved. In some cases additional explanatory notes are provided. The "official" albums — those that also appear in the illustrated discography — are rated for quality, from one star * (completists only) to five stars ***** (must-have).

DAVID ACKLES

ALBUMS
David Ackles *****
Elektra EKL 4022 mono, EKS 74022 stereo
Released 1968
'The Road To Cairo' / 'When Love Is Gone' / 'Sonny Come Home' / 'Blue Ribbons' / 'What A Happy Day' / 'Down River' / 'Laissez-Faire' / 'Lotus Man' / 'His Name Is Andrew' / 'Be My Friend'.
David Ackles piano, vocal; Michael Fonfara organ; Doug Hastings guitar; John Keliehor percussion; Jerry Penrod bass; Danny Weiss guitar.
Produced by David Anderle and Russ Miller. Engineered by Bruce Botnick.
Re-released later as The Road To Cairo.

Subway To The Country ****
Elektra EKS 74060
Released 1969
'Mainline Saloon' / 'That's No Reason To Cry' / 'Candy Man' / 'Out On The Road' / 'Cabin On The Mountain' / 'Woman River' / 'Inmates Of The Institution'.
David Ackles piano, vocal; John Audino horns; Gary Coleman percussion; Victor Feldman percussion; Don Gallucci harmonica; Jim Gordon drums; William Green flute, saxophone; Doug Hastings guitar; Jim Horn saxophone; Larry Knetchel bass; Lonnie Mack guitar; Gordon Marron violin; Lew McCreary horns; Ollie Mitchell horns; Fred Myrow arrangements; Clifford Shank saxophone; Louie Shelton guitar; Sheridan Stokes flute; Anthony Terran horns; Craig Woodson drums; plus Meyer Rubin, Raymond Triscari and William Ulyate, unknown instruments.
Produced by Russ Miller.

American Gothic *****
Elektra EKS 75032
Released 1972
'American Gothic' / 'Love's Enough' / 'Ballad Of The Ship Of State' / 'One night Stand' / 'Oh California' / 'Another Friday Night' / 'Family Band' / 'Midnight Carousel' / 'Waiting For The Moving Van' / 'Blues For Billie Whitecloud' / 'Montana Song'.
David Ackles arrangements, piano, vocal; Robert Kirby conductor; orchestral musicians unknown.
Produced by Bernie Taupin. Recorded at IBC studios, London, England.

Five And Dime ***
Columbia KC 32466
Released 1973

'Everybody Has A Story' / 'I've been Loved' / 'Jenna Saves' / 'Surf's Down' / 'Berry Tree' / 'One Good Woman's Man' / 'Run Pony Run' / 'Aberfan' / 'House Above The Strand' / 'Photograph Of You' / 'Such A Woman' / 'Postcards'.
David Ackles piano, vocal; Robert L. Adcock cello; Donald Ambroson violin; Colin Bailey drums, vibraphone; Bobby Bruce violin; Gene Cipriano saxophone; Cynthia Cole Daley violin; John Daley trombone; Earl Dumler English horn, oboe; Douglas Graham vocal; Janice Graham guitar; Robert Henderson French horn; Zigmant Kanstul trumpet; James Kanter clarinet; Russell Kidd trumpet; Bruce Langhorne bass, guitar; Todd Millar French horn; Georgia Mohammer flute; Lou Anne Neill harp; Loren Pickford flute, guitar, saxophone; Red Rhodes pedal steel guitar; Patrick Smith double bass; Barbara Thomason viola; Dean Torrance vocal; Dawn Weiss piccolo; Edmond Welter tuba.
Produced by David Ackles. Recorded at Ackles's home; additional recording at Paramount Recording Studios. Los Angeles, CA.

SINGLES
'Down River' / 'La Route A Chicago'
Elektra EKSN 45039
Released 1968
The b-side of this British single release is a French-language version of 'Road To Cairo', unavailable on any album.

'David Ackles Talking About Subway To The Country' / 'Subway To the Country'
Elektra EKS 45676
Released 1969
A promotional single intended for radio stations, given away with the Subway To The Country *album. It features Ackles talking about the writing of the title track, and is backed with the song itself.*

DAVID BLUE

ALBUMS
David Blue *
Elektra EKL 4003 mono, EKS 74003 stereo
Released 1966
'The Gasman Won't Buy Your Love' / 'About My Love' / 'So Easy She Goes By' / 'If Your Monkey Can't Get It' / 'Midnight Through Morning' / 'It Ain't The Rain That Sweeps The Highway Clean' / 'Arcade Love Machine' / 'Grand Hotel' / 'Justine' / 'I'd Like to Know' / 'The Street' / 'It Tastes Like Candy'.
David Blue guitar, vocal; Harvey Brooks bass; Monte Dunn guitar; Paul Harris organ; Herb Lovell drums; Buddy Salzman drums.
Produced by Arthur Gorson.

These 23 Days In September ***

Reprise R6296 mono, RS 6296 stereo

Released 1968

'These Twenty-three Days In September' / 'Ambitious Anna' / 'You Need A Change' / 'The Grand Hotel' / 'The Sailor's Lament' / 'You Will Come Back Again' / 'Scales For A Window Thief' / 'Slow And Easy' / 'The Fifth One'.

David Blue guitar, vocal; Gabriel Mekler piano; Bob Rafkin guitar, musical director.

Produced by Gabriel Mekler.

Me, S. David Cohen ***

(Credited to S. David Cohen, not David Blue.)

Reprise RS 6375

Released 1970

'Mama Tried' / 'Lady Fair' / 'Atlanta Farewell' / 'Turning Towards You' / 'Isn't That The Way It's Supposed to Be' / 'Beautiful Susan' / 'He Holds The Wings She Wore' / 'Better Off Free' / 'Me And Patty On The Moon' / 'How Much My Life Marks Time' / 'Sara'.

David Blue guitar, vocal; Charlie McCoy harmonica; other musicians not credited.

Produced by Paul Tannen. Recorded in Nashville.

Stories ****

Asylum SD 5052

Released 1972

'Looking For A Friend' / 'Sister Rose' / 'Another One Like Me' / 'House Of Changing Faces' / 'Marianne' / 'Fire In The Morning' / 'Come On John' / 'The Blues (All Night Long)'.

John Barbata drums; David Blue guitar, piano, vocal; Ry Cooder slide guitar; Rita Coolidge vocal; Chris Ethridge bass; Milt Holland percussion; Pete Jolly accordion; James Karstein drums; Russ Kunkel drums; Jack Nitzsche string arrangement; Bob Rafkin bass, guitar; Ralph Schuckett keyboards.

Produced by David Blue, Bob Rafkin and Henry Lewy. Engineered by Henry Lewy. Recorded and mixed at A&M Studios, Los Angeles, CA.

Nice Baby And The Angel ****

Asylum SYL 9009

Released June 1973

'Outlaw Man' / 'Lady O' Lady' / 'True To You' / 'On Sunday, Any Sunday' / 'Darlin' Jenny' / 'Dancing Girl' / 'Yesterday's Lady' / 'Nice Baby And The Angel' / 'Troubadour Song' / 'Train To Anaheim'.

Terry Adams cello; John Barbata drums; David Blue guitar, piano, vocal; Chris Ethridge bass; Glenn Frey vocal; David Lindley guitar, mandolin, viola, violin, zither; Dave Mason guitar, vocal; Graham Nash guitar, electric piano, vocal; Bob Rafkin guitar; Jennifer Warren vocal.

Produced by Graham Nash. Recorded at Nash's home studio.

Com'n Back For More *

Asylum SYL 9025

Released 1975

'Com'n Back For More' / 'Oooh Mama' / 'When The Rains Came' / 'Who Love' / 'Save Something (For Me Tonight)' / 'Lover, Lover, Lover' / 'Hollywood Babies' / '23 Days #2' / 'Any Love At All' / 'Where Did It Go'.

Jerry Beckley vocal; Ben Benay guitar; Max Bennett bass; David Blue guitar, vocal; Dewey Bunnell vocal; Kreag Caffey harmonica; Larry Carlton guitar; Carol Carmichael vocal; Bob Dylan harmonica; Don Felder guitar; Robben Ford guitar; John Guerin drums, vocal; Dick Hamilton synthesiser; Tom Hensley piano; Ben Keith pedal steel guitar; Danny Kootch guitar; Karin Lamm vocal; Joni Mitchell vocal; Larry Nash piano; Dan Peek vocal; Reinie Press bass.

Produced and arranged by John Guerin, engineered by Roger Mayer. Recorded at Elektra Sound Recorders, Los Angeles, CA.

Cupid's Arrow **

Asylum 7E-1077

Released 1976

'Run Run Run' / 'The Ballad Of Jennifer Lee' / 'Tom's Song' / 'I Feel Bad' / 'Cordelia' / 'Maria Maria' / 'Cupid's Arrow' / 'Primeval Tune' / 'She's Got You'.

Mike Baird drums; Auburn Barrell Jr guitar; David Blue guitar, vocal; Patti Brooks vocal; Phyllis Brown vocal; Jesse Ed Davis guitar; Donald "Duck" Dunn bass; Barry Goldberg keyboards; Levon Helm drums; David Lindley guitar, violin; Jackie Lomax vocal; Bill Schwartz vocal.

Produced by Barry Goldberg.

SINGLES

'Outlaw Man' / 'Troubadour Song'

Asylum YAYM 519

Released 1973

COMPILATIONS

Singer-Songwriter Project

Elektra EKL 299 mono, EKS 7299 stereo

Released 1965

David Cohen: 'I Like To Sleep Late In The Morning' / 'It's Alright With Me' / 'Don't Get Caught In A Storm'.

This set included Blue's first commercial releases, credited to David Cohen; Blue's three songs shared space with others from Richard Fariña, Bruce Murdoch and Patrick Sky.

TIM BUCKLEY

ALBUMS

Tim Buckley ***

Elektra EKL 4004 mono, EKS 74004 stereo

Released October 1966

'I Can't See You' / 'Wings' / 'Song Of The Magician' / 'Strange Street Affair Under Blue'/ 'Valentine Melody' / 'Aren't You The Girl' / 'Song Slowly Sung' / 'It Happens Every Time' / 'Song For Jainie' / 'Grief In My Soul' / 'She Is' / 'Understand Your Man'.

Tim Buckley guitar, vocal; Jim Fielder bass; Billy Mundi drums; Van Dyke Parks piano; Lee Underwood guitar, keyboards.

Produced by Paul Rothchild and Jac Holzman.

Goodbye And Hello ****

Elektra EKL 318 mono, EKS 7318 stereo

Released October 1967

'No Man Can Find The Warm' / 'Carnival Song' / 'Pleasant Street' / 'Hallucinations' / 'I Never Asked To Be Your Mountain' / 'Once I Was' / Phantasmagoria In Two' / 'Knight Errant' / 'Morning Glory' / Goodbye And Hello'.

Jimmy Bond bass; Tim Buckley guitar, vocal; Carter "CC" Collins congas; John Farsha guitar; Jim Fielder bass; Dave Guard percussion; Brian Hartzler guitar; Eddie Hoh percussion; Don Randi keyboards; Lee Underwood guitar, keyboards; Jerry Yester keyboards; uncredited orchestra.

Produced by Jerry Yester.

Happy/Sad *****

Elektra EKS 74045

Released April 1969

'Strange Feeling' / 'Love From Room 109 At The Islander' / 'On Pacific Coast Highway' / 'Dream Letter' / 'Buzzin' Fly' / 'Gypsy Woman' / 'Sing A Song For You'.

Tim Buckley guitar, vocal; Carter "CC" Collins congas; David Friedman percussion, vibraphone; John Miller bass; Lee Underwood guitar, keyboards..

Produced by Jerry Yester and Zal Yanovsky.

Blue Afternoon ****

Straight STS 1060

Released February 1970

'Happy Time' / 'Chase The Blues Away' / 'I Must Have Been Blind' / 'The River' / 'So Lonely' / 'Café' / 'Blue Melody' / 'Train'.

John Balkin bass; Tim Buckley guitar, vocal; Carter "CC" Collins congas; David Friedman percussion, vibraphone; Jimmy Madison drums; John Miller bass; Lee Underwood guitar, keyboards.

Produced by Tim Buckley.

Lorca ****

Elektra EKS 74074

Released October 1970

'Lorca' / 'Anonymous Proposition' / 'I Had A Talk With A Woman' / 'Driftin' / 'Nobody Walkin'.

John Balkin bass, organ; Tim Buckley guitar, vocal; Carter "CC" Collins congas; Lee Underwood guitar, keyboards.

Produced by Dick Kunc.

Starsailor ****

Straight STS 1064

Released 1970

'Come Here Woman' / 'I Woke Up' / 'Monterey' / 'Moulin Rouge' / 'Song To The Siren' / 'Jungle Fire' / 'Starsailor' / 'The Healing Festival' / 'Down By The Borderline'.

Maury Baker percussion; John Balkin bass; Tim Buckley guitar, vocal; Bunk Gardner horns; Buzz Gardner horns; Lee Underwood guitar, keyboards.

"Executive Producer" Herb Cohen.

Greetings From LA ***

Warner Bros K46176

Released October 1972

'Move With Me' / 'Get On Top' / 'Sweet Surrender' / 'Nighthawkin" / 'Devil Eyes' / 'Hong Kong Bar' / 'Make It Right'.

Alena "dancer"; Tim Buckley guitar, vocal; Carter "CC" Collins conga; Jesse Ehrlich cello; King Errison conga; Joe Falsia guitar, arrangement; Venetta Fields vocal; Jerry Goldstein hand-clap, arrangements; Ed Greene drums; Harry Hymas viola; Kevin Kelly organ, piano; Louis Kievman violin; Clydie King vocal; Robert Konrad violin; William Kurasch violin; Paul Ross Novros saxophone; Reinie Press bass; Chuck Rainey bass; Ralph Schaffer viola; Eugene Siegel saxophone; Lee Underwood guitar, keyboards; Lorna Maxine Willard vocal.

Produced by Jerry Goldstein. Engineered by Stan Agol, Chris Huston. Recorded at Far Out Studios, Hollywood, CA.

Sefronia **

Discreet K49201

Released May 1974

'Dolphins' / 'Honey Man' / 'Because Of You' / 'Martha' / 'Peanut Man' / 'Quicksand' / 'I Know I'd Recognise Your Face' / 'Stone In Love' / 'Sefronia – After Askipiades, After Kafka; Sefronia – The King's Chain' / 'Sally Go Round The Roses'.

Sharon Beard vocal; Tim Buckley guitar, vocal; Larry Bunker percussion; Eric Dumler horns; Joe Falsia guitar; Buddy Helm drums; Myrna Matthews vocal; Bernie Mysior bass; Reinie Press bass; Bob Rafkin guitar; Denny Randell keyboards, percussion;

Lisa Roberts vocal; Tom Scott saxophone; Fred Seldon flute; Mark Tiernan keyboards; Marcia Waldorf vocal; Ken Watson percussion; plus uncredited orchestra.
Produced by Denny Randell.

Look at the Fool *
Discreet K59204
Released November 1974
'Look At The Fool' / 'Bring It On Up' / 'Helpless' / 'Freeway Blues' / 'Tijuana Moon' / 'Ain't It Peculiar' / 'Who Could Deny You' / 'Mexicali Voodoo' / 'Down The Street' / 'Wanda Lu'.
David Bluefield keyboards; Tim Buckley guitar, vocal; Gary Coleman percussion; Jesse Ehrlich cello; Joe Falsia guitar; Jim Fielder bass; Vanetta Fields vocal; Terry Harrington saxophone; Jim Hughart bass; Clydie King vocal; Shirley Matthews vocal; Mike Melvoin piano; Richard Nash horns; Earl Palmer drums; Bill Peterson horns; Chuck Rainey bass; John Rotella horns; Anthony Terran horns; Mark Tiernan keyboards; Lee Underwood guitar, keyboards.
Produced by Joe Falsia.

POSTHUMOUS ALBUMS
There have been several posthumous Tim Buckley albums containing previously unissued material. The first was 1990's *Dream Letter*. Most consist of live recordings and radio sessions, and are of varying quality and interest. A selection is listed here.

Dream Letter – Live In London 1968
Demon D-Fiend 200
Released June 1990
'Buzzin' Fly' / 'Phantasmagoria In Two' / 'Morning Glory' / 'Dolphins' / 'I've Been Out Walking' / 'The Earth Is Broken' / 'Who Do You Love' / 'Pleasant Street; You Keep Me Hanging On; Love From Room 109; Strange Feelin'' / 'Carnival Song; Hi Lily Hi Lo' / 'Hallucinations' / 'Troubadour' / 'Dream Letter; Happy Time' / 'Wayfaring Stranger; You Got Me Runnin'' / 'Once I Was'.
Tim Buckley guitar, vocal; David Friedman vibraphone; Danny Thompson double bass; Lee Underwood guitar.
Produced by Bill Inglot and Lee Hammond.
Features live versions of songs drawn from Buckley's first three albums, plus previously unavailable material. It was recorded at The Queen Elizabeth Hall, London, on October 7th 1968. British bassist Danny Thompson only performed with Buckley during this UK visit.

The Copenhagen Tapes
PLR PLRCD018
Released 2000
'I Don't Need It To Rain' / 'Buzzin' Fly' / 'Strange Feelin'' / 'Gypsy

Woman'. Tim Buckley guitar, vocal; David Friedman vibraphone; Niels Henning double bass; Lee Underwood guitar.
Similar to Dream Letter *but of less good sound quality. It was recorded in Copenhagen on December 10th 1968. Niels Henning replaced Danny Thompson on bass. It includes a 21-minute version of the non-album song 'I Don't Need It To Rain'.*

TIM HARDIN

ALBUMS
Tim Hardin 1 ****
Verve Forecast FTS 3004
Released July 1966
'Don't Make Promises' / 'Green Rocky Road' / 'Smugglin' Man' / "How Long' / 'While You're On Your Way' / 'It'll Never Happen Again' / 'Reason To Believe' / 'Never Too Far' / 'Part Of The Wind' / 'Ain't Gonna Do Without' / 'Misty Roses' / 'How Can We Hang On To A Dream'.
Gary Burton vibraphone; Bob Bushnell bass; Artie Butler string arrangements; Tim Hardin piano, guitar, vocal; Phil Krauss vibraphone; Earl Palmer drums; Buddy Saltzman drums; John Sebastian harmonica; Walter Yost bass.
Produced by Eric Jacobsen. Engineered by Val Valentin.
Tim Hardin 1 *and* Tim Hardin 2 *were reissued as a vinyl double pack (Verve 2683 048) in 1974, and later on CD by Repertoire (IMS 7030) in 1995.*

Tim Hardin 2 *****
Verve Forecast FTS 3022
Released April 1967
'If I Were A Carpenter' / 'Red Balloon' / 'Black Sheep Boy' / 'Lady Came From Baltimore' / 'Baby Close Its Eyes' / 'You Upset The Grace Of Living When You Lie' / 'Speak Like A Child' / 'See Where You Are And Get Out' / 'It's Hard To Believe In Love For Long' / 'Tribute To Hank Williams'.
Tim Hardin guitar, piano, vocal; other musicians not credited.
Produced by Eric Jacobsen, Charles Koppelman and Don Rubin.
Tim Hardin 1 *and* Tim Hardin 2 *were reissued as a vinyl double pack (Verve 2683 048) in 1974, and later on CD by Repertoire (IMS 7030) in 1995.*

This Is Tim Hardin **
Atco SD 33 210
Released September 1967.
'I Can't Slow Down' / 'Blues On The Ceiling' / 'I'm Your Hoochie Coochie Man' / 'Stagger Lee' / 'I've Been Working On The Railroad' / 'House Of The Rising Sun' / 'Fast Freight' / 'Cocaine Bill' / 'You

Got To Have More Than One Woman' / 'Danville Dame'.
Tim Hardin guitar, vocal; other musicians not credited.
Produced by Eric Jacobsen.

Tim Hardin 3 – Live In Concert ***
Verve Forecast FTS 3049
Released September 1968
'Lady Came From Baltimore' / 'Reason To Believe' / 'You Upset
The Grace Of Living When You Lie' / 'Misty Roses' / 'Black Sheep
Boy' / 'Lenny's Tune' / 'Don't Make Promises' / 'Danville Dame' / 'If I
Were A Carpenter' / 'Red Balloon' / 'Tribute To Hank Williams' /
'Smugglin' Man'.
Tim Hardin guitar, piano, vocal; Warren Bernhardt clavinet, piano;
Daniel Hankin guitar; Mike Maineiri vibraphone; Eddie Gomez bass;
Donald McDonald drums.
Produced by Gary Klein. Recorded live at Town Hall, New York
City, New York, April 10th 1968.
*A CD release of this album in the 1990s added three previously
unissued tracks, namely 'If I Knew', 'Last Sweet Moment' and
'Turn The Page'.*

Tim Hardin 4 **
Verve Forecast FTS 3064
Released May 1969
'Airmobile' / 'Whiskey Whiskey' / 'Seventh Son' / 'How Long' /
'Danville Dame' / 'Ain't Gonna Do Without (Part I)' / 'Ain't Gonna Do
Without (Part II)' / 'House Of The Rising Sun' / 'Bo Diddley' / 'I Can't
Slow Down' / 'Hello Baby'.
Tim Hardin guitar, vocal; Warren Bernhardt keyboards; Eddie
Gomez bass; Daniel Hankin guitar; Mike Maineiri vibraphone;
Donald McDonald drums.
Produced by Eric Jacobsen. Engineered by Val Valentin.

Suite For Susan Moore And Damion – We Are One, One, All In One **
Columbia CS 9787
Released June 1969
'First Love Song' / 'Everything Good Becomes More True' /
'Question Of Birth' / 'Once-touched By Flame' / 'Last Sweet
Moments' / 'Magician' / 'Loneliness She Knows' / 'The Country I'm
Living In' / 'One, One, The Perfect Sum' / 'Susan'.
Tim Hardin guitar, piano, vocal; Warren Bernhardt keyboards;
Monte Dunn guitar; Buzz Gardner celeste; David (no surname)
saxophone; Keith (no surname) trumpet; Gary Klein keyboards;
Donald McDonald drums; Philipe conga.
Produced by Gary Klein.
Suite For Susan Moore… *and* Bird On A Wire *were reissued as a
double-pack CD by BGO (BGO 470) in 1999.*

Bird On A Wire ****
Columbia CS 30551
Released August 1971
'Bird On A Wire' / 'Moonshiner' / 'Southern Butterfly' / 'A Satisfied
Mind' / 'Soft Summer Breeze' / 'Hoboin' / 'Georgia On My Mind' /
'André Johray' / 'If I Knew' / 'Love Hymn'.
Warren Bernhardt keyboards; Richard Bock cello; Sam Brown
guitar; The Canby Singers vocal; Bill Chelf keyboards; Monte Dunn
guitar; Ed Freeman guitar, string/horn arrangements; Steve Haas
drums, percussion; Tim Hardin guitar, piano, vocal; Paul Hornsby
keyboards; Bill Keith pedal steel guitar; Tony Levin bass; Ralph
MacDonald drums, percussion; Mike Mainieri vibraphone; Glen
Moore bass; Alphonse Mouzon drums, percussion; Natoga drums,
percussion; Robert Popwell bass, percussion; George Ricci cello;
Margaret Ross harp; Robbie Rothstein bass; Joe Rudd guitar; Bill
Stewart drums, percussion; Ralph Towner guitar; Miroslav Vitous
bass; Colin Wolcott vibraphone; Joe Zawinul keyboards.
Produced by Ed Freeman. Engineered by Wayne Tarnowski, Doug
Pomeroy, Jim Greene, Lacy O'Neal.
Bird On A Wire *and* Suite For Susan Moore… *were reissued as a
double-pack CD by BGO (BGO 470) in 1999.*

Painted Head *
Columbia KC 31764
Released January 1973
'You Can't Judge A Book By The Cover' / 'Midnight Caller' /
'Yankee Lady' / 'Lonesome Valley' / 'Sweet Lady' / 'Do The Do' /
'Perfection' / 'Till We Meet Again' / 'I'll Be Home' / 'Nobody Knows
You When You're Down And Out'.
Rebop Kwaku Baah percussion; Don Brooks harmonica; Tony Carr
percussion; Alun Davies guitar; Peter Frampton guitar; Tristan Fry
vibraphone; Tim Hardin guitar, piano, vocal; Cissy Houston vocal;
Dennis Lopez percussion; Tony Meehan drums, percussion; Rod
Murfield percussion; Larry Packer violin; Alan Ross guitar, mandolin;
Jean Roussel keyboards; Bruce Rowlands drums; Jeff Schwartz
steel guitar; Neil Sheppard keyboards; Chris Stewart bass; Liza
Strike vocal; Bobbie Whitaker violin.
Produced by Tony Meehan.

Nine **
GM Records GM 1004 (UK), Antilles AN 7023 (US)
Released June 1973 (UK), 1976 (US)
'Shiloh Town' / 'Never Too Far' / 'Rags And Old Iron' / 'Look Our
Love Over' / 'Person To Person' / 'Darling Girl' / 'Blues On My
Ceiling' / 'Is There No Rest For The Weary' / 'Fire And Rain' / 'While
You're On Your Way'.
Madeline Bell vocal; Andy Bown bass; Bob Cohen guitar; Mike
Driscoll drums; Lesley Duncan vocal; Peter Frampton guitar; Susan

Glover vocal; Tim Hardin guitar, piano, vocal; Jimmy Horowitz piano, organ, conductor; David Katz string arrangements; John Mealing piano, electric piano; Liza Strike vocal.
Produced by Jimmy Horowitz. Engineered by Andy Knight, Hugh Jones. Recorded at IBC Studios, London.

POSTHUMOUS ALBUMS
The Homecoming Concert
Kamera KAM 004
Released 1981
'Black Sheep Boy' / 'Misty Roses' / 'Reason To Believe' / 'Lady Came From Baltimore' / 'Old Blue Jeans' / 'Hang On To A Dream' / 'If I Were A Carpenter' / 'Tribute To Hank Williams' / 'Smugglin' Man' / 'Speak Like A Child' / 'Red Balloon' / 'Amen'.
Tim Hardin guitar, piano, vocal.
Produced by Phil Freeman. Recorded live at The Community Center For The Performing Arts, Eugene, OR, January 17th 1980.
This live album is a recording of the only performance Hardin ever gave at his hometown of Eugene, Oregon. The concert took place a year before Hardin died.

Unforgiven
San Francisco Records SFS 10810 or SFS 24810
Released 1981
'Unforgiven' / 'Luna Cariba' / 'Mercy Wind' / 'If I Were Still with You' / 'Judge And Jury' / 'Partly Yours' / 'Sweet Feeling' / 'Secret'.
Tim Hardin guitar, piano, vocal; other musicians unknown
Produced by Don Rubin.
This was a partially completed album that Hardin was working on at the time of his death. It consists of eight songs, two of which are finished studio recordings. The other six are home or studio demos in varying stages of completion. It was released in very limited numbers in 1981, and recently was made available again on Warrior. Joe Cocker recorded the title track in the early 1980s.

COMPILATIONS
Hang On To A Dream – The Verve Recordings
Polydor CD 314 521 583-2
Released 1994
This double-CD compilation includes Tim Hardin 1, 2 and 4 in their entirety, plus much previously unavailable material.

Simple Songs Of Freedom – The Tim Hardin Collection
Sony Legacy Series CD 485108-2
Released 1996
This compilation draws on Hardin's later Columbia material. It includes previously unreleased recordings and his sole US hit single, 'Simple Song of Freedom'.

Woodstock – The Lost Performances
WEA 12202
Released 1991
Hardin has one song, 'If I Were A Carpenter', featured on this latter-day Woodstock compilation.

SINGLES
'Hang On To A Dream' / 'Misty Roses'
Verve VS 1504
Released May 1967 (UK)
Reached number 50 in the UK charts in January 1967.

'Simple Song Of Freedom' / 'Question Of Birth'
Columbia 44920
Released September 1969
Produced by Gary Klein
Reached number 50 in the US charts in late summer 1969.

FRED NEIL

ALBUMS
Vince Martin & Fred Neil Tear Down The Walls **
Elektra EKL 248 mono, EKS 7248 stereo
Released 1964
'I Know You Rider' / 'Red Flowers' / 'Tear Down The Walls' / 'Weary Blues' / 'Toy Balloon' / 'Baby' / 'Morning Dew' / 'I'm A Drifter' / 'Linin' Track' / 'I Got 'Em' / 'Wild Child In A World Of Trouble' / 'Dade County Jail Lonesome Valley'.
Vince Martin guitar, vocal; Fred Neil guitar, vocal; Felix Pappalardi bass; John Sebastian harmonica.
Produced by Paul Rothchild.

Bleecker And MacDougal ****
Elektra EKL 293 mono, EKS 7293 stereo
Released 1965
'Bleecker And MacDougal' . 'Blues On The Ceiling' / 'Sweet Mama' / 'Little Bit Of Rain' / 'Country Boy' / 'Other Side Of This Life' / 'Mississippi Train' / 'Travelin' Shoes' / 'Water Is Wide' / 'Yonder Comes The Blues' / 'Candy Man' / 'Handful Of Gimme' / 'Gone Again'.
Pete Childs guitar; Douglas Hatfield bass; Fred Neil guitar, vocal; Felix Pappalardi bass, guitar; John Sebastian harmonica.
Produced by Paul Rothchild.
Reissued (new sleeve) as Little Bit Of Rain *(Elektra EKS 74073) 1970.*

Fred Neil *****
Capitol ST 2665
Released 1967
'The Dolphins' / 'I've Got A Secret (Didn't We Shake Sugaree)' /

'That's The Bag I'm In' / 'Dadi-Da' / 'Faretheewell (Fred's Tune)' / 'Everybody's Talkin'' / 'Everything Happens' / 'Sweet Cocaine' / 'Green Rocky Road' / 'Cynicrustpetefredjohn Raga'.
James E Bond double bass; Pete Childs guitar; Cyrus Faryar guitar; Rusty Faryar finger cymbals; John T Forsha guitar; Billy Mundi drums; Fred Neil guitar, vocal; Al Wilson harmonica.
Produced by Nik Venet.
This album was reissued later retitled as Everybody's Talkin' *to capitalise on the success of the song in* Midnight Cowboy.

Sessions **
Capitol ST 2862
Released 1968
'Felicity' / 'Please Send Me Someone To Love' / 'Merry Go Round' / 'Look Over Yonder' / 'Fools Are A long Time Coming' / 'Looks Like Rain' / 'Roll On Rosie'.
James E Bond double bass; Pete Childs guitar; Cyrus Faryar guitar;.Eric Glen Hord guitar; Bruce Langhorne guitar; Fred Neil guitar, vocal.
Produced by Nik Venet.

Other Side Of This Life **
Capitol E-ST 657 MB checking
Released 1971
'The Other Side Of This Life' / 'The Dolphins' / 'That's The Bag I'm In' / 'Sweet Cocaine' / 'Everybody's Talkin'' / 'Come Back Baby' / 'Ba-De-Da' / 'Prettiest Train' / 'Ya Don't Miss Your Water'.
Monte Dunn guitar; Vince Martin guitar; Les McCann piano; Fred Neil guitar, vocal; Gram Parsons piano, vocal; plus a number of other uncredited musicians.
Produced by Howard L Solomon and Nik Venet.

COMPILATIONS
The Many Sides Of Fred Neil
EMI Collector's Choice CCM-070-2
Released 1998
This double-CD collection includes all three of Neil's Capitol albums, a further six previously unreleased recordings dating from the late 1960s, and both sides of a rare 1963 single with The Nashville Street Singers.

Hootenanny Live At The Bitter End
FM LP 309
Released c.1965
A very rare live compilation album recorded at the famous Greenwich Village coffee-house, The Bitter End. Neil has three songs featured on the record: 'Linin' Track', 'That's The Bag I'm In' and 'The Sky Is Falling'.

PHIL OCHS

ALBUMS
All The News That's Fit To Sing ***
Elektra EKL 269 mono, EKS 7269 stereo
Released November 1964
'The Power And The Glory' / 'Too Many Martyrs' / 'One More Parade' / 'The Thresher' / 'Talking Vietnam' / 'Lou Marsh' / 'The Bells' / 'Celia' / 'Automation Song' / 'Ballad Of William Worthy' / 'Bound For Glory' / 'Knock On The Door' / 'Talking Cuban Crisis' / 'What's That I Hear'.
Danny Kelb guitar; Phil Ochs guitar, vocal.
Produced by Paul Rothchild.

I Ain't Marching Anymore ***
Elektra EKL287 mono, EKS 7287 stereo
Released February 1965
'I Ain't Marching Anymore' / 'That Was The President' / 'Here's To The State Of Mississippi' / 'In The Heat Of The Summer' / 'Draft Dodger Rag' / 'That's What I Want To Hear' / 'Iron Lady' / 'The Highway Man' / 'Links On The Chain' / 'Hills Of West Virginia' / 'The Men Behind The Guns' / 'Talking Birmingham Jam' / 'Ballad Of The Carpenter' / 'Days Of Decision'.
Phil Ochs guitar, vocal.
Produced by Paul Rothchild.

Phil Ochs In Concert ***
Elektra EKL310 mono, EKS 7310 stereo
Released March 1966
'I'm Going To Say It Now' / 'Bracero' / 'Ringing Of Revolution' / 'Is There Anybody Here' / 'Canons Of Christianity' / 'There But for Fortune' / 'Cops Of The World' / 'Santo Domingo' / 'Changes' / 'Love Me, I'm A Liberal' / 'When I'm Gone'.
Phil Ochs guitar, vocal.
Produced by Mark Abramson and Jac Holzman.

Pleasures Of The Harbor ****
A&M SP 4133
Released August 1967
'Cross My Heart' / 'Flower Lady' / 'Outside Of A Small Circle Of Friends' / 'I've Had Her' / 'Miranda' / 'The Party' / 'Pleasures Of The Harbor' / 'The Crucifixion'.
Phil Ochs guitar, vocal. Produced by Larry Marks.

Tape From California ****
A&M SP 4138
Released July 1968
'Tape From California' / 'White Boots Marching In A Yellow Land' /

'Half A Century High' / 'Joe Hill' / 'The War Is Over' / 'The Harder
They Fall' / 'When In Rome' / 'Floods Of Florence'.
Jack Elliot guitar, vocal; Lincoln Mayorga piano; Phil Ochs guitar,
vocal; Van Dyke Parks keyboards.
Produced by Larry Marks.

Rehearsals For Retirement ****
A&M SP 4181
Released 1968
'Pretty Smart On My Part' / 'The Doll House' / 'I Kill Therefore I Am' /
'William Butler Yeats Visits London Park And Escapes Unscathed' /
''My Life' / 'The Scorpion Departs But Never Returns' / 'The World
Begun In Eden Ended In Los Angeles' / 'Doesn't Lenny Live Here
Anymore' / 'Another Age' / 'Rehearsals For Retirement'.
Phil Ochs guitar, vocal.
Produced by Larry Marks.

Phil Ochs Greatest Hits ***
A&M SP 4253
Released March 1970
'Chords Of Fame' / 'Gas Station Women' / 'Boy In Ohio' / 'One
Way Ticket Home' / 'Jim Dean Of Indiana' / 'Ten Cents A Coup' /
'No More Songs' / 'My Kingdom For A Car' / 'Bach, Beethoven,
Mozart And Me' / 'Basket In The Pool'.
Laurindo Almeida guitar; Bobby Bruce violin; James Burton guitar;
Merry Clayton vocal; Gary Coleman percussion; Ry Cooder guitar;
Chris Ethridge bass; Anne Gordon cello; Clydie King vocal; Shirley
Matthews vocal; Phil Ochs guitar, vocal; Gene Parsons drums; Bob
Rafkin guitar; Don Rich violin; Richard Rosmini guitar; Mike Rubini
guitar, keyboards; Tom Scott saxophone; Clarence White guitar.
Produced by Van Dyke Parks.

Gunfight At Carnegie Hall ***
A&M SP 9010
Released 1975
'Mona Lisa' / 'I Ain't Marching Anymore' / 'Okie From Muskogee' /
'Chords Of Fame' / 'Buddy Holly Medley: Not Fade Away; I'm
Gonna Love You Too, Think It Over, Oh Boy, Everyday, Not Fade
Away' / 'Pleasures Of The Harbor' / 'Tape From California' / 'Elvis
Presley Medley: My Baby Left Me, I'm Ready, Heartbreak Hotel. All
Shook Up, Are You Lonesome Tonight, My Baby Left Me, A Fool
Such As I'.
Kenny Kaufman bass; Kevin Kelley drums; Lincoln Mayorga piano;
Phil Ochs guitar, vocal; Bob Rafkin guitar.
Produced by Phil Ochs.
*This was a recording of the famous "gold-suit" concert at the
New York venue, and in the first instance it was only released
in Canada.*

COMPILATIONS
In addition to the records listed here, Ochs appeared on several
early-1960s folk compilations released on the Broadside and
Folkways labels.

Chords Of Fame
A&M SP4599
Released 1976
*This posthumous tribute was compiled by Phil's brother Michael
Ochs, with the co-operation of Elektra Records. It includes the
following tracks which at the time were not available on any other
albums: single versions of 'The Power And The Glory' and 'Here's
To The State Of Richard Nixon', an electric version of 'I Ain't
Marching Anymore' and an acoustic version of 'Crucifixion'.*

A Toast To Those Who Are Gone
Rhino 70080
Released 1986
*A compilation of "lost" recordings – mostly early, previously
unreleased material, and some songs from earlier folk compilations.*

The Best Of Phil Ochs – The War Is Over
A&M CD-5215
Released 1989
*A compilation selected from the A&M albums, including one
previously unreleased song, a live version of 'I Ain't Marching
Anymore' recorded in Canada in 1968.*

American Troubadour
A&M 540 728-2
Released 1999
*A double-CD compilation of A&M material and assorted rarities
compiled by Sid Griffin, who also contributed sleevenotes. It
marked the first Western release for Ochs's African-recorded single
'Bwatue' / 'Niko Mchumba Ngombe', and also includes an
unreleased song from the Carnegie Hall concert, 'School Days'.*

SINGLES
'I Ain't Marching Anymore' / 'That Was The President'
Elektra EKSN 45002
Released December 1965
*This was an electric version of Ochs's popular anthem, originally
released in the UK. It later appeared as a "paper" record in Sing
Out magazine.*

'Kansas City Bomber' / 'Gas Station Women'
A&M 1376
Released 1973

The a-side of this single, recorded in Australia, was intended for the film of the same name, although it was never used for that purpose.

'Bwatue' / 'Niko Mchumba Ngombe'
A&M
Released 1973
Recorded in Kenya and released in Africa only. It was later re-pressed in small numbers by the Canadian Phil Ochs fan club, on the Sparkle label.

'The Power And The Glory' / 'Here's To The State Of Richard Nixon'
A&M 1509
Released February 1974
Re-recordings of two earlier songs, here with full band arrangements, released to coincide with the Watergate scandal.

OTHERS
Interviews With Phil Ochs
Folkways FH-532
Released 1976

TOM RAPP / PEARLS BEFORE SWINE

ALBUMS
Pearls Before Swine *One Nation Underground* ****
ESP DISK 1054
Released 1967
'Another Time' / 'Playmate' / 'Balled To An Amber Lady' / '(Oh Dear) Miss Morse' / 'Drop Out' / 'Morning Song' / 'Regions Of May' / 'Uncle John' / 'I Shall Not Care' / 'The Surrealist Waltz'.
Roger Crissinger organ, harpsichord, clavioline; Wayne Harley audio oscillator, autoharp, banjo, mandolin, vibraphone, vocal; Lane Lederer bass, celeste, finger cymbals, guitar, English horn, sarangi, "swinehorn", vocal; Tom Rapp guitar, vocal; Warren Smith drums.
Produced by Richard Alderson. Recorded at Impact studio, NY.

Pearls Before Swine *Balaklava* ****
ESP DISK 1075
Released 1968
'Trumpeter Landfrey' / 'Translucent Carriages' / 'Images Of April' / 'There Was A Man' / 'I Saw The World' / 'Guardian Angels' / 'Suzanne' / 'Lepers And Roses' / 'Florence Nightingale' / 'Ring Thing'.
Jim Bohannon clavinet, marimba, organ, piano; Lee Crabtree flute, organ, flute; Joe Farrell English horn, flute; Wayne Harley banjo, vocal; Lane Lederer bass, guitar, "swinehorn"; Tom Rapp guitar, vocal; William Salter bass; Al Shackman guitar.
Produced by Richard Alderson. Recorded at Impact studio, NY.

Pearls Before Swine *These Things Too* ****
Reprise RSLP 6364
Released 1969
'Footnote' / 'Sail Away' / 'Look Into Her Eyes' / 'I Shall Be Released' / 'Frog In The Window' / 'I'm Going To City' / 'Man In The Tree' / 'If You Don't Want To (I Don't Mind)' / 'Green And Blue' / 'Mon Amour' / 'Wizard Of Is' / 'Frog In The Window' / 'When I Was A Child' / ''These Things Too'.
Jim Fairs celeste, guitar, vocal; Richard Greene electric violin; Wayne Harley banjo, vocal; Elisabeth Rapp vocal; Tom Rapp guitar, vocal; Bill Salter bass; Grady Tate drums.
Produced by Richard Alderson with Jim Fairs. Engineered by Danford Griffiths. Recorded at Impact Sound, New York and at RKO studio.

Pearls Before Swine *The Use Of Ashes* ****
Reprise RSLP 6405
Released 1970
'The Jeweler' / 'From The Movie' / 'Rocket Man' / 'God Save The Child' / 'Song About A rose' / 'Tell Me Why' / 'Margery' / 'The old Man' / 'Riegal' / 'When The War Began'.
David Briggs piano, harpsichord; Kenny Buttrey drums; Hutch Davie keyboards; John Duke flute, oboe; Mac Gayden guitar; Charlie McCoy bass, guitar, harmonica; Bill Pippin flute, oboe; Norbert Putnam bass; Elisabeth Rapp vocal; Tom Rapp guitar, vocal; Buddy Spicher cello, viola, violin.
Produced by Peter H Edmiston. Engineered by Rick Horton, Brooks Arthur. Recorded at Woodland Studios, Nashville, TN, March 1970.

Thos. Rapp – Pearls Before Swine *City Of Gold* ***
Reprise RSLP 6442
Released 1971
'Sonnet #65' / 'Once Upon A Time' / 'Raindrops' / 'City Of Gold' / 'Nancy' / 'Seasons In The Sun' / 'My Father' / 'The Man' / 'Casablanca' / 'Wedding' / 'Did You Dream Of'.
David Noyes violin, vocal; Elisabeth Rapp vocal; Tom Rapp guitar, vocal. Produced by Tom Rapp. Recorded in New York and Nashville during fall 1970.

Tom Rapp/Pearls Before Swine *...beautiful lies you could live in* ***
Reprise RSLP 6467
Released 1971
'Snow Queen' / 'A Life' / 'Butterflies' / 'Simple Things' / 'Everybody's Got A Pain' / 'Bird On A Wire' / 'Island Lady' / 'Come To Me' / 'Freedom' / 'She's Gone' / 'Epitaph'.
Morrie E Brown bass; Bob Dorough piano; Amos Garrett guitar;

Steven Alan Grable organ, piano; Gordon Hayes bass; Jerry
Jermott bass; Michael Krawitz piano; Herb Lovell drums; Billy
Mundi drums; Elisabeth Rapp vocal; Tom Rapp guitar, vocal; Stu
Scharf guitar; Grady Tate drums; Jon Tooker guitar.
Produced by Peter H Edmiston. Engineered by Mark Harman.
Recorded at A&R Studios, NY; Aura Sound, NY; Bearsville Studios,
Woodstock, NY.

Tom Rapp *Familiar Songs* *
Reprise MS 2069
Released 1972
'Grace Street' / 'The Jeweler' / 'Rocket Man' / 'Snow Queen' / 'If
You Don't Want To (I Don't Mind)' / 'Charley And The Lady' /
'Margery Medley: Full Phantom Five and I Shall Not Care' / 'These
Things Too' / 'Sail Away'.
Musicians, production and recording details unknown.

Tom Rapp *Stardancer* ****
Blue Thumb BTS 44
Released 1973
'Fourth Day Of July' / 'For The Dead In Space' / 'The Baptist' /
'Summer Of '55' / 'Tiny Song' / 'Stardancer' / 'Marshall' / 'Touch
Tripping' / 'Why Should I Care' / 'Les Ans'.
David Briggs keyboards; Jim Colvard Dobro, guitar; Art Ellis
congas, flute, vocal; Jim Isbell drums, percussion; Mike Leech
bass; Steve McCord guitar; Charlie McCoy guitar, harmonica,
keyboards, vocal; Weldon Myrick pedal steel guitar; Harry Orlove
guitar, mandolin, vocal; Bill Rollins cello; Tom Rapp guitar, vocal;
Buddy Spicher violin; Florence Warner vocal; Bobby Wood
percussion; Reggie Young piano. Uncredited string section.
Produced by Peter H Edmiston.

Tom Rapp *Sunforest* ***
Blue Thumb BTS 56
Released 1973
'Comin' Back' ./ 'Prayers Of Action' / 'Forbidden City' / 'Love/Sex' /
'Harding Street' / 'Blind River' / 'Some Place To Belong' /
'Sunforest' / 'Sunshine & Charles'.
David Briggs keyboards; Kenny Buttrey drums; James Cason
bass; Chuck Cochran piano; Jim Colvard Dobro, guitar; Bob
Dorough piano; Art Ellis congas, flute, vocal; Diane Harris vocal;
Karl Himmel drums; Mike Leech bass; Steve McCord guitar;
Charlie McCoy guitar, harmonica, keyboards, vocal; Bob Moore
piano; Farrell Morris percussion; Bill Rollins cello; Tom Rapp guitar,
vocal; William Salter bass; Warren Smith percussion; Buddy
Spicher violin; Bobby Thompson banjo, guitar; Bobby Wood
percussion; Chip Young guitar; Reggie Young piano.
Produced by Larry Butler.

OTHERS
Tom Rapp *A Journal Of The Plague Year*
Woronzow WOO 35
Released August 1999
*This came out on a UK independent label associated with the
Ptolemaic Terrascope fanzine and was Rapp's first new album
since 1973's Sunforest. It was recorded in the studio of American
independent duo Damon & Naomi, and featured contributions from
them and Nick Saloman, main-man of the Bevis Frond and owner
of Woronzow.*

TIM ROSE

ALBUMS
Tim Rose *****
Columbia CS 9577
Released 1967
'I Got A Loneliness' / 'I'm Gonna Be Strong' / 'I Gotta Do Things My
Way' / 'Fare Thee Well' / 'Eat, Drink And Be Merry' / 'Hey Joe' /
'Morning Dew' / 'Where Was I' / 'You're Slipping Away From Me' /
'Long Time Man' / 'Come Away Melinda'.
Jay Berliner guitar; Patti Bown keyboards; Artie Butler keyboards;
Jim Fischoff percussion; Ernie Hayes keyboards; Richard Hussan
bass; Bob Jones percussion; Richard Kilgore drums; Hugh
McCracken guitar; Felix Pappalardi bass; Bernard Purdie drums;
Chuck Rainey bass; Tim Rose guitar, vocal; Joey Scott piano;
Charles Smalls piano; Eric Weissberg bass.
Produced by David Rubinson.
*This album has been reissued several times under the title Morning
Dew. It was also reissued in 1997 by BGO Records together with
Through Rose Colored Glasses on a single CD (BGOCD378).*

Through Rose Colored Glasses ***
Columbia CS 9772
Released July 1969
'The Days Back When' / 'Roanoke' / 'Hello Sunshine' / 'When I
Was A Young Man' / 'Whatcha Gonna Do' / 'Maman' / 'Let There
Be Love' / 'Baby Do You Turn Me On' / 'Apple Truck Swamper' /
'Angela' / 'You'd Laugh' / 'You Ain't My Girl No More'.
Musicians unknown.
Produced by Jack Tracy. Engineered by Sy Mitchell, Jerry Hochman.
Through Rose Colored Glasses *and* Tim Rose *were reissued in
1997 by BGO Records on a single CD (BGOCD378).*

Love – A Kind Of Hate Story **
Capitol ST 22673
Released November 1970
'I've Gotta Get A Message To You' / 'Dimlight' / 'Where Do You Go

To My Lovely' / 'You Can't Stop Yourself' / 'Sad Song' / 'Georgia By Morning' / 'Ode To An Old Ball' / 'Sympathy' / 'I Know These Two People' / 'Jamie Sue'.

Herbie Flowers bass; Clem Cattini drums; Alan Hawkshaw keyboards; Peter Lee Stirling vocal; Tim Rose guitar, vocal; Alan Parker guitar.

Produced by Shel Talmy.

Both the original Love – A Kind Of Hate Story *and* Tim Rose *albums were reissued together in 1999 by RPM Records on a single CD (RPM 192).*

Tim Rose **

Playboy PB 101

Released 1972

'It Takes A Little Longer' / 'You Can't Keep Me' / 'Hide Your Love Away' / 'Boogie Boogie' / 'If I Were A Carpenter' / 'Cryin' Shame' / 'Darling You Were All That I Had' / 'Cotton Growin' Man' / 'Goin' Down In Hollywood'.

Bryson Graham drums; Mick Jones guitar; Archie Leggett bass; Tim Rose guitar, vocal; Gary Wright organ, piano.

Produced by Gary Wright. Engineered by Chris Kimsey. Recorded at Olympic Studios, London.

Both the original Tim Rose *and* Love – A Kind Of Hate Story *albums were reissued together in 1999 by RPM Records on a single CD (RPM 192).*

The Musician *

Atlantic K50183

Released 1975

'7.30: Song' / 'Small Town Talk' / 'The Musician' / 'Loving Arms' / 'Old Man' / 'It's Not My Life That's Been Changin'' / 'The Day I Spent With You' / 'Second Avenue' / 'Now You're A Lady' / 'Where Is The Good Life'.

Richard Burgess drums; Dave Charles drums; Paul Cobbold bass; BJ Cole pedal steel guitar; Tommy Eyre keyboards; Ken Freeman synthesiser; Lee Jackson keyboards; Ray Martinez guitar; Jonathan Rowlands percussion; Andy Summers guitar; Roger Sutton bass; John Verity guitar;

Produced by Jonathan Rowlands, Hugh Murphy and Tim Rose. Engineered by Dave Charles, Piers Ford-Crush, Mike Gardner, Damon Lyon-Shaw. Recorded at Eden Studios, London; IBC Studios, London; Rockfield Studios, Gwent, Wales.

COMPILATIONS

The Rock Machine Turns You On

Columbia 484 439 2

Released 1967

Tim Rose has one track featured, 'Come Away Melinda'.

The Big Three, Featuring Mama Cass

Sequel NEMCD 755

Released 1995

This is a compilation drawn from The Big Three's two albums recorded for the FM label in the early 1960s.

OTHERS

Unfinished Song

Tiger Lily TL 14055

Released 1976

This is an album of questionable legitimacy. A raw, guitar-based collection lasting a mere 26 minutes and featuring Andy Summers, it was recorded in 1970 but never released with Rose's permission. The tapes came into the possession of the owner of the small Tiger Lily label in 1976, and the album was released without Rose's prior knowledge.

The Gambler

President PCOM 1117

Released November 1991

Recorded in 1977 for Atlantic. The company liked the songs as demos but considered the finished masters over-produced, and declined to release the album. This precipitated Rose returning to the US and dropping out of music for two decades.

Haunted **

Best Dressed Records Skirt 51

Released 1997

A combination of live re-recordings of some of his best known songs and low-budget recordings of new material, released on a tiny British independent label.

TOM RUSH

ALBUMS

Got A Mind To Ramble **

Prestige/Folklore 14003

Released 1963

'Duncan And Brady' / 'I Don't Want Your Millions Mister' / 'San Francisco Bay Blues' / 'Mole's Moan' / 'Orphans Blues' / 'Rye Whiskey' / 'Big Fat Woman' / 'Nine Pound Hammer' / 'Diamond Joe' / 'Just A Closer Walk With Thee' / 'Mobile-Texas Line' / 'Joe Turner' / 'Every Day In The Week'.

Tom Rush guitar, vocal; Fritz Richmond washtub bass.

Produced by Paul Rothchild. Recorded May 1963.

Got A Mind To Ramble *and* Blues, Songs And Ballads *were released by Transatlantic/Xtra in the UK. They were packaged as a double-album on Fantasy in 1972 (Fantasy 24709).*

Blues, Songs And Ballads **

Prestige 7374

Released 1965

'Alabama Bound' / 'More Pretty Girls' / 'Sister Kate' / 'Original Talking Blues' / 'Pallet On The Floor' / 'Drop Down Mama' / 'Rag Mama' / 'Barb'ry Allen' / 'Cocaine' / 'Come Back Baby' / 'Stackerlee' / 'Baby Please Don't Go'.

Tom Rush guitar, vocal; Fritz Richmond washtub bass.
Produced by Sam Charters. Recorded in New York.

Blues, Songs And Ballads and Got A Mind To Ramble were released by Transatlantic/Xtra in the UK. They were packaged as a double-album on Fantasy in 1972 (Fantasy 24709).

Tom Rush ***

Elektra EKL 288 mono, EKS 7288 stereo

Released 1965

'Long John' / 'If Your Man Gets Busted' / 'Do-Re-Mi' / 'Milk Cow Blues' / 'The Cuckoo' / 'Black Mountain Blues' / 'Poor Man' / 'Solid Gone' / 'When She Wants Good Lovin'' / 'I'd Like To Know' / 'Jelly Roll Baker' / 'Windy Bill' / 'Panama Limited'.

John "Daddy Bones" Herrald guitar; Ramblin' Jack Elliot guitar, vocal; Bill Lee bass; Felix Pappalardi guitarr' / 'Poor Man' / 'Solid Gone' / 'When She Wants Good Lovin'' / 'I'd Like To KnowProduced by Paul Rothchild.

Take A Little Walk With Me ***

Elektra EKL 308 mono, EKS 7308 stereo

Released June 1966

'You Can't Tell A Book By The Cover' / 'Who Do You Love' / 'Love's Made A Fool Of You' / 'Too Much Monkey Business' / 'Money Honey' / 'On The Road Again' / 'Joshua Gone Barbados' / 'Statesboro Blues' / 'Turn Your Money Green' / 'Sugar Babe' / 'Galveston Flood'.

John "Daddy Bones" Herrald guitar; Harvey Brooks bass; Roosevelt Gook piano; Bobby Gregg drums; Al Kooper guitar, keyboards; Bruce Langhorne guitar; Bill Lee bass; Felix Pappalardi guitar; Tom Rush guitar, vocal; John Sebastian harmonica.
Produced by Mark Abramson.

The Circle Game *****

Elektra EKL 4018 mono, EKS 74018 stereo

Released 1968

'Tin Angel' / 'Something In The Way She Moves' / 'Urge For Going' / 'Sunshine Sunshine' / 'Glory Of Love' / 'Shadow Dream Song' / 'The Circle Game' / 'So Long' / 'Rockport Sunday' / 'No Regrets'.

Bob Bushnell bass; Eric Gale guitar; Joe Grimm saxophone; Paul Harris keyboards; Bruce Langhorne guitar; Herb Lovell drums; Buddy Lucas saxophone; Joe Mack bass; Hugh McCracken

guitar; Bernard Purdie drums; Jonathan Raskin bass, guitar; Richie Ritz drums; Tom Rush guitar, vocal; Don Thomas guitar.
Produced by Arthur Gorson.

Tom Rush ****

Columbia CS 9972

Released 1970

'Driving Wheel' / 'Rainy Day Man' / 'Drop Down Mama' /. 'Old Man Song' / 'Lullaby' / 'These Days' / 'Wild Child (World Of Trouble)' / 'Colors Of The Sun' / 'Livin' In The Country' / 'Child's Song' / 'Wrong End Of The Rainbow'.

Duke Bardwell bass; Warren Bernhardt keyboards; David Bromberg guitar, steel guitar; Ron Carter bass; Ed Freeman guitar; Paul Griffin keyboards; Herb Lovell drums; Red Rhodes pedal steel guitar; Tom Rush guitar, vocal; Trevor Veitch guitar, mandolin, vocal.
Produced by Ed Freeman.

Tom Rush and Wrong End Of The Rainbow were released on one CD in 1997 by Beat Goes On (BGOCD361).

Wrong End Of The Rainbow ****

Columbia CS 30402

Released 1970

'Biloxi' / 'Merrimac County' / 'Riding On A Railroad' / 'Came To See Me Yesterday In The Merry Month Of' / 'Starlight' / 'Sweet Baby James' / 'Rotunda' / 'Jazzman' / 'Gnostic Serenade'.

Paul Armin violin, string arrangements; Bob Boucher bass; David Bromberg guitar, steel guitar; Bob Bushnell bass; Eric Gale guitar; Joe Grimm saxophone; Paul Harris keyboards; Bruce Langhorne guitar; Dave Lewis percussion; John Locke keyboards; Herb Lovell drums; Buddy Lucas saxophone; Joe Mack bass; Hugh McCracken guitar; Bernard Purdie drums; Jonathan Raskin bass, guitar; Richie Ritz drums; Eric Robertson keyboards; Tom Rush guitar, vocal; Don Thomas guitar; Brent Titcomb harmonica; Trevor Veitch guitar, mandolin, vocal.
Produced by David Briggs.

Wrong End Of The Rainbow and Tom Rush were released on one CD in 1997 by Beat Goes On (BGOCD361).

Merrimack County ***

Columbia CS 31306

Released 1972

'Kids These Days' / 'Mink Julip' / 'Mother Earth' / 'Jamaica Say You Will' / 'Merrimack County II' / 'Gypsy Boy' / 'Wind On The Water' / 'Roll Away The Grey' / 'Seems The Songs' / 'Gone Down River'.

Paul Armin violin; Ed Freeman conductor, string arrangements; Gary Mallaber drums, percussion, vibes; Kathryn Moses flute; Eric Robertson organ, piano; James Rolleston bass, vocal; Tom Rush guitar, vocal; John Savage drums; Bill Stevenson piano; Trevor

Veitch guitar, mandocello, vocal.
Produced by Tom Rush. Engineered by Jay Messina.

Ladies Love Outlaws **
Columbia KC 33054
Released 1974
'Ladies Love Outlaws' / 'Hobo's Mandolin' / 'Indian Woman From
Wichita' / 'Maggie' / 'Desperados Waiting For The Train' / 'Claim On
Me' / 'Jenny :Lynn' / 'Black Magic Gun' / 'No Regrets' / 'One Day I
Walk'.
Paul Armin violin, string arrangements; Bob Babitt bass; Jeff Baxter
guitar, pedal steel guitar; Bob Boucher bass; David Bromberg
guitar, steel guitar; Jackson Browne vocal; George Devens
percussion; Jerry Friedman guitar; Jack Hale trombone; Carl Hall
vocal; Rupert Holmes string/woodwind arrangements, vocal;
Wayne Jackson trumpet; Dave Lewis percussion; John Locke
keyboards; Ed Logan flute, saxophone; Andrew Love saxophone;
Jeff Miranov guitar; James Mitchell saxophone; Leon Pendarvis
electric piano, piano; Elliott Randall guitar; Eric Robertson
keyboards; Tom Rush guitar, vocal; Tim Schmit vocal; Allan
Schwartzberg drums; Carly Simon vocal; Andrew Smith drums;
James Taylor vocal; Tasha Thomas vocal; Brent Titcomb
harmonica; Trevor Veitch guitar, mandolin, vocal; Harold Wheeler
organ, piano.
Produced by Mark Spector. Engineered by Alan Varner, Terry
Rosiello, Lou Sclossberg. Recorded at Mediasound, New York, NY.

COMPILATIONS
No Regrets – The Very Best of Tom Rush
Columbia Legacy SNY 658602
Released 1999
*A collection compiled by Rush himself, this spans his 37-year
recording career. It includes a song from* Live At The Unicorn *and
selections from his Elektra and Columbia albums, plus some of his
own-label material from the 1980s and 1990s. There is one new
piece, 'River Song', unavailable elsewhere. Two previous best-ofs
appeared, 1971's* Classic Rush *(Elektra EKS 74062) and 1976's*
The Best Of Tom Rush *(Columbia KC 33907).*

OTHERS
Tom Rush Live At The Unicorn
Released 1962
'Ramblin' On My Mind' / 'San Francisco Bay Blues' / 'The Old '97' /
'Every Night When The Sun Goes Down' / 'Walkin' Blues' / 'Make
Love To You' / 'Poor Man' / 'Orphan's Blues' / 'Pretty Boy Floyd' /
'Julie's Blues' / 'Talking Dust Bowl' / 'Old Blue'.
Tom Rush guitar, vocal.
Produced by Dan Flickinger.

*This album was released as a private pressing in Boston in 1962
and sold at concerts. It was reissued by Rush's own label, Night
Light, in 1986.*

New Year
Night Light 28011
Released 1982
'Anna' / 'Louisiana Eyes' / 'Merrimack County' / 'Gold On The River'
/ 'The Dreamer' / 'Joshua Gone Barbados' / 'Kind Kind Lovin'' /
'Drivin' Wheel' / 'Wasn't That A Mighty Storm' / 'Urge For Going'.
*This and the two following records were released on Rush's own
label, Night Light.* New Year *celebrated his 20th anniversary and
was a live recording, as was* Late Night Radio, *while* Work In
Progress *was a six-song cassette-only release of incomplete
sketches of new material.*

Late Night Radio
Night Light 48001
Released 1984
'Late Night Radio' / 'Blow Whistle Blow' / 'Annette' / 'The Boy With
The Violin' / 'Beam Me Up Scotty' / 'Old New England' / 'Jazzman'
/ 'Jonah' / 'Swallow Song' / 'City Of New Orleans' / 'Jamaica Say
You Will' / 'On The Road Again'.
Mimi Fariña vocal; Steve Goodman vocal; Beverly Rush vocal; Tom
Rush guitar, vocal.

Work In Progress
Night Light
Released c.1987
'All A Man Can Do' / 'I Believe In You' / 'Shoo-rah Shoo-rah' / 'Wild
Irish Rose' / 'No One Else But You' / 'Who Do You Love'.
Tom Rush guitar, vocal.

KEY TO OTHER PEOPLE

KEY FIGURES
These are some of the influential musicians, managers, producers
and record company executives whose careers became
interwoven in the stories told in this book. In different ways, they all
left their mark on the music.

Area Code 615
Group of assured country session-players who started to record
on their own after backing Dylan during the 1960s. Charlie McCoy
(harmonica), Kenny Buttrey (drums) and others recorded with
David Blue, Tim Rose and Pearls Before Swine.

Warren Bernhardt

Tim Hardin's keyboard player for a period in the late 1960s/early 1970s. He also played on Tom Rush's first Columbia album.

Harvey Brooks

Bassist who played on albums by Tom Rush and David Blue in the 1960s, as well as releasing a tuition album *How To Play Electric Bass* on Elektra. In the 1970s he played on some as-yet-unreleased Fred Neil recordings.

Clive Davis

Chairman of Columbia Records from the late 1960s to the early 1970s. During his tenure, Tim Rose, Tom Rush, Tim Hardin and David Ackles recorded for the label.

Ed Freeman

Columbia producer/arranger in the early 1970s. He worked in both capacities on successive sessions on Tim Hardin's *Bird On A Wire* and Tom Rush's eponymous Columbia debut.

Arthur Gorson

Started the 1960s as a student political activist, and while chairman of Campus Americans For Democratic Action he came into contact with Phil Ochs. Impressed with Gorson's organisational abilities, Ochs persuaded him to become his manager. Arthur H Gorson Management eventually had Ochs, David Blue, Tom Rush and Eric Andersen on its books. These acts and others were grouped together for folk package-tours in smaller clubs and colleges. Gorson also became involved in record production, with one of his first producer's credits on David Blue's eponymous debut album. Gorson later graduated to Tom Rush's *Circle Game,* one of the definitive singer-songwriter records. Rush recalls Gorson's involvement as more organisational than creative.

Jac Holzman

Founded Elektra Records in 1951 and remained a dominant force in the company until 1973. Originally concentrating on traditional folk records and albums of sound effects, Holzman was by the early 1960s beginning to build a significant roster of folk-based singer-songwriters. At various times David Ackles, David Blue, Tim Buckley, Phil Ochs, Fred Neil and Tom Rush recorded for the label. In the mid 1960s Holzman began signing rock acts like Love and The Doors, and their success partially eclipsed the singer-songwriters – while also providing sufficient funds for Holzman to continue to record poor-selling mavericks like Buckley and Ackles. Although some, like Ochs, criticised what they felt to be the restrictive financial terms of Holzman's contract, most of his artists remember their time at Elektra with affection and gratitude. After

leaving Elektra, Holzman continued to be active in the media and music industries. In 1998 he published with Gavan Daws a memoir of his time at Elektra, *Follow The Music.*

Al Kooper

Guitarist, songwriter, organist and producer, famed for playing the primitive organ lines on Dylan's 'Like A Rolling Stone'. Kooper worked on Tom Rush's second Elektra album, made an abortive attempt to record David Ackles's second Elektra LP, and produced the classic, rare Tim Rose single 'Long Haired Boy'.

Bruce Langhorne

Prolific session guitarist, renowned for his work with Bob Dylan. He played on albums by Fred Neil, Tom Rush and David Ackles.

Herb Lovelle

Played drums with David Blue, Tom Rush and Pearls Before Swine.

Billy Mundi

One of many drummers to pass through the ranks of Frank Zappa's Mothers of Invention, but also played at various times with Tim Buckley, Fred Neil and Pearls Before Swine.

Felix Pappalardi

One-time Mountain bassist and producer of Cream, Pappalardi had started his career as a session bassist in New York. He played on early recordings by Tim Hardin, Tim Rose, Fred Neil and Tom Rush. Pappalardi was shot dead in the early 1980s. His wife Gail Collins, with whom he and Eric Clapton had co-written Cream's 'Strange Brew', was charged with his murder.

Van Dyke Parks

Writer of inscrutable lyrics for The Beach Boys and an eccentric solo artist in his own right. The former child actor played on records by Tim Buckley and Phil Ochs, and also produced Ochs's last studio album. He still writes, records, performs and produces.

Bernard Purdie

Still an in-demand session drummer, "Pretty" Purdie played on Tom Rush's seminal *Circle Game* album, Tim Hardin's only US hit single, 'Simple Song of Freedom', and Tim Rose's solo debut. According to Rose, during sessions for the latter the drummer displayed a sign by the drum booth: "Bernard Purdie will solve your rhythm problems."

Bob Rafkin

Guitarist who worked on most of David Blue's albums. He also recorded with Phil Ochs and Tim Buckley.

Paul Rothchild

Started his career at Prestige Records where he recorded Tom Rush. When he moved to Elektra, Rothchild persuaded Rush to join him, and produced Rush's first Elektra recordings. Rothchild went on to work with most of the great Elektra acts of the 1960s. He died of cancer in 1995.

John Sebastian

Best remembered as the singer, songwriter and guitarist with The Lovin' Spoonful who enjoyed considerable commercial success in the mid 1960s. Prior to the Spoonful's breakthrough he was active on the Greenwich Village circuit and played harmonica on recordings by Fred Neil, Tom Rush and Tim Hardin. Since the Spoonful's late-1960s demise Sebastian has had a fitful solo career. Despite throat problems that affected his voice, he still performs.

OTHER ARTISTS

The folk revival and the ensuing singer-songwriter movement threw up dozens of artists of note. Some have been dealt with in more detail in the body of this book, but here are a few of the other main players.

Eric Andersen

(b. Pittsburgh, PA, February 14th 1943) Arriving in Greenwich Village in 1964, Andersen was soon absorbed into the burgeoning folk singer-songwriter scene. Renowned for his pretty-boy looks, he recorded for Vanguard in the mid 1960s and occasionally thereafter for various other labels. Two of his most famous songs, 'Thirsty Boots' and 'Violets Of Dawn', were on his second album *'Bout Changes And Things* (1966). He made a bizarre effort to jump on the folk-rock bandwagon by releasing an electric version of the same album a year later. He is still active, and spends much of his time in Norway.

Ramblin' Jack Elliott

(b. New York, NY, August 1st 1931) Elliott met Woody Guthrie in 1949, and Guthrie became his mentor and a major influence. After touring Europe in the 1950s, Elliott had by the early 1960s settled in New York where he was an inspiration to a young Bob Dylan and many others. He later guested on albums by Tom Rush and Phil Ochs, and joined Dylan's Rolling Thunder Revue. He still performs.

Richard Fariña

(b. New York, NY, 1937; d. Carmel, CA, April 30th 1966) Born in New York of Irish/Cuban parents, Fariña is reputed to have smuggled guns for the IRA in the mid 1950s when that seemed like a bohemian thing to do. He was connected to the folk revival by virtue of marriage to Mimi Baez, the younger sister of Joan. After travelling widely in the late 1950s and early 1960s he recorded as a solo artist, notably on Elektra's 1965 *Singer-Songwriter Project* compilation, and as a duo with Mimi, playing guitar, zither and dulcimer as well as singing and writing songs. His novel *Been Down So Long, It Looks Like Up To Me* was heralded in some quarters as a latter-day beat classic. He died in a motorcycle crash in April 1966, just as the book was due to be published.

Richie Havens

(b. New York, NY, January 21st 1941) Active in Greenwich Village from the early 1960s, Havens was one of relatively few blacks operating in what at the time was a predominantly white middle-class idiom. He was a unique guitar stylist whose percussive strumming accompanied his vocals to great effect, and he often created unusual interpretations of well-known songs by Dylan, The Beatles and others. Havens is widely remembered for opening the Woodstock festival, and his appearance is strongly featured in the film of the event. He has maintained a recording career since the mid 1960s. In recent years he has supplemented his earnings from his musical career with lucrative work as a voiceover artist. He also paints, writes and sculpts, and continues to be involved in political and humanitarian activities.

Bob Neuwirth

(b. Akron, OH, June 20th 1939) Neuwirth began performing in Boston at a time when Joan Baez and Tom Rush were rising to prominence. He met Bob Dylan in 1961 and came to occupy an ill-defined position as his road manager, sidekick, henchman and "verbal assassin". His debut album appeared in 1974, making him the last of his generation of folk singers to launch a recording career, which has continued intermittently ever since.

Tom Paxton

(b. Chicago, IL, October 31st 1937) Something of an elder statesman in Greenwich Village, being several years older than most other singers, Paxton signed to Elektra in 1964 for his first album *Ramblin' Boy,* and has continued to record and tour ever since. Although highly regarded among his contemporaries as a singer and songwriting craftsman, he always seemed in spirit, at least, to belong more to the earlier liberal-leaning, topical-songwriting generation personified by Pete Seeger.

Pete Seeger

(b. New York, NY, May 3rd 1919) Seeger was a primary link between Woody Guthrie and the new generation of singers of the late 1950s and early 1960s. He had sung with the Almanac Singers alongside Guthrie, and later with The Weavers. By the late

1950s he was a leading spokesman of the humanitarian, liberal-left folk community. He was scandalised by Dylan's electric conversion, but later softened his stance. He remained active as a performer, recording artist and activist into old age.

Patrick Sky

(b. Atlanta, GA, October 2nd 1940) He first came to attention touring with Buffy Sainte-Marie. Like her, Sky had Native American blood and has spent much of his career fighting for the rights of the cause of the indigenous American population. A lesser light on the Greenwich Village scene, he was one of four artists on Elektra's *Singer Songwriter Project* compilation. His recording career has been sporadic, and more recently he has been employed as a musical-instrument maker.

Dave Van Ronk

(b. New York, NY, June 30th 1936) Van Ronk played jazz guitar

before becoming involved in folk music in 1957. He recorded for Folkways, Lyrichord, Prestige and Mercury from the late 1950s onward. He joined Phil Ochs and Bob Dylan for 'Blowin' In The Wind' during the Evening With Salvador Allende concert in 1974.

Eric Von Schmidt

(b. Westport, CT, May 29th 1930) A leading figure on the Boston/Cambridge circuit, Von Schmidt was a guitarist, singer, songwriter and artist. Tom Rush recorded several of his songs. In the early 1960s Von Schmidt and Richard Fariña recorded an album in the cellar of Dobell's jazz record shop in London; the record featured an appearance by Bob Dylan under the pseudonym of Blind Boy Grunt. One of Von Schmidt's albums can be seen in the front-cover photograph on Bob Dylan's *Bringing It All Back Home*. Von Schmidt co-wrote *Baby Let Me Follow You Down*, a book about the Boston/Cambridge scene.

ACKNOWLEDGEMENTS

*The author would like to thank: David
Ackles, Tom Rapp, Tim Rose, Tom
Rush, Janice Vogel-Ackles, Keith
Badman, Tony Bacon, Nigel
Osborne, Brian Mathieson, Geoff
Gough, Ian Wood, Geoff Smith,
Steve Turner, Madeleine Brend and
Phil Smee.*

PHOTOGRAPHS Supplied by the
following (number indicates page;
source in *italics*): 2 Troubadour *Phil
Smee/Strange Things*; 18 vaudeville
pair *Janice Vogel-Ackles*; 18 Ackles
doorway *Janice Vogel-Ackles*; 18
Ackles waistcoat *Redfern's*; 19
Ackles live *Redfern's*; 19 Ackles
recent *Janice Vogel-Ackles*; 21 Blue
live *Redfern's*; 22 Buckley portraits x2
Redfern's; 23 Buckley portrait
Pictorial Press; 24-25 Buckley
Redfern's; 26 Hardin with guitar
Pictorial Press; 27 Hardin live
Redfern's; 28 Hardin live *Pictorial
Press*; 29 Hardin live *Redfern's*; 30
Martin and Neil *Phil Smee/Strange
Things*; 31 Neil live *Redfern's*; 32-33
Neil live x3 *Redfern's*; 34 Ochs street
Redfern's; 34 Ochs live *Redfern's*; 35

Ochs live *Pictorial Press*; 36
Ginsberg/Ochs *Phil Smee/Strange
Things*; 36 Dylan etc *Phil
Smee/Strange Things*; 37 Ochs
Michael Ochs; 38 Rapp close-up *Phil
Smee/Strange Things*; 38 Pearls *Tom
Rapp*; 39 Pearls (top) *Tom Rapp*; 39
Pearls (bottom) *Phil Smee/Strange
Things*; 40-41 Rapp *Tom Rapp*; 42
Rose with guitar *Phil Smee/Strange
Things*; 42 Rose posing *Pictorial
Press*; 42 Rose/Kooper *Tony Bacon*;
43 Rose portrait *Pictorial Press*; Rose
recent *Redfern's*; 44 Rush Elektra
shot *Phil Smee/Strange Things*; 45
Rush portrait *Pictorial Press*; 46 Rush
with guitar *Pictorial Press*; Rush at
mirror *Phil Smee/Strange Things*; 47
Rush with jacket *Redfern's*; 47 Rush
with guitar *Phil Smee/Strange Things*;
Rush recent *Tom Rush*. 49 Ackles
Redfern's; 69 Buckley *Redfern's*; 79
Hardin *Pictorial Press*; 90 Neil
Redfern's; 99 Ochs *Redfern's*; 112
Rapp *Tom Rapp*; 123 Rose *Pictorial
Press*; 135 Rush *Redfern's*.
Other illustrated items including
advertisements, posters and record
sleeves came from the collections of:
Tony Bacon; Mark Brend; Tom Rapp;
Phil Smee/Strange Things.

BIBLIOGRAPHY

David Browne *Dream Brother: The
Lives And Music Of Jeff And Tim
Buckley* (Fourth Estate 2001); Donald
Clarke (ed) *The Penguin
Encyclopedia Of Popular Music*
(Penguin 1998); Marc Eliot *Phil Ochs:
Death of a Rebel* (Omnibus 1990);
Phil Hardy & Dave Laing *The
Encyclopedia of Rock – Volume 2:
From Liverpool To San Francisco*
(Panther 1976); Jac Holzman &
Gavan Daws *Follow the Music*
(FirstMedia 1998); Terry Hounsome
Rock Record 7 (Record Researcher
1997); Colin Larkin (ed) *The
Guinness Who's Who Of Blues*
(Guinness 1995); Colin Larkin (ed)
*The Guinness Who's Who Of Folk
Music* (Guinness 1993); Rough
Guides *Rock: The Rough Guide*
(Rough Guides 1999); Robert
Shelton *No Direction Home: The Life
and Music of Bob Dylan* (Penguin
1987); MC Strong *The Great Rock
Discography* (Canongate 1995);
Richie Unterberger *Urban Spacemen
And Wayfaring Strangers* (Miller
Freeman 2000); Jacques Vassal
Electric Children (Taplinger c1972);
Eric Von Schmidt & Jim Rooney *Baby

Let Me Follow You Down* (University
of Massachusetts Press 1994); Mike
Watkinson & Pete Anderson *Scott
Walker: A Deep Shade of Blue* (Virgin
1994); Robbie Woliver *Hoot! A 25-
Year History Of The Greenwich
Village Music Scene* (Pantheon
1986).

Periodicals: *Acoustic Guitar World*;
Beat Instrumental; *Broadside*; *Disc &
Music Echo*; *The Guardian*; *Guitar
Player*; *The Independent*; *The Los
Angeles Free Press*; *Melody Maker*;
Mojo; *New Musical Express*;
Ptolemaic Terrascope; *Q*; *Record
Mirror*; *Rolling Stone*; *Sing Out*;
Sounds; *Strange Things Are
Happening*; *The Times*; *ZigZag*.

At a loose end in a record store?
Consider that you only need seven
records to have every five-star album
in this book's discography: *David
Ackles* and *American Gothic* by
David Ackles; *Happy/Sad* by Tim
Buckley; *Tim Hardin 2*; *Fred Neil* (later
retitled *Everybody's Talkin'*); *Tim Rose*
(Columbia); and *The Circle Game* by
Tom Rush.

"They mean what they mean."
Tim Hardin